PYTHON FOR BEGINNERS

A practical introduction

Hafed Benteftifa, PhD

Lecturer, Information Technology

Collège de Bois-de-Boulogne, Montréal, Canada

Published by: Hafed Benteftifa.

Legal deposit – Library and Archives Canada / Bibliothèque et Archives Canada and Bibliothèque et Archives nationales du Québec, 2023

Issued in print and electronic formats.

ISBN printed version: 978-1-7380627-0-6

ISBN electronic version: 978-1-7380627-1-3

In memory of my parents:

Fatma-Zohra and *Sid'Ahmed*

To my children:

Malia and *Moncef*

and to my wife:

Assia

Acknowledgments

I would like to extend my heartfelt appreciation to all my colleagues and the countless students whose efforts and feedback have enriched this book.

A special thanks goes to Mrs. Halia Ferhat, a longstanding colleague, whose unwavering trust and dedication to innovative educational projects have been a constant source of inspiration.

I am also grateful to Mrs. Sabine Boufenara, academic coordinator at Bois-de-Boulogne, for her enthusiasm, commitment, and perseverance, which were vital to the successful completion of this complex endeavor.

I extend my thanks to Mrs. Soraya Ferdenache, Mr. Sabri Benferhat, and Mr. Hacine Benchoubane for their encouragement, stimulating discussions, and interest in this project.

Lastly, I would like to express my sincere gratitude to all the individuals involved, including Mr. Simon Delamarre, the director of continuing education at Collège de Bois-de-Boulogne, whose collaboration and dedication were instrumental in bringing this project to fruition. Their support made this endeavor a reality.

Contents in brief

1	Introduction	1
2	Basic Syntax	25
3	Decision Structures	53
4	Repetition Structures	69
5	Functions	87
6	Sequences and Collections	111
7	Classes and Objects	147
8	Inheritance	171
9	Files	203
10	Exception Handling	227
11	Graphical User interfaces	247
12	Integration Project	279
13	Debugging with PyCharm	297

A Operator Precedence 305

B Quiz Solutions 309

C Answers for Selected Problems 311

Contents

Why this book? xvii
What this book covers xviii
What you need to do the exercises xix
Audience for this book xx
Conventions xx
Source code xxi
Errata xxi
Questions and feedback xxi

1 Introduction **1**
1.1 Python's versions 1
1.2 Python as a programming language 2
1.3 Development flow 2
1.3.1 Step 1: Understand the requirements 2
1.3.2 Step 2: Create the algorithm 3
1.3.3 Step 3: Use a programming language to create the program . . . 3
1.4 Software production steps 4
1.5 Procedural languages 5
1.6 Object-oriented languages 5
1.6.1 What is an object? 6
1.6.2 What is a class? 7
1.6.3 Class members 8
1.7 Development phases in Python 8
1.8 Read and write instructions 9
1.9 Quiz 11
1.10 Laboratory: Setting up the development environment 13
1.10.1 Manipulation 1: Python installation 14
1.10.2 Manipulation 2: Installing the PyCharm IDE 17
1.10.3 Manipulation 3: Getting started with the PyCharm IDE 21
1.10.4 Manipulation 4: Modifying output instructions 24

2 Basic Syntax **25**

2.1 Python programs . . . 25
2.1.1 Comments . . . 26
2.1.2 Declaration or assignment of variables . . . 26
2.1.3 Declaration of constants . . . 27
2.2 Data types in Python . . . 28
2.2.1 Data type – Boolean . . . 28
2.2.2 Data type – None . . . 29
2.2.3 Data type – Numeric . . . 29
2.2.4 Data Type - `str` . . . 30
2.3 Python essentials . . . 30
2.3.1 Naming conventions . . . 31
2.3.2 Python statements . . . 31
2.3.3 Concatenation of strings . . . 32
2.3.4 Blocks of instructions and indentation . . . 32
2.3.5 Delimiters . . . 33
2.3.6 Python keywords . . . 33
2.3.7 Python expressions and operators . . . 34
2.4 Operators . . . 34
2.4.1 Arithmetic operators . . . 34
2.4.2 Arithmetic operators - precedence . . . 36
2.4.3 Relational-comparison operators . . . 36
2.4.4 Logical operators . . . 37
2.4.5 Truth table . . . 38
2.5 Explicit conversion . . . 40
2.6 Other useful notations in Python . . . 41
2.6.1 Functions . . . 42
2.6.2 Formatting strings . . . 43
2.7 Quick summary . . . 46
2.8 Quiz . . . 47
2.9 Practice problems . . . 49
2.10 Programming problems . . . 51

3 Decision Structures 53
3.1 Introduction . . . 53
3.2 The simple if structure (One-way) . . . 54
3.2.1 Logic of simple or One-way if structure . . . 55
3.3 The if-else structure (Two-way) . . . 56
3.3.1 Logic of the `if-else` structure . . . 57
3.4 The complex if-elif-else structure (Multi-way) . . . 59
3.5 The conditional operator . . . 59
3.6 Quick summary . . . 60
3.7 Quiz . . . 61
3.8 Practice problems . . . 64
3.9 Programming problems . . . 66

4 Repetition Structures **69**
4.1 Introduction 69
4.2 The `while` loop 70
4.2.1 Logic of the `while` Loop 70
4.3 The `for` Loop 72
4.3.1 The `range()` function 73
4.4 Transfer of control 74
4.4.1 Break statement 74
4.4.2 Continue statement 75
4.5 Quick summary 76
4.6 Quiz 77
4.7 Practice problems 80
4.8 Programming problems 83

5 Functions **87**
5.1 Introduction 87
5.1.1 Why should we use functions? 88
5.1.2 Definition 88
5.1.3 Syntax 89
5.1.4 Docstrings 90
5.1.5 Calling a function 91
5.2 Scope of a variable 93
5.2.1 Local variables 93
5.2.2 Global variables 93
5.3 Using parameters 94
5.3.1 Using keywords 94
5.3.2 Default values 94
5.3.3 Using * in the header 95
5.3.4 Using ** in the header 96
5.4 Parameter typing 96
5.5 Quick summary 98
5.6 Quiz 99
5.7 Practice problems 102
5.7.1 Function declaration and call 102
5.7.2 Modifying a global variable inside a function, using the global keyword 103
5.8 Programming problems 106

6 Sequences and Collections **111**
6.1 Introduction 111
6.2 Lists 112
6.3 Tuples 116
6.4 Sets 119
6.5 Dictionaries 122
6.6 Quick summary 129

6.7 Quiz . . . 131
6.8 Practice problems . . . 133
6.8.1 Practice: Manipulating Lists . . . 133
6.8.2 Practice: Manipulating Tuples . . . 138
6.8.3 Practice: Manipulating Sets . . . 139
6.8.4 Practice: Manipulating Dictionaries . . . 140
6.9 Programming problems . . . 144

7 Classes and Objects 147
7.1 Introduction . . . 147
7.2 Structure of a class . . . 148
7.2.1 Terminology . . . 148
7.2.2 Classes in Python . . . 149
7.2.3 Class members . . . 151
7.3 Objects in Python . . . 151
7.3.1 What is an object? . . . 151
7.3.2 Notion of object in Python . . . 151
7.3.3 Constructors and initializers . . . 152
7.4 Methods . . . 153
7.4.1 Encapsulation – Visibility . . . 153
7.4.2 Service methods . . . 153
7.4.3 Utility methods . . . 154
7.4.4 Parameters of a method . . . 154
7.4.5 Returning values from a method . . . 154
7.5 Case study . . . 157
7.6 Quick summary . . . 162
7.7 Quiz . . . 163
7.8 Practice problems . . . 165
7.9 Programming problems . . . 168

8 Inheritance 171
8.1 Introduction . . . 171
8.1.1 Declaration syntax . . . 174
8.1.2 How to determine the type or parent of an object? . . . 188
8.2 Case study . . . 190
8.3 Quick summary . . . 194
8.4 Quiz . . . 195
8.5 Practice problems . . . 198
8.6 Programming problems . . . 201

9 Files 203
9.1 Input and output files . . . 203
9.1.1 File types . . . 204
9.1.2 Types of access . . . 204
9.2 File manipulation . . . 205

9.2.1 Opening a file 205
9.2.2 Reading from a file 206
9.2.3 The `read()` method 207
9.2.4 The `readline()` method 208
9.2.5 The `readlines()` method 209
9.2.6 Writing to a file 209
9.2.7 Closing a file 210
9.3 String slicing 211
9.3.1 Splitting a string into tokens 212
9.4 Using the `csv` module 212
9.4.1 Reading from a file 212
9.4.2 Using `DictReader` 215
9.4.3 Writing to a file 217
9.4.4 Using `DictWriter` 219
9.5 Quick summary 220
9.6 Quiz 221
9.7 Practice problems 223
9.8 Programming problems 224

10 Exception Handling 227
10.1 Introduction 227
10.2 The try-except-finally structure 229
10.2.1 The else clause 232
10.2.2 The finally Clause 233
10.3 Exception propagation 233
10.4 Exception hierarchy 234
10.5 Creating a custom exception class 235
10.6 Quick summary 236
10.7 Quiz 238
10.8 Practice problems 240
10.9 Programming problems 244

11 Graphical User interfaces 247
11.1 The tkinter module 247
11.1.1 Developing a GUI 248
11.2 Components or Widgets 250
11.3 Events 257
11.3.1 Command binding 259
11.3.2 Event binding 261
11.4 Quick summary 263
11.5 Quiz 264
11.6 Laboratories 266
11.6.1 Developing a Graphical Interface 266
11.6.2 Integration of Functions in a Graphical Interface 269
11.7 Practice problems 272

11.8 Programming problems 274

12 Integration Project **279**
12.1 Context 279
12.2 Basic module: BMI calculator 281
12.3 Tests and loops 282
12.3.1 Tests, display of risk and classification 282
12.3.2 Loops, input validation 284
12.4 Functions 286
12.5 Class 288
12.6 Files 290
12.7 GUI Interface with tkinter 292

13 Debugging with PyCharm **297**
13.1 Introduction 297
13.2 Debugging with breakpoints 298
13.3 Using a watch on a variable 301

A Operator Precedence **305**

B Quiz Solutions **309**

C Answers for Selected Problems **311**

List of Figures

1 Introduction

1.1 Basic algorithm flowchart. 3
1.2 Procedural approach. 5
1.3 Object-oriented approach. 6
1.4 Objects in a program. 7
1.5 Model classes. 7
1.6 Producing Python vs Java code. 8
1.7 Processing instructions with Python. 9
1.8 Python download link. 14
1.9 Python installation screen. 15
1.10 Confirmation of Python installation. 15
1.11 Confirmation of the installed Python version. 16
1.12 Launching the Python interpreter. 16
1.13 Executing a basic instruction. 16
1.14 Download link for the Python Pycharm IDE. 17
1.15 Pycharm installation ccreen. 18
1.16 Pycharm installation screen, selecting an installation path. 18
1.17 Associating the .py extension with Python files. 19
1.18 Confirmation of the installation. 20
1.19 Creating a project. 21
1.20 Project location. 22
1.21 Creating a module in Pycharm. 22
1.22 Module name. 22
1.23 Project structure. 23
1.24 Basic print statement. 23
1.25 Console output. 23

2 Basic Syntax

2.1 Unauthorized use of a keyword as a variable name. 33

3 Decision Structures
3.1 If Structure one-way. 55
3.2 Logic of the simple One-way `if` structure. 56
3.3 Logic of the `if` two-way structure. 58

4 Repetition Structures
4.1 Logic of the `while` loop. 71

5 Functions
5.1 Function call with value return. 88
5.2 Function call without returning values. 89

7 Classes and Objects
7.1 Basic classes. 158
7.2 Basic classes with attributes. 158
7.3 Basic classes with attributes and methods. 159

8 Inheritance
8.1 Parent class. 174
8.2 Inheritance - Parent and Child. 176
8.3 Inheritance hierarchy. 179
8.4 Method redefinition in subclasses. 183
8.5 Multiple inheritance hierarchy. 186
8.6 Base classes with attributes and methods. 190
8.7 Basic classes with attributes and methods. 191

9 Files
9.1 Stream in read mode. 206
9.2 Stream in write mode. 210

10 Exception Handling
10.1 Error stack. 228
10.2 Exception hierarchy in Python. 234

11 Graphical User interfaces
11.1 Structure of a GUI interface. 249
11.2 Prototype of the input window. 253
11.3 Resulting prototype. 253
11.4 Final prototype. 254
11.5 Prototype using grid manager. 256

11.6 Prototype with the grid layout manager. 258
11.7 Using callbacks. 260
11.8 Result obtained after using the callback. 260
11.9 Using callback with event binding. 262
11.10Entry widget. 273
11.11Initial window. 274
11.12Action on the button. 275
11.13Initial window with Combobox. 275
11.14Window displaying the selection result. 275
11.15Initial window with radio buttons. 276
11.16Window with the expected result. 276
11.17Window with the Scale widget. 277

12 Integration Project
12.1 BMI calculator. 280
12.2 The final GUI interface. 292

13 Debugging with PyCharm
13.1 Breakpoint before the function call. 298
13.2 Starting a debug session through the menu. 299
13.3 Starting a debug session through the toolbar icon. 299
13.4 Stopping at a breakpoint. 299
13.5 Accessing the debugging icons through the toolbar. 299
13.6 Adding a watch on a variable. 300
13.7 Checking the watch on variables. 301
13.8 Checking the watch on variables. 301
13.9 Checking watches on variables. 302
13.10Checking watches on variables. 302
13.11Breakpoint on the while loop. 302
13.12Checking watches on variables. 303
13.13Checking watches on variables. 303
13.14Checking watches on variables. 304
13.15Adding a watch for the logical expression. 304

List of Tables

1 Introduction

1.1 Python development toolchain. 9
1.2 Read and write operations. 10

2 Basic Syntax

2.1 Arithmetic operators. 35
2.2 Operator precedence. 36
2.3 Relational operators. 37
2.4 Logical operators. 38
2.5 The `not` operator. 38
2.6 The `and` operator. 39
2.7 The `or` operator. 40
2.8 Augmented operator and equivalence. 42

5 Functions

5.1 Postage rates for letter, postcards, and standard cards. 107

6 Sequences and Collections

6.1 Dictionary properties. 124
6.2 Dictionary methods. 128

9 Files

9.1 File opening modes according to type. 205
9.2 File opening modes for reading and writing. 206
9.3 File reading methods. 207
9.4 Student grades File. 213

10 Exception Handling
10.1 Examples of exception classes. 235

11 Graphical User interfaces
11.1 Parameters for the `pack` layout manager. 252
11.2 Parameters for the `grid` layout manager. 257
11.3 Events related to event binding. 262

12 Integration Project
12.1 Classification and Risk. 279

FOREWORD

Why this book?

For many years, I have been teaching two introductory Python courses. The first one, lasting 24 hours, is offered to students who have completed an introductory course in algorithms as a prerequisite. The second 14-hour course is designed for individuals with prior experience in another programming language like Java or C++.

Python is a versatile and easy-to-learn programming language, making it an excellent choice for beginners. It finds extensive application in web development, data analysis, artificial intelligence, internet of things, and much more. Python's clear and concise syntax enables writing readable and understandable code, facilitating an effective pedagogical approach.

Based on this foundation, the content of this book has been adapted to enable beginners to acquire basic Python programming skills, regardless of their current level of programming experience. Each concept in this book is accompanied by at least one simple demonstration example.

The book's content can be adapted for a shorter training duration of 3 or 4 days while covering a significant number of Python language concepts. It is important to note that the examples provided are purely educational and not intended as references for real-world production cases.

The book follows a deliberate approach in its subject matter and structure. It starts with a procedural approach in the early chapters in order to familiarize beginners with Python's basic syntax. Subsequently, it introduces object-oriented programming progressively to help beginners grasp the concept of object collaboration in problem-solving.

For those already familiar with this programming approach in other languages, the initial chapters might seem straightforward. Advanced concepts will be covered in another volume of this series.

While there are many excellent Python programming books available on the market, very few cater to true beginners and include practice and programming problems. It is precisely this gap that this book aims to fill, as it offers a wide array of practice and programming problems. Answers to many of these are provided in the appendix and can also be found on the book's GitHub repository. Moreover, a companion book containing over 100 programming problems with detailed solutions is also available.

Python is a pleasant language and it was a real pleasure to write this book. I hope it will give you as much pleasure.

What this book covers

Chapter 1
This chapter introduces the different versions of Python available in the market. Additionally, it presents various programming paradigms that can be employed with Python. The process of installing the PyCharm development environment is also described within this chapter.

Chapter 2
This chapter covers the basic syntax of Python and introduces the fundamental data types of integers, floating-point numbers, strings, and booleans. We also review the different types of operators.

Chapter 3
Here, we introduce the control structures that modify the sequential execution flow of a program. We illustrate the if, if-else, and if-elif-else structures with examples.

Chapter 4
Similar to Chapter 3, we introduce the repetition or loop structures that also modify the sequential execution flow of a program. The `while` and `for` structures are illustrated with examples.

Chapter 5
This chapter introduces the notion of program units or functions. We will explore how to build functions from a set of instructions. Additionally, we will introduce the concepts of local variables and global variables.

Chapter 6
In this chapter, we cover Python's basic data structures or collections, namely `list`, `tuple`, `set` and `dict`.

Chapter 7
We introduce here the concept of object-oriented programming with the notion of classes and objects. We explore the basic structure of a class from the point of view of Python, including the initializer, the constructor, and the methods.

Chapter 8

We continue here with the concept of object-oriented programming by introducing inheritance in the design of parent and child (or base and derived) classes. We also explore the concepts of generalization and specialization.

Chapter 9
Given that we manipulate the input and output data of a program, we introduce in this chapter reading and writing from textual and binary files.

Chapter 10
In order to make Python scripts and programs robust, it is important to introduce effective exception handling. This chapter shows how to integrate robust exception handling into Python code.

Chapter 11
We review here the basic techniques for creating graphical interfaces in Python. We will use the native `tkinter` module available in the standard Python library.

Chapter 12
A practical laboratory for the implementation of a complete Python program in several stages is offered in this chapter.

Chapter 13
In this chapter, we explore how to debug basic code with a typical example by using the debugging features of the development environment used in this book.

Appendix A
This appendix elaborates on the rules of precedence for operators, whether logical, relational, or arithmetic.

Appendix B
This appendix provides the solutions for the quizzes offered at the end of each chapter.

Appendix C
Solutions for some of the problems in each chapter are provided in this appendix.

What you need to do the exercises

All the examples, exercises, and problems proposed in this book have been carried out with version 3.11 of Python. The development environment used is PyCharm, powered by JetBrains, specifically PyCharm 2022. Other environments such as Eclipse PyDev, Visual Studio Code, Jupyter Anaconda, and others can be used to practice the examples in this book.

Audience for this book

This book was written especially for individuals wishing to acquire the basic notions of the Python language. If you have ever programmed in a computer language such as Java, C++, or others, certain notions will be familiar. On the other hand, if you are new to programming, this book will lead you to understand the basic syntax of Python and provide you with an introduction to structured (procedural) and object-oriented programming.

Conventions

In this book, a number of text styles have been adopted to alert you to the importance of a word or phrase. The conventions are as follows:

Python code
Everything attached to instructions, variables, functions, classes or other elements of Python code will be in the form:

```
#Code python
print('An example')
```

Different text styles have been adopted to enhance the explanatory nature of the content:

Python Syntax: For Python-specific syntax and code examples, we use the COURIER font. For instance, `print("Hello, World!")` is an example of Python syntax.

Defined Elements: Class names, such as **Employee**, are shown in bold to distinguish them from other elements.

Additional explanations are illustrated by a series of pictograms.

Alert
This will be used to draw your attention to a potential problem that may occurr.

Alert
Your attention is drawn here.

Information
This will be used to provide additional information for those who want to go further.

Additional information

information related to the section is presented here.

Source code

All the solutions to the programming problems in this book can be downloaded from the companion website `https://www.github.com/degenio/python_book`.

The pictogram shown within a problem indicates that the solution for the problem is available on the companion website.

Errata

We have taken all necessary precautions to validate the accuracy of the content in this book. The source code has been thoroughly verified with the most recent version of Python.

However, we understand that errors may still occur. If you happen to come across any mistakes in the content or the source code, we kindly request that you reach out to us via email at info@degenio.com, providing specific details about the error, including the page number, section, and the nature of the issue.

Upon receipt of your feedback, we will promptly review and validate the reported errors. Subsequently, we will update the errata section of the book, ensuring that any identified issues are addressed. You can find the updated errata section on our GitHub repository: `https://www.github.com/degenio/python_book/errata`.

We greatly appreciate your help in making this book as accurate and reliable as possible. Your feedback is invaluable to us, and we are committed to delivering the best possible learning experience for our readers.

Questions and feedback

For any questions related to this book, please contact us at info@degenio.com

Chapter 1

Introduction

Contents of this chapter

Objectives

- To describe a development flow in Python
- To explain the notion of a procedural language
- To understand the meaning of object-oriented programming
- To understand the notion of object
- To understand the notion of class
- To setup the Pycharm development environment
- To write a simple Python program

1.1 Python's versions

Python is a programming language developed by Guido Van Rossum in the late 20th century. Its initial release, Version 0.9.0, took place in 1991. Currently, two main versions are prevalent in the market: version 2.X and version 3.X. Python 2.0 was introduced in 2000, with the latest update being released in late 2019. Despite its popularity in certain industries, this version is not actively maintained anymore.

In 2008, Python version 3 was introduced, marking a significant overhaul and even considered a language overhaul in many respects. Python 2.X and 3.X are not directly compatible, necessitating careful consideration while transitioning between them.

The core philosophy behind Python is to make code readable like prose and to ensure ease of development. Python is highly versatile, allowing programmers to write and execute code on various operating systems, including Linux, Windows, Unix, MacOS, and more.

1.2 Python as a programming language

Python is a highly versatile language that is extensively used in various scenarios. Depending on your specific requirements, you can utilize Python in the following ways:

- **Python Script Development**: For smaller projects that require specific functionalities, you can develop Python scripts. These scripts focus on achieving precise tasks. For instance, you could create a script to retrieve data from a text file downloaded from the internet.
- **Python Application Development**: For more extensive projects that encompass multiple functionalities, Python is well-suited for application development. In this context, you can build complete programs to achieve a set of specific tasks. For example, you could develop a media application like a music player.

Before diving into Python development, it is crucial to understand the approach to follow. This includes comprehending the development process for both scripts and larger applications, based on your particular needs.

1.3 Development flow

For the sake of simplicity, the development of a script or program can be broken down into the following steps:

1.3.1 Step 1: Understand the requirements

To develop a program effectively, it is essential to conduct a requirements analysis. For simplicity, this analysis should concentrate on identifying the input data and the desired output data. The main goal is to create one or more procedures that can manipulate the input data to produce the desired output data.

In conclusion, this step can be summarized in the following points:

- There is a need
- The program uses data and applies a given treatment to them
- A specific result is expected

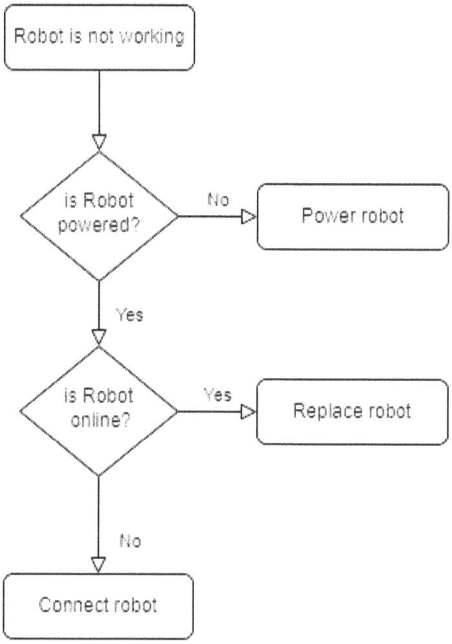

Figure 1.1: Basic algorithm flowchart.

1.3.2 Step 2: Create the algorithm

In this step, we develop the algorithm that will allow us to reach the desired result. We do this by identifying a series of instructions in pseudocode. Pseudocode is a notation that allows us to express these instructions in a logical manner. Alternatively, we can use flowcharts like the one shown in figure 1.1, which incorporate pictograms to represent the basic instructions visually.

To summarize, this step can be broken down into the following three points:

- Identify the data needed
- Know the result to be achieved
- Know how to pass data to the result, which is the algorithm itself.

1.3.3 Step 3: Use a programming language to create the program

In practice, algorithms cannot be executed directly on a processing unit, such as a computer or a micro-controller. They must first be translated into an executable form. This is done by choosing a programming language, such as Python, and then writing code that implements the algorithm. The code can then be executed on the processing unit.

In summary, this step can be broken down into the following three points:

- Choose a programming language.
- Write code that implements the algorithm.
- Execute the code on the processing unit.

1.4 Software production steps

In software development, we refer to the software development life cycle (SDLC). This is a set of steps that are followed to create a software product, such as a script or program.

- **Understanding requirements**: Clearly define the objectives and functionalities the script or program should fulfill. Gather all necessary information and specifications.
- **Planning and design**: Create a high-level plan for the structure and flow of the script or program. This includes defining functions, classes, and the overall architecture.
- **Writing code**: Begin coding based on the established plan. Implement the logic and algorithms needed to achieve the desired functionalities. One or more programming languages are used in this phase.
- **Testing and debugging**: Thoroughly test the script or program to identify and fix any errors or issues. Verify that it meets the specified requirements.
- **Documentation**: Document the code thoroughly to aid future maintenance and understanding.
- **Deployment**: Prepare the script or program for deployment on the intended platform or system.
- **Maintenance**: Continuously maintain the script or program, making necessary updates and improvements as needed.

Before coding a program, we must choose a programming paradigm. Three popular paradigms among developers are:

- Procedural
- Object-oriented
- Functional

The good news is that all three paradigms can be used to develop Python code.

In the following, we will review the procedural and object-oriented approaches, and identify popular languages on the market that use these approaches.

1.5 Procedural languages

A procedural program is made up of several processing units called procedures and functions. These units perform processing on data.

- **Procedure**: Performs processing on data without returning values.
- **Function**: Performs processing on data and return a value after it is invoked.

Figure 1.2 shows examples of treatments that are applied to data.

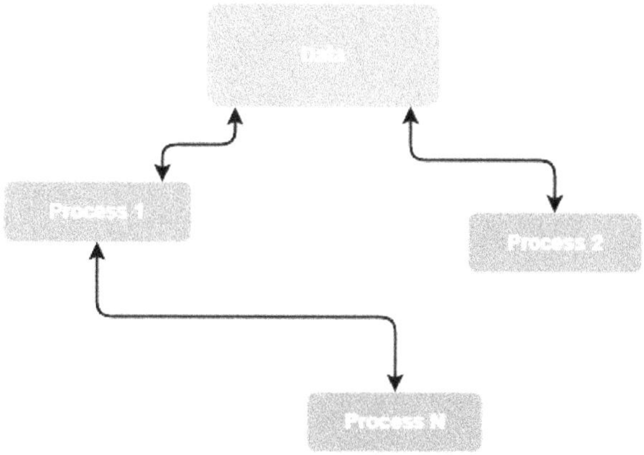

Figure 1.2: Procedural approach.

Languages that can be used with this approach include Fortran, Python and C.

1.6 Object-oriented languages

As shown in figure 1.3, an object-oriented program is made up of several objects. Each object contains:

- Internal data, which is data that is specific to the object.
- Processing, which is code that allows the object to manipulate its internal data or other data.

The interactions between objects are the very essence of the program. An object's data is stored in its attributes, and its processes are its methods (or operations).

Languages that can be used with this approach include Java, C++ and Python.

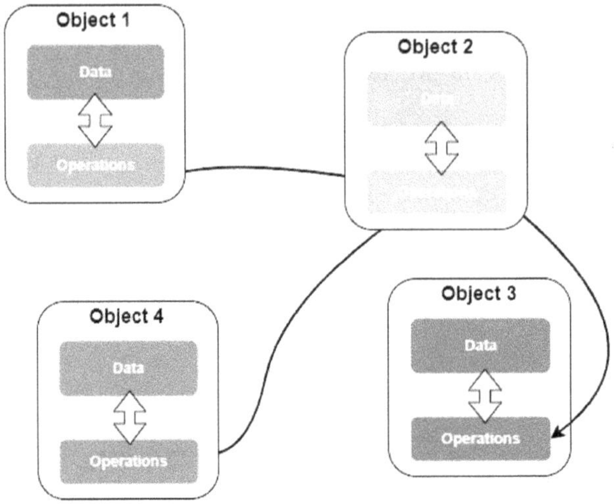

Figure 1.3: Object-oriented approach.

1.6.1 What is an object?

In a procedural approach, the focus is on the actions that the program should perform. In an object-oriented approach, the focus is on the objects that the program will consist of.

For example, in a procedural approach, we might ask "What should my program do to sell a computer?" In an object-oriented approach, we might ask "What objects will my program need to sell a computer?"

Taking the computer store in figure 1.4 as an example, we can identify several objects that would be involved in selling a computer, such as a customer, a salesperson, a computer, and a payment. These objects can be similar or different depending on their role in the sale. For example, all customers are similar in that they want to buy a computer, but salespeople and computers can be different depending on their specific roles.

The object-oriented approach is often seen as a more natural way to model the world, as it allows us to think about the objects that are involved in a problem and the relationships between them.

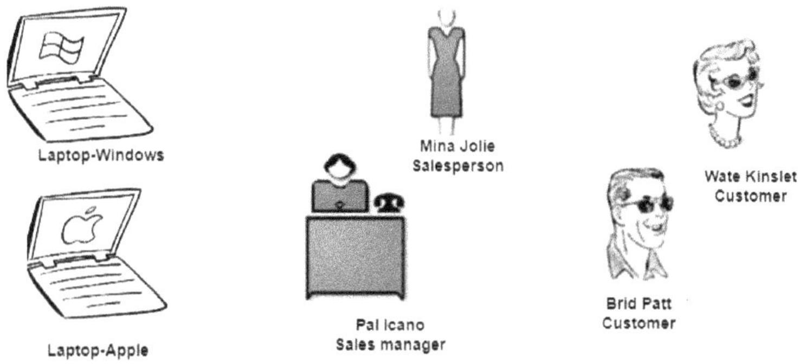

Figure 1.4: Objects in a program.

1.6.2 What is a class?

Based on the example in figure 1.4, similar objects can be described by the same abstraction, which we will call a class.

A class contains structures for data storage and operations or methods.

Figure 1.5 shows the possible classes that can be isolated: the **Customer** class, the **Employee** class, and the **Laptop** class.

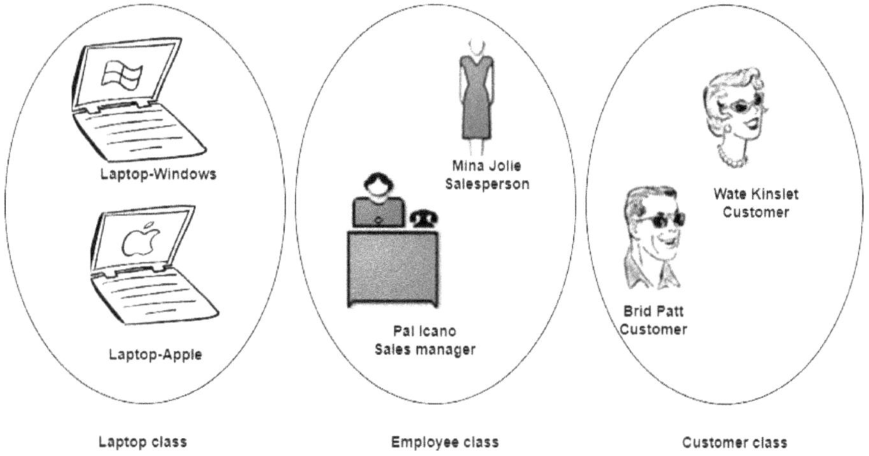

Figure 1.5: Model classes.

For each object that is created from a class, we will have to define the data that is specific to that object.

1.6.3 Class members

A class is made up of several members, each of which is either:

- **An attribute**: A typed variable that stores data about the class.
- **A method**: A set of processing statements that defines the behavior of the class.

Chapter 7 discusses in detail the concept of classes and objects in the context of object-oriented programming.

1.7 Development phases in Python

Python is an interpreted language, which means that the instructions in a Python script are translated into machine code one at a time as they are executed. This is in contrast to compiled languages, in which the entire program is translated into machine code before it is executed.

Figure 1.6 shows the difference between Python, an interpreted language, and Java, a compiled language.

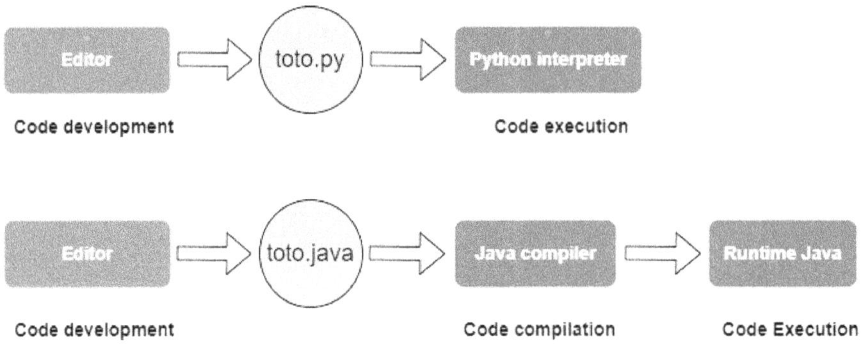

Figure 1.6: Producing Python vs Java code.

As an interpreted language, Python has both advantages and disadvantages.

One advantage is that the code is portable, meaning that it can be run on different platforms without having to be recompiled. This is because the instructions are interpreted by the Python interpreter, rather than being compiled into machine code for a specific platform.

Another advantage is that it is easier to debug, since the interpreter can provide feedback on errors as they occur.

However, interpreted languages in general can be slower than compiled languages, since the instructions need to be interpreted every time they are executed. Future versions of Python are supposed to be much faster.

In general, Python is a good choice for rapid prototyping and scripting, where speed is not the most important factor. However, for performance-critical applications, a compiled language may be a better choice.

Task	Tool	Output
Editing	Notepad or IDLE or IDE such as PyCharm	File with extension *.py
Running	Python Interpreter	Output

Table 1.1: Python development toolchain.

The editing tools shown in table 1.1 include PyCharm from JetBrains, IDLE, which comes with Python or Microsoft's Visual Studio with Python extensions, and PyDev on Eclipse. In this book, we adopted PyCharm for its ease of use. However, you can use other IDEs (integrated development environments) as you see it fit.

1.8 Read and write instructions

To get started with Python, we'll learn the basic read and write instructions. We can think of our program as receiving input data through a reading system, performing some processing, and then sending the processed output to a writing system.

The diagram in figure 1.7 shows this concept.

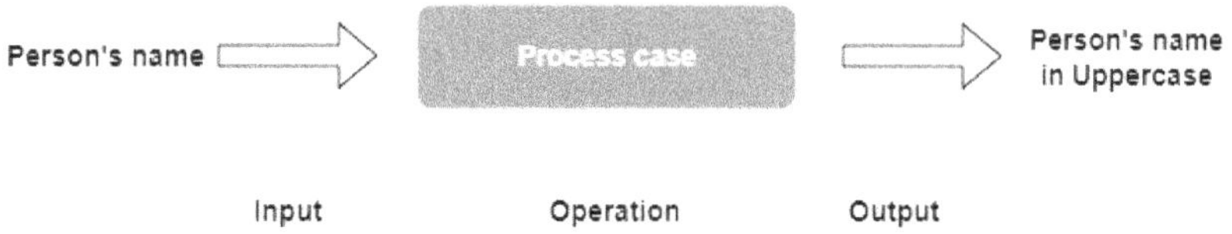

Figure 1.7: Processing instructions with Python.

In this case, we receive the name of the person as data. This is the input step. We then process the data by transforming it into uppercase. Finally, we output the processed data.

For most of the problems in this book, we will use the reading and writing systems listed in table 1.2. Python has built-in functions that allow us to perform these operations. Table 1.2 lists the systems and functions that we will use.

System	Operation	Python function
Read	Keyboard	`input()`
Write	Screen-console	`print()`

Table 1.2: Read and write operations.

In order to store the data, we will use variables. These are special memory storage unit that will be defined in Chapter 2.

The code used to perform the read operation is described in listing 1.1.

Listing 1.1: Reading and writing data.

```
name = input('Please enter your name:')
print('Your name is:', name)
```

After the name is entered, the output is:

Output in execution mode

```
Please enter your name: Flouflou
Your name is: Flouflou
```

1.9 Quiz

Please answer the following questions. There may be one or more correct answers.

1. Python is an interpreted language:
   (a) True
   (b) False

2. Among the programming approaches that can be used in Python, we have the:
   (a) Declarative
   (b) Object-oriented
   (c) Procedural
   (d) Functional

3. Some of the steps used in software production are:
   (a) Analysis
   (b) Coding
   (c) Drawing
   (d) Test

4. To indicate a certain code structure in a script or program, Python uses indentation:
   (a) True
   (b) False

5. If a script developed with version 3 of Python requires the use of a module that only exists in version 2 of Python, we can integrate it directly into the script:
   (a) True
   (b) False

6. If a Python script is developed on a Windows machine, it can also be run on a Linux machine:
   (a) True
   (b) False

7. Python can be used in many areas including:
   (a) All areas of Science

(b) Data visualization
(c) Artificial intelligence
(d) All of the above

8. IDLE is an integrated code editor provided with Python:
   (a) True
   (b) Falase

9. One can program and run Python code on the following operating systems:
   (a) Linux
   (b) Windows
   (c) MacOS
   (d) All of the above

10. A program developed according to a procedural approach uses objects and method calls:
    (a) True
    (b) False

1.10 Laboratory: Setting up the development environment

Manipulations

- Manipulation 1: Installing Python
- Manipulation 2: Installation of the Pycharm IDE
- Manipulation 3: Getting started with the Pycharm IDE
- Manipulation 4: Modifying output instructions
- Manipulation 5: Modifying display instructions

1.10.1 Manipulation 1: Python installation

Objective

Install Python.

Context

Access to the internet to download the Python installer.

Procedure

Python is available for a wide range of platforms including Windows, Mac, and Linux. The main download site is `https://www.python.org`

The download link is accessible through the main menu on python.org, as shown in figure 1.8. The following shows the installation procedure for Windows.

Figure 1.8: Python download link.

- Click on the download button or link. The version shown is the one available in December 2022, which is version 3.11. It is possible that when you visit the link, a new version is available. In this case, the installation steps should be the same.
- Once the installer has been downloaded, proceed to launch it. The installation screen is similar to the one shown in figure 1.9. You will have a different installation path in your case.
  The installation path in figure 1.9 is for the user named degenio2020.
- Click on the **Install Now** option. If there is a user account control prompt, click on **Yes** to continue the installation.

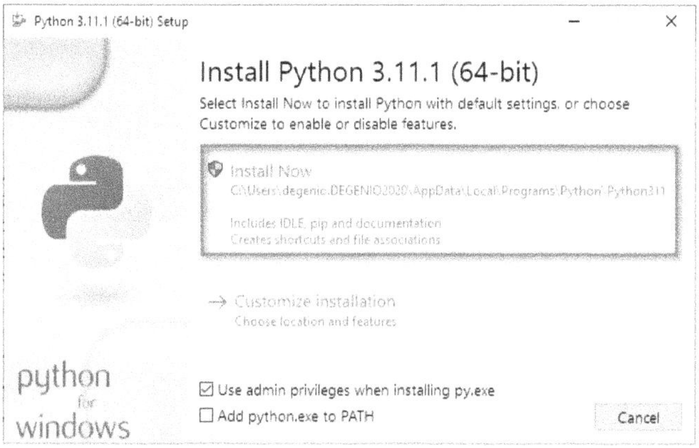

Figure 1.9: Python installation screen.

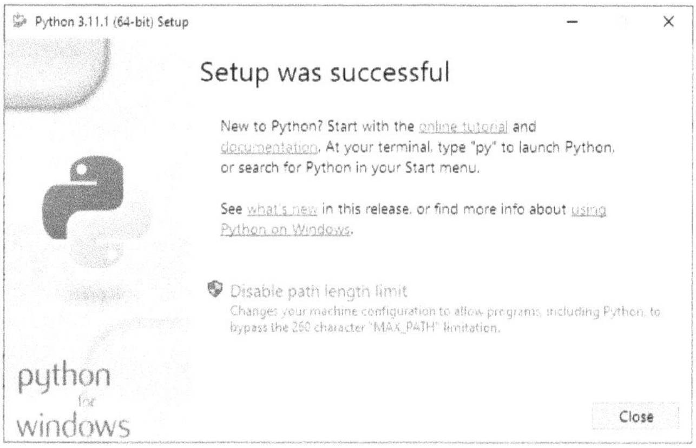

Figure 1.10: Confirmation of Python installation.

The installation will take a few minutes and a confirmation screen will appear at the end, as shown in figure 1.10.

- Now, we will check the version of Python installed on your machine. Open a DOS window. This can be launched by using the command **CMD** in the Windows search bar.
  Next, run the command **python –version** as shown in figure1.11. It should display the current version of Python that you just installed.
- To validate the installation, we will run a display command through Python. This is the famous **Hello World** of programming. First, launch the Python interpreter by typing the command **python** followed by the **Enter** key. We will see the prompt >>> appear as shown in figure 1.12.
- Type the command `print("Hello World")` function. We will also indicate the string to be displayed. The string is enclosed in double or single quotes. Press

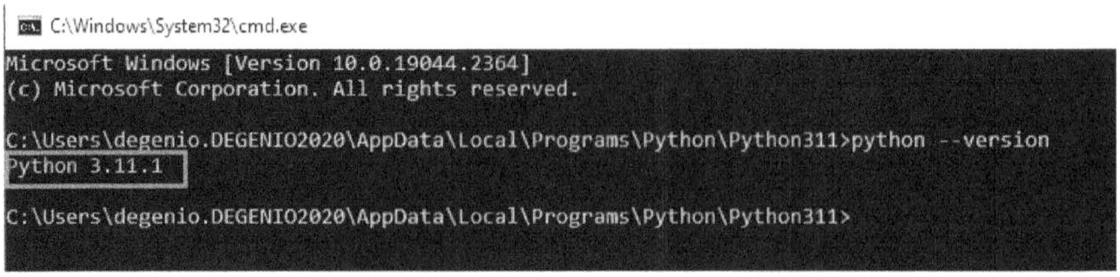

Figure 1.11: Confirmation of the installed Python version.

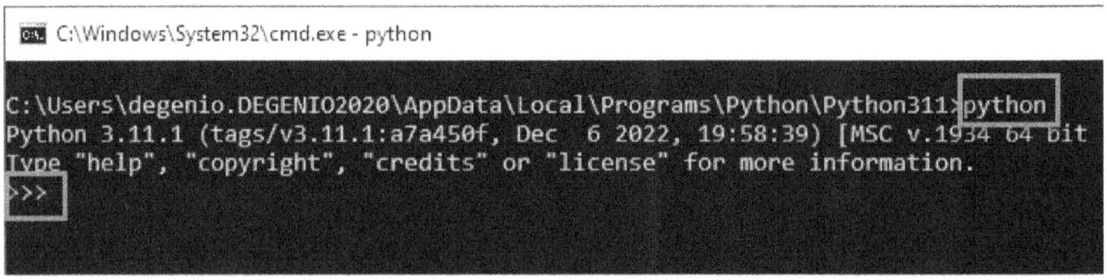

Figure 1.12: Launching the Python interpreter.

Enter to execute the command. This gives the result shown in figure 1.13.

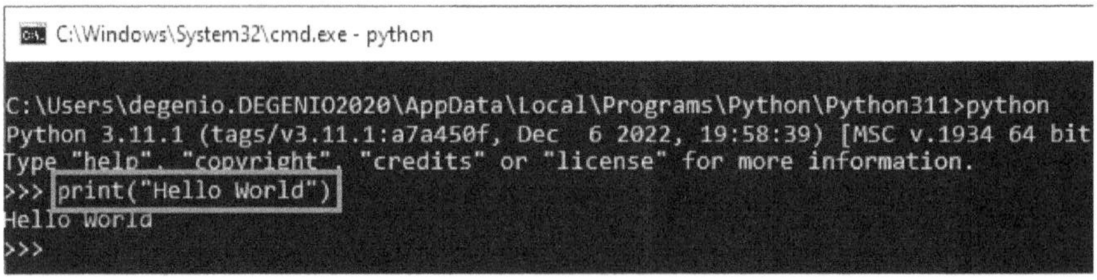

Figure 1.13: Executing a basic instruction.

- To exit the interpreter, press **Ctrl+Z** and then press **Enter**. Alternatively, you can always type the command `exit()` to exit.

1.10.2 Manipulation 2: Installing the PyCharm IDE

Objective

Install PyCharm IDE.

Context

Internet access is available to download the PyCharm IDE installer.

Procedure

The PyCharm Integrated Development Environment (IDE) is provided by JetBrains. The company has put on the market a number of development environments, including IntelliJ and AndroidStudio. In the case of Python, it offers the **PyCharm** environment. It is available in two versions, the Professional Edition and the Community Edition.

A major difference between the two versions is the support for the development of web applications with Python, which is natively offered in the Professional Edition. In this book, we will use the Community Edition. It is frequently updated and you should not see any major differences when installing your version.

The download link is available on `https://www.jetbrains.com/pycharm/download/` as shown in figure 1.14.

Figure 1.14: Download link for the Python Pycharm IDE.

The following steps show the installation procedure for Windows. The steps should be the same for Linux or MacOS.

- Click on the specified download button or link. The version shown is the one available in December 2022, which is version 2022.3.1. It is possible that a newer version is available in your case. However, the process should be very similar, and the installation steps should remain the same.

Figure 1.15: Pycharm installation ccreen.

- Once the PyCharm installer program has been downloaded, proceed to launch it. The installation screen will be similar to the one shown in figure 1.15.

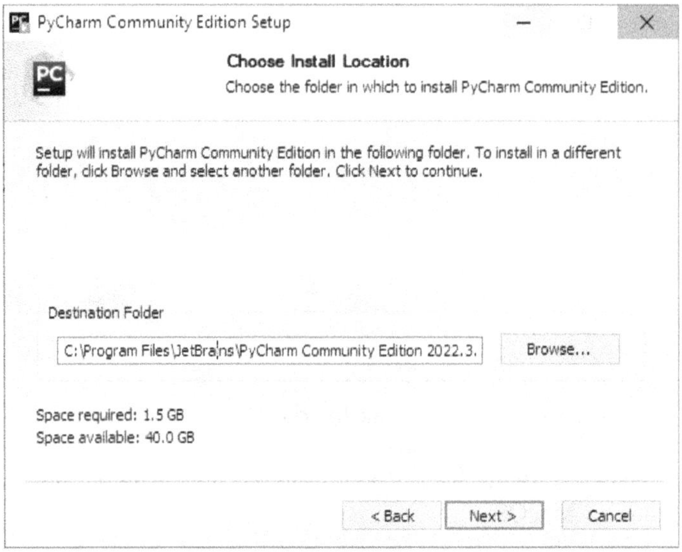

Figure 1.16: Pycharm installation screen, selecting an installation path.

- On the following screen, you will need to verify and choose the installation path.

In figure 1.16, the path shown is for users who are administrators of the machine. If you are not the administrator, it will prompt you to install PyCharm in your personal profile.

- Click the **Next** button.

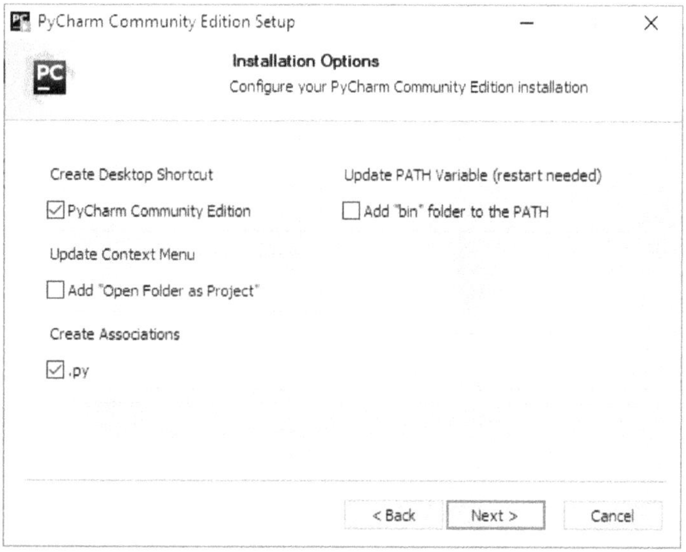

Figure 1.17: Associating the .py extension with Python files.

- As illustrated in figure 1.17, you can associate the *.py* extension with Python files.
- On the following screen, leave the options as default and click the **Install** button.

Figure 1.18: Confirmation of the installation.

- The installation process will take a few minutes, and a confirmation screen will appear at the end, as shown in figure 1.18.

By following these steps, PyCharm will be successfully installed on your Windows system. The same steps should be followed for MacOS or Linux.

1.10.3 Manipulation 3: Getting started with the PyCharm IDE

Objective

Write and run a simple program.

Context

The PyCharm IDE and Python 3.X are available.

Procedure

Follow the instructions below to create a project for this laboratory.

- Create a new project as shown in the following screen. Note that the screen may be different in your case. What is important for you is to find the **New project** button.

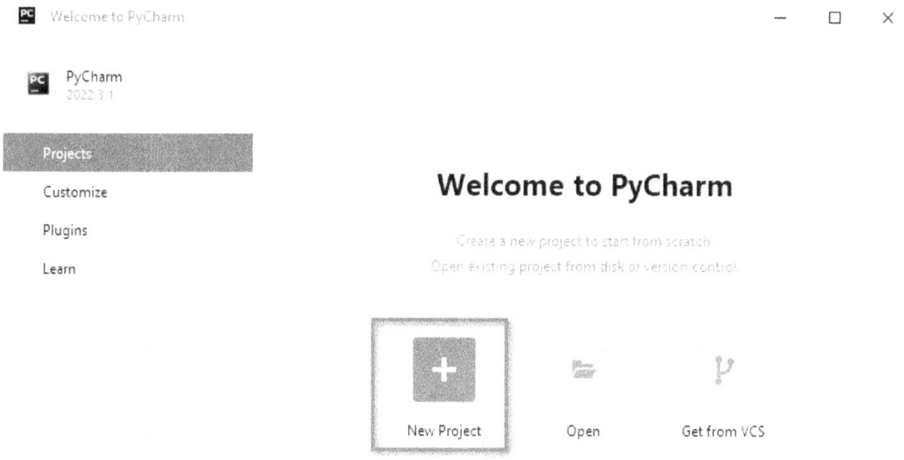

Figure 1.19: Creating a project.

- Specify the project location and the interpreter that will be used for the project. Note that we will use Python version 3.11 (or newer). The project should be named **lab1_part1**. We don't want to create a **main** module for the time being so you should uncheck the checkbox as shown in figure 1.20.
- A Python project in PyCharm will contain modules or files. Packages or directories are used to organize the source code. For now, we will not create a package.
- Create your first Python module. Right-click and select the "Create Python file" option as shown in figure 1.21.

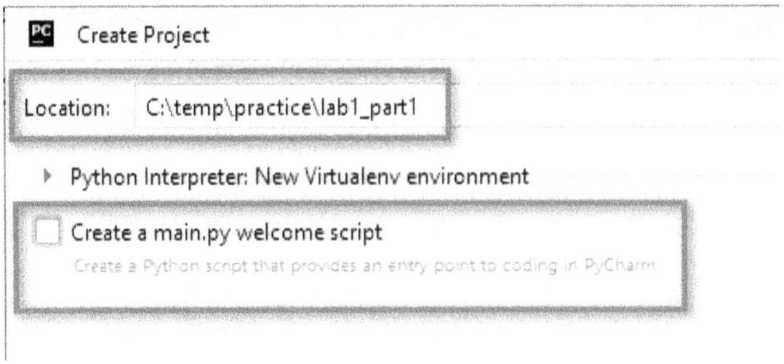

Figure 1.20: Project location.

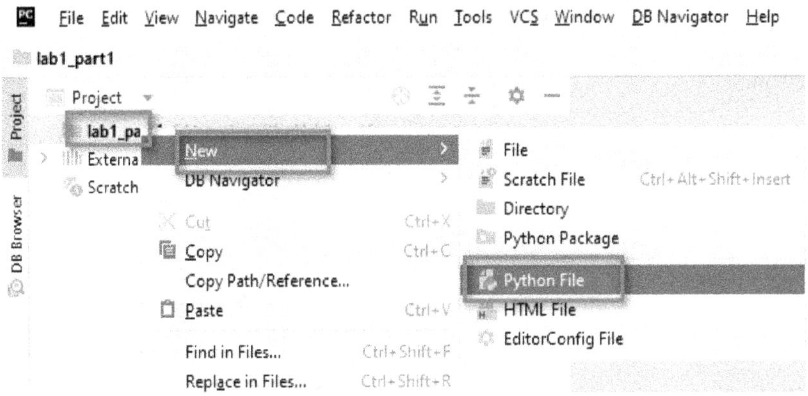

Figure 1.21: Creating a module in Pycharm.

- A good convention to adopt is to prefix modules with **mod_**. This will avoid circular references (during import operations) if by mistake you give your module the same name of a module you are trying to import.
- Name your module **mod_world.py**.

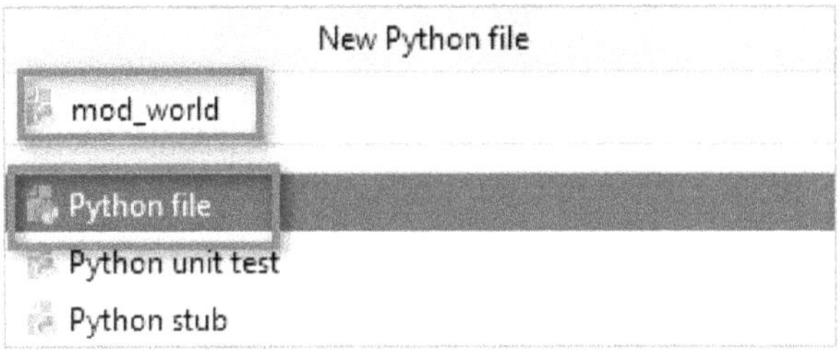

Figure 1.22: Module name.

- The final project structure in PyCharm should look like figure 1.23. Depending on the exact version of Pycharm, you might have the **venv** directory. This is the virtual environment or directory that will be used for the libraries and other modules that you may import into your project. For now, you don't need to worry about this environment.

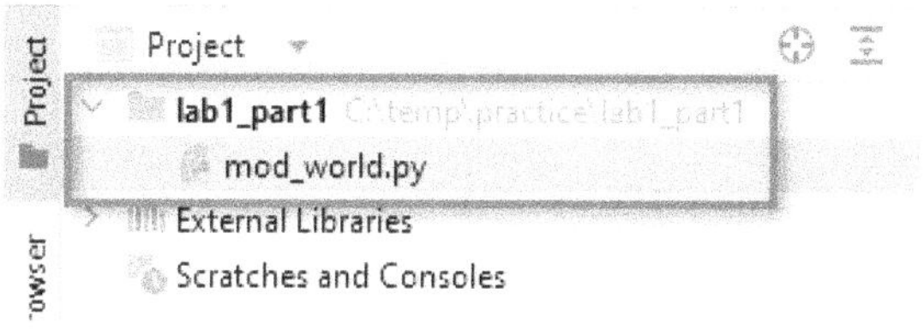

Figure 1.23: Project structure.

- Write the code indicated in figure 1.24 as is. This code will display the string of characters at the console level.

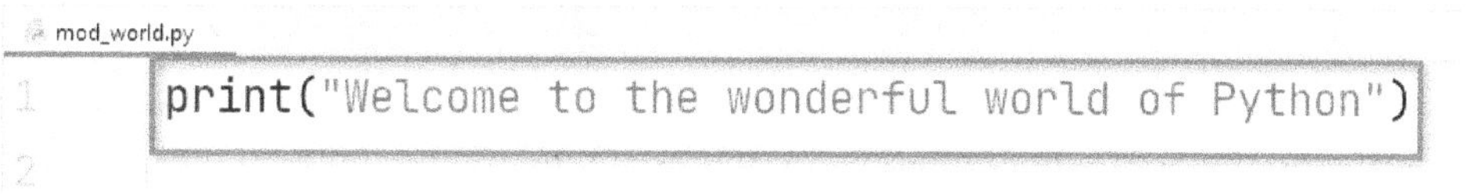

Figure 1.24: Basic print statement.

- Execute your program by clicking on **Run** in the menu or by pressing the keys **CTRL+SHIFT+F10**.
- If you have no errors, you will see the output shown in figure 1.25 in the console.

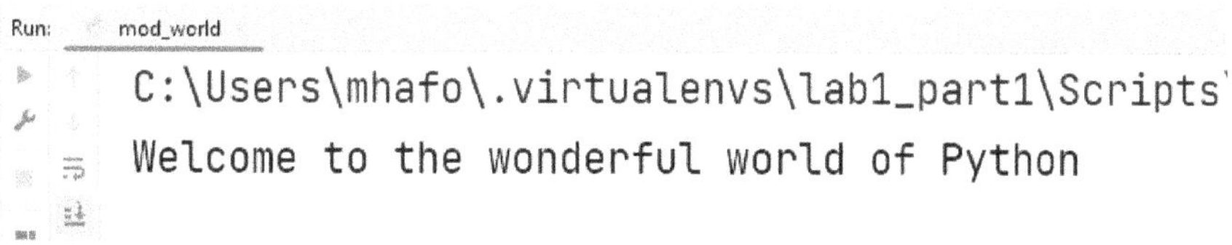

Figure 1.25: Console output.

- Change your code by adding a print statement that displays the message **Goodbye and see you soon**. Run your program.

Resetting the PyCharm interface to its initial state

If your IDE no longer looks the same as it did when you first started it, you can reset it by clicking on the Window-Restore Default Layout *option in the menu bar.*

1.10.4 Manipulation 4: Modifying output instructions

Objective

Modify and run a simple program.

Context

The PyCharm IDE and Python 3.X are available.

Procedure

- Create a new project. We will not use the string directly in the `print()` function, as shown in listing 1.2:

Listing 1.2: Basic print statement

```
print('Welcome to the wonderful world of Python')
```

- We will use a variable as indicated in listing 1.3:

Listing 1.3: Code using a variable.

```
message = 'Welcome to the wonderful world of Python'
print(message)
```

- Run your program. Note the messages you get in the Output tab.
- What do you notice?

Chapter 2

Basic Syntax

Contents of this chapter

Objectives:

- To understand the structure of a Python program
- To use variables to store data
- To identify and use data types in Python
- To use naming conventions
- To identify operators in Python
- To cast the value of one type to another type
- To write Python programs to perform basic computations

2.1 Python programs

The source code of a Python program is contained in one or more files with the **.py** extension. Ideally, file names should be lowercase to avoid casing issues when running code on case-sensitive machines like Linux. The file may contain instructions, functions, classes, or other constructs written in Python.

From the point of view of Python terminology, a file corresponds to a module.

2.1.1 Comments

A comment is a text that can be added to the code to explain a line or a set of lines of code. Comments are included to make the code easier to read in the future. Note that a comment will be ignored by the Python interpreter at runtime.

To put a line in a comment, you can use the # symbol at the beginning of the line. A shortcut to comment out lines of code in Pycharm is **CTL** followed by /.

For multiple lines of comments, you can use the triple-quote notation `'''`. The triple-quotes must be closed with another `'''`.

Listing 2.1: Example of comments in a Python script

```
'''My comments
spanning multiple lines'''
# Single-line comment by Alain Flouclair

def main():
    print('Hello World')
```

2.1.2 Declaration or assignment of variables

Variables can be used to store data that is needed by the program. They can also be used to pass data between functions.

In Python, a variable is a reference to a value stored in memory. The variable name can be composed of upper and lower case letters (A-Z, a-z), numbers (0-9), and the underscore character _. The name cannot start with a number, and Python is case-sensitive. Thus, **Name**, **name** and **NAME** do not designate the same variable.

Unlike other languages, Python does not require a declaration of the type of data to be stored in the variable. To create a variable in Python, we proceed by assigning a value to this variable.

A variable can contain for example:

- A number
- An object or function
- A string

Listing 2.2: Assigning a value to a variable

```
# Assignment
name = 'Alain Flouflou'
```

Following this assignment, a **name** variable will be created and will reference the value

'Alain Flouflou'.

Each variable will have a unique identifier called **id** and an associated **type**. They can be obtained using the `id()` and `type()` functions as shown in the following code:

Listing 2.3: Identifying a variable

```
name = 'Alain Flouflou'
# Display the type
print(type(name))
# Display the identity or id
print(id(name))
```

Note: The **id** obtained when you run your own code will most likely be different from the one shown in listing 2.4.

Listing 2.4: Execution output

```
<class 'str'>
12993504
```

2.1.3 Declaration of constants

In Python, there is no concept of a constant in the traditional sense. However, it is common practice to use variables whose values are not expected to change during the execution of the program. These variables are often called pseudo-constants.

The name of a pseudo-constant is typically written in all uppercase letters, by convention. This helps to distinguish pseudo-constants from other variables in the code.

For example, the following code defines a pseudo-constant called **PI**:

```
PI = 3.14159
```

The value of **PI** is not explicitly declared as a constant in Python. However, the convention of writing the name in all uppercase letters helps to indicate that the value of **PI** should not be changed during the execution of the program.

It is important to note that the value of a pseudo-constant can still be changed by the programmer. However, this is not recommended, as it can lead to errors in the program.

Initialization of a constant

A constant will be initialized in the same manner as a variable.

```
CONSTANT_NAME = value1
```

Example

```
INTEREST_RATE = 0.12
```

2.2 Data types in Python

In Python, you can work with various data types, such as numeric types, character strings, complex numbers, dates, and more.

Python has a set of built-in data types that are available by default. These data types include numeric types, character strings, complex numbers, dates, and booleans. There's no need to import any additional modules to use these fundamental types.

2.2.1 Data type – Boolean

The boolean data type, also known as `bool`, represents a variable that can have one of two possible values: `True` or `False`.

The significance of this representation will become clearer within the context of repetitive and decision structures. In these situations, we use boolean expressions or variables to determine whether a particular condition exists.

Origin of the word Boolean

In the nineteenth century, English mathematician George Boole invented the concept of `True` and `False` in mathematical calculations.

What becomes essential is identifying either the `True` value, signifying the occurrence of an event, for example, or its opposite, the `False` value, indicating the non-occurrence of the event of interest.

In listing 2.5, we assess whether a student has a passing grade or not by setting the passing limit to 60.

Listing 2.5: Using a boolean

```
final_grade = int(input('Enter your final grade:'))
if final_grade >= 60:
    result = True
else:
    result = False
```

The control variable which is **result** can now be used to make a decision, for example displaying a congratulatory message as shown in listing 2.6.

Listing 2.6: Using a boolean flag variable

```
final_grade = int(input('Enter your final grade:'))
if final_grade >= 60:
    result = True
else:
    result = False

if result:
    print('Congratulations, you have passed the course!')
```

Note: in listing 2.6, we don't really need to compare the value of **result** to `True`. In addition, we did not display any message when the condition is `False`.

2.2.2 Data type – None

The `None` type is a special value that signifies:

- Non-existence
- Unknown
- Empty

Listing 2.7: Type None

```
def fun():
    pass

print (fun())
```

This feature proves to be particularly valuable in situations where a function returns no value.

2.2.3 Data type – Numeric

This data type can represent the following types of numbers:

- integers
- real numbers
- complex numbers

Listing 2.8: Integer numeric type

```
val1 = 11
val2 = 34
```

```
# total
total = val1 + val2
# Display the result
print('Total:', total)
```

Listing 2.9: Output in execution mode

```
Total: 45
```

Numbers are stored differently in memory based on their nature, and their type is determined following these rules:

- If a numeric value is written without a decimal point, it will be considered an `int` type. For example, the numbers `11`, `300`, and `2456` are considered `int` .
- If a numeric value is written with a decimal point, it will be considered a `float` type. The decimal representation must use a period as a separator. For instance, the numbers `11.5`, `300.24`, and `2456.17` are considered `float`.
- When a variable is initialized in the form `2+5j`, including both a real part and an imaginary part, it represents a complex number.

2.2.4 Data Type - `str`

This data type is used to represent textual data or character strings. Variables of type `str` can be created using the following symbols:

- `'`
- `"`
- Multi-line string: `'''` or `"""`

Listing 2.10 shows the different ways to declare a string.

Listing 2.10: Strings

```
a = "Alain flouflou"
b = 'Flouclair'
c = ''' His name
is Abdel Flouclair
'''
```

2.3 Python essentials

In this section, we will cover the fundamental elements of the Python language, including naming conventions, various operators, and other essential elements.

2.3.1 Naming conventions

Maintaining a consistent naming convention for variables and constants is crucial to any script or program. Furthermore, these conventions also extend to other constructs within our program, such as functions, classes, packages, etc.

In most programming languages, you can choose from the following three approaches:

- **CamelCase**: The first letter is lowercase, and each subsequent word begins with a capital letter.
  - Example: `myInterestRate`
- **SnakeCase**: All words are in lowercase and separated by the symbol `_`.
  - Example: `my_interest_rate`
- **PascalCase**: The first letter of each word is capitalized.
  - Example: `FinanceExtra`

The Python language specification includes precise guidelines for naming conventions, known as `PEP` 8[1]. This document outlines the recommended conventions for writing Python code.

Regarding variable names, it is suggested to follow the snake case convention. However, when employing object-oriented programming, adopting CamelCase or PascalCase conventions is preferred.

2.3.2 Python statements

Python code consists of a series of instructions. These can be on one or more lines.

Listing 2.11: Block of instructions

```
import time

current_time = time.time()
# seconds
total_seconds = int(current_time)
print('Total:', total_seconds)
```

Output in execution mode

```
Total: 1586011389
```

[1] `https://www.python.org/dev/peps/pep-0008/`

2.3.3 Concatenation of strings

There are different ways to combine strings in Python, as shown in the following examples:

Listing 2.12: Concatenation of strings

```
# Example 1: Repeating a string multiple times using the * operator
result = 'apple ' * 3
print(result)

# Example 2: Joining two strings without any space in between
result = 'Apple ' 'MacIntosh'
print(result)

# Example 3: Combining multiple strings using the + operator
result = 'Apple ' + 'Mc ' + 'Intosh'
print(result)
```

Output in execution mode

```
apple apple apple
Apple MacIntosh
Apple Mc Intosh
```

In the first example, we use the * operator to repeat the string 'apple ' three times, resulting in 'apple apple apple'.

In the second example, we simply join the strings 'Apple ' and 'MacIntosh' without any space in between, giving us 'Apple MacIntosh'.

Finally, in the third example, we combine the strings 'Apple ', 'Mc ', and 'Intosh' using the + operator, which gives us 'Apple Mc Intosh'.

String concatenation is a useful technique for creating customized messages, greetings, or even manipulating text in your Python programs.

2.3.4 Blocks of instructions and indentation

A block of instructions in Python is delimited using indentation. An increase in indentation occurs after certain statements like `if`. This means that you are now within a specific scope. A decrease in indentation indicates the end of the current block or exiting the scope. In Python, four spaces are recommended for indentation. Typically, your IDE allows you to configure the number of spaces for indentation.

Listing 2.13: Indentation in a conditional structure

```
if age > 18:
    print('Adult person')
```

2.3.5 Delimiters

Delimiters are markers consisting of one or more characters used to specify the boundary between different regions in text or other structures. The following delimiters are commonly used in Python.

```
( ) [ ] { }
, : . ` = ;
+= -= *= /= //= %=
<= |= ^= >>= <<= **=
' " \ @
```

They are helpful in constructing expressions, strings, dictionaries, lists, etc.

2.3.6 Python keywords

Like all programming languages, Python has the following keywords (version 3.11):

```
False      await      else       import     pass
None       break      except     in         raise
True       class      finally    is         return
and        continue   for        lambda     try
as         def        from       nonlocal   while
assert     del        global     not        with
async      elif       if         or         yield
```

Please note that you cannot use them as variable names in your code. For example, figure 2.1 shows the error that happens when trying to use `and` as a variable name.

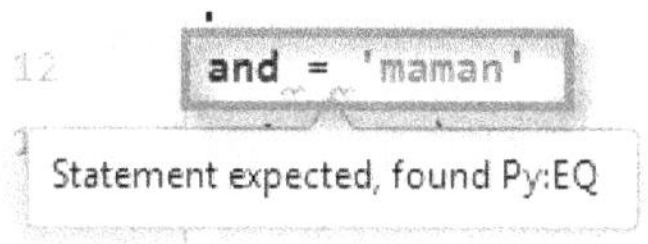

Figure 2.1: Unauthorized use of a keyword as a variable name.

How to Find the Keywords in your version of Python?

In PyCharm, you can use the following command `help('keywords')` *to display the list of keywords corresponding to your version of Python.*

2.3.7 Python expressions and operators

The Python language provides numerous operators for performing arithmetic operations, as well as comparison operations among others.

An operator is used to perform an operation on one or more operands. An operand can be a value, such as the numeric `5`, the string `'Flouflou'`, or a variable referencing a value in memory.

```
a = 12
b = 15
result = a + b
```

In the previous example, we used the arithmetic addition operator, the assignment operator, and two operands.

The assignment operator in Python is represented by the symbol `=`, and it's important to remember that the destination can be a variable, multiple variables, or constants. The expression on the right-hand side of the assignment can be a variable, a constant, or a combination of variables and constants connected by operators.

2.4 Operators

An operator is a symbol used to perform an action on a certain value. The operator can be unary, binary, or ternary.

- **Unary**: The operation involves only one operand.
- **Binary**: The operation involves two operands.
- **Ternary**: The operation involves three operands.

In Python programming, you will encounter various unary and binary operators that allow you to perform different types of operations on values and variables. Understanding and using these operators is essential for writing effective Python code.

2.4.1 Arithmetic operators

The arithmetic operators available in Python are the ones commonly used in regular mathematical operations. However, it is important to note that floor division works differently from regular division.

The arithmetic operators available in Python are given in table 2.1.

Operator	Operation	Example
+	Addition	`a + b`
-	Subtraction	`a - b`
*	Multiplication	`a * b`
**	Exponentiation	`a ** b`
/	Division	`a / b`
//	Floor Division: quotient rounded to the nearest integer	`a // b`
%	Modulo: remainder of the division	`a % b`

Table 2.1: Arithmetic operators.

Listing 2.14: Python operators

```
a = 15
b = 2
#Addition
resa = a + b
#Subtraction
ress = a - b
#Multiplication
resm = a * b
#Exponentiation
rese = a ** b
#Floor division
resd = a / b
#Division
resde = a // b
#Modulo
resmo = a % b
```

If we were to display the results of the previous operations, we would add the `print()` function call for each of the output variables.

Output in execution mode

```
17
13
30
225
7.5
7
1
```

2.4.2 Arithmetic operators - precedence

Table 2.2 provides the order of precedence for arithmetic operators. In case of ambiguity in the evaluation order, it is advisable to use parentheses to group the necessary operations together. Appendix A provides more details on the use of operator precedence.

Operator	Operation	Evaluation Order
( )	Allows grouping	Left to Right
*, /, //, %	Multiplication, division, floor division, modulo	Left to Right
+, -	Addition, subtraction	Left to Right
=	Assignment	Right to Left

Table 2.2: Operator precedence.

2.4.3 Relational-comparison operators

This type of operator allows us to compare two operands. The result is a boolean value that can be `True` or `False`.

These operators are useful in the repetitive and decision structures that we will see later.

Listing 2.15: Relational operators

```
a = 15
b = 2
# equal to
print(a == b)
# not equal to
print(a != b)
```

```
# less than
print(a < b)
# greater than
print(a > b)
# less than or equal to
print(a <= b)
# greater than or equal to
print(a >= b)
```

If we were to display the results of the previous operations, we would have:

Output in execution mode

```
False
True
False
True
False
True
```

The available relational operators in Python are given in table 2.3.

Operator	Operation	Example
`==`	equal to	`a == b`
`!=`	not equal to	`a != b`
`<`	less than	`a < b`
`>`	greater than	`a > b`
`<=`	less than or equal to	`a <= b`
`>=`	greater than or equal to à	`a >= b`

Table 2.3: Relational operators.

2.4.4 Logical operators

Let's imagine that we have the possibility of two events **a** and **b** occurring. If the event happens, we assign the value `True` to it. Otherwise, we assign the value `False`.

If we are interested in evaluating the simultaneous occurrence of both events **a** and **b**, we will use the `and` operator to connect the expressions **a** and **b**.

We would evaluate the combined expression `a and b`.

Now, if we are interested in the occurrence of either event **a** or **b**, we will use the `or` operator to connect the expressions **a** and **b**.

Operator	Operation	Example
`not`	`True` if the operand is `False`. `False` if the operand is `True`	`not a`
`and`	`True` if both operands are `True`. `False` if one of the operands is `False`	`a and b`
`or`	`True` if at least one of the operands is `True`. `False` if both operands are `False`	`a or b`

Table 2.4: Logical operators.

In this case, we would evaluate the combined expression `a or b`.

On the other hand, if we are interested in the non-occurrence of an event, we will use the unary `not` operator . For example, the non-occurrence of event **a** would be evaluated by the expression `not a`.

These operators will be useful in the repetitive and decision structures that we will see later.

2.4.5 Truth table

When working with logical operators, we use what is called the truth table. This table lists expressions showing all possible combinations of `True` and `False` related to the logical operator.

The `not` Operator

With this operator, the output result is the inverse of what we receive as input.

a	Expression Value
`True`	`False`
`False`	`True`

Table 2.5: The `not` operator.

Listing 2.16 shows the effect of the `not` operator on variables **a** and **b**.

Listing 2.16: The not operator

```
a = True
#not a
print(not a)
b = False
#not b
print(not b)
```

If we were to print the results of the previous operations, the output would be:

Output in execution mode

```
False
True
```

The `and` operator

For this operator, the output is `True` only if both operands are `True`. Moreover, if the first operand, **a**, is `False`, the output is automatically `False`, and in this case, there is no need to evaluate the operand **b**.

a	b	Expression Value
True	False	False
False	True	False
False	False	False
True	True	True

Table 2.6: The `and` operator.

An example of using the `and` operator is shown in listing 2.17.

Listing 2.17: The and operator

```
a = True
b = False
#and
print(a and b)
```

If we were to print the result of the previous operation, the output would be:

Output in execution mode

```
False
```

The or operator

The output for the or operator is True when either of the two operands is True. Moreover, if the first operand, **a**, is True, the output is automatically True, and in this case, there is no need to evaluate the operand **b**. The output is False when both operands are False.

a	b	Expression Value
True	False	True
False	True	True
False	False	False
True	True	True

Table 2.7: The or operator.

An example of using the or operator is shown in listing 2.18.

Listing 2.18: The or operator

```
a = True
b = False
#or
print(a or b)
```

If we were to print the result of the previous operation, the output would be:

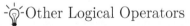

Output in execution mode

```
True
```

Other Logical Operators

Python also provides Bitwise OR, Bitwise XOR, and Bitwise AND operators.

2.5 Explicit conversion

When we need to convert data from one type to another, we use explicit conversion or cast. The Python syntax for this conversion is as follows:

```
Type (expression)
```

where Type is a specific Python data type, such as int, for example.

Listing 2.19: Explicit cast

```
import time
current_time = time.time()
# seconds
total_seconds = int(current_time)
print(total_seconds)
```

Output in execution mode

```
1586012219
```

In the code example, we import the time module to work with time-related functions. The time.time() function returns the current time in seconds as a floating-point number. By using int() to explicitly convert this value to an integer, we get the total number of seconds since a specific reference point (epoch). The converted value is then printed, showing the total number of seconds.

2.6 Other useful notations in Python

In the case of an assignment operation where a variable appears on both sides of the = operator, as in the following example:

```
a = 15
a = a + 13
```

we can use a much shorter but equivalent notation:

```
a = 15
a += 13
```

Of course, if the expression on the right-hand side of the assignment operator is more complex, involving references to other variables in addition to the variable on the left-hand side of the assignment, we can still use the same notation:

```
b = 7
a = 15
a = a + b + 13
a += b + 13#shorter version
```

This technique applies to other operators as summarized in table 2.8.

Example	Operator	Equivalence
`x += 5`	`+=`	`x = x + 5`
`x -= 5`	`-=`	`x = x - 5`
`x *= 5`	`*=`	`x = x * 5`
`x /= 5`	`/=`	`x = x / 5`
`x %= 5`	`%=`	`x = x % 5`

Table 2.8: Augmented operator and equivalence.

This notation provides a convenient way to simplify expressions and make the code more concise and readable.

2.6.1 Functions

In Python, a function groups a set of instructions to perform a specific task. We use the keyword `def` to declare a function. Later in Chapter 5, we will go through different ways to declare and use or call functions.

Subsequently in chapter 7, we will explore the concept of methods, which are similar to functions but are defined within a class. A method can have parameters, just like a function, and they follow the same naming rules.

By convention, the name of a function or method always starts with a lowercase letter. Understanding functions and methods is fundamental to writing organized and efficient Python code.

Listing 2.20: Basic Python function

```
import tkinter as tk

def display_message(message):
    # Basic GUI interface
    root = tk.Tk()  # Create the container window
    # Label with our message
    labelo = tk.Label(root, text=message)
    labelo.pack()
    root.mainloop()
```

The function call will be made using its name, like this:

```
display_message('Welcome')
```

The following example defines the function and the call is made by passing the string of characters that will be used as the label.

Listing 2.21: Function call

```
import tkinter as tk

def display_message(message):
    # Basic GUI interface
    root = tk.Tk()  # Create the container window
    # Label with our message
    labelo = tk.Label(root, text=message)
    labelo.pack()
    root.mainloop()

display_message('Welcome')
```

Output in execution mode

2.6.2 Formatting strings

In Python, the are several ways to format and print a string.

Using the `print()` function without formatting the string

This is the basic approach for printing strings. In this case, variables are passed to the `print()` function.

Listing 2.22: Using the print() function

```
name = input('Please enter your name:')
print("Hello:",name)
```

If there more than one value, we will separate them with the comma as shown in the following code.

Listing 2.23: Using the print() function with two values

```
name = input('Please enter your name:')
age = int(input('Please enter your age:'))
print("Hello:",name, age)
```

Using the % operator for string formatting

The % operator, also known as modulo, can be utilized for string formatting. When using the syntax `'astring' % values`, any occurrences of % in the string are replaced with zero or more elements from the variables **values**.

Listing 2.24: Basic usage of % operator

```
name = input('Please enter you name:')
print('Hello, %s!' % name)
```

Listing 2.25: Basic usage of % operator with two or more variables

```
name = input('Please enter you name:')
age = int(input('Please enter you age:'))
print('Hello, %s, your age is  %d !' % (name, age))
```

There is additional information in the python documentation[2] regarding the specific format to use for strings, integer and floats. In the code shown here, we used `%s` and `%d` to format a string and an integer.

Using the `format()` method for string formatting (available in Python 2.6+ and 3.x)

The basic usage of the string `format()` method is as follows:

Listing 2.26: Basic usage of the format() function.

```
name = input('Please enter you name:')
age = int(input('Please enter you age:'))
print('Hello, {}, your age is:{}!'.format(name, age))
```

The curly brackets and the characters within them (known as format fields) get replaced with the variables passed into the `format()` method. A number inside the brackets can be used to reference the position of the object passed into the method.

Listing 2.27: Basic usage of the format() function with positional parameters

```
name = input('Please enter you name:')
age = int(input('Please enter you age:'))
print('Hello, {0}, your age is:{1}!'.format(name, age))
```

We can include special formatting for strings, integer and float that are used with the string.

[2] https://docs.python.org/3/library/stdtypes.html#old-string-formatting

Listing 2.28: Basic usage of the format() function with positional parameters and formatting

```
name = input('Please enter you name:')
age = int(input('Please enter you age:'))
salary=float(input('Please enter your salary:'))
print('Hello, {0:10s}, your age is:{1:3d}, your salary
↪   is:{2:7.2f}!'.format(name, age, salary))
```

When using keyword arguments in the `format()` method, their values are accessed by using the name of the argument.

Listing 2.29: Basic usage of the format() function with keyword arguments and formatting

```
name = input('Please enter you name:')
age = int(input('Please enter you age:'))
salary=float(input('Please enter your salary:'))
print('Hello, {last_name:10s}, your age is:{age:3d}, your salary
↪   is:{sal:7.2f}!'.format(
    last_name=name, age=age, sal=salary))
```

Using f-strings or String literals (available in Python 3.6+)

Formatted string literals, also known as f-strings let us embed the value of Python expressions within a string. To create an f-string, we simply prefix the string with the letter **f** or **F** and include expressions inside curly braces, like this: **f'Special format to be used {expression}'**.

In addition, we can use an optional format specifier like the ones used in the `format()` method after the expression, which gives us greater control over the formatting of the value.

Listing 2.30: Using f-strings without format specifier

```
name = input('Please enter you name:')
print(f'Hello, {name}!')
```

Listing 2.31: Using f-strings with format specifier

```
name = input('Please enter you name:')
print(f'Hello, {name:10s}!')
```

2.7 Quick summary

This quick summary highlights the essential concepts in Python programming, providing a concise overview of the key elements you have learned:

- A Python program consists of one or multiple modules.
- A variable is used to store data in Python.
- Python has several data types.
- Python has arithmetic, relational, and logical operators.
- Functions can be created and used in Python.
- Python supports classes and objects.

2.8 Quiz

Please answer the following questions. There may be one or more correct answers.

1. Variable names in Python are case-sensitive:
   (a) True
   (b) False

2. We use variables to:
   (a) Store data
   (b) Indicate an action
   (c) Perform operations

3. To use strings in Python code, we need a variable of type:
   (a) String
   (b) str
   (c) Chain

4. Python has special variables called constants:
   (a) True
   (b) False

5. In Python, we must explicitly declare variables before starting to use them:
   (a) True
   (b) False

6. The following code:

```
counter = 1
print(counter++)
```

   leads to the result:
   (a) 1
   (b) 2
   (c) error

7. The operator // is used for:
   (a) Floor division
   (b) Integer division
   (c) Modulo operation

8. The following code:

```
a = True
b = 0
print(a or b)
```

gives us:
(a) error
(b) 0
(c) True

9. The following code:

```
a = True
b = 0
print(a and b)
```

gives us:
(a) error
(b) 0
(c) False

10. The following code:

```
a = 5
b = 2
print(a % b)
```

gives us:
(a) 2
(b) 1
(c) 0

2.9 Practice problems

PROBLEM 2.1

Concatenate the two strings 'Hello' and 'Flouflou'

```
valx = 'Hello'
valy = ' Flouflou'
print(valx + valy)
```

PROBLEM 2.2

Assign the string **Welcome to college and I hope you have a good semester.** in a way that it is saved as:

```
Welcome to college
and I hope you have a good semester.
```

Thus, it will be on two lines.

The `'''...'''` triple quotes are used to surround the string. Triple quotes allow you to write a string on multiple lines without having to use a newline character.

```
valx='''Welcome to college
and I hope you have a good semester. '''
print(valx)
```

PROBLEM 2.3

Consider problem 2.2 but using double quotes for the string.

```
valx="""Welcome to college
and I hope you have a good semester. """
print(valx)
```

PROBLEM 2.4

Display the length of the string **Hello Alain flouflou** using the built-in function `len()`.

```
#string length
my_str = 'Hello Alain flouflou'
print(len(my_str))
```

PROBLEM 2.5

Let's consider the string **Hello Alain flouflou**:

- Obtain the character at position 4 of the string.
- Obtain the character at position 4 from the end of the string.
- Obtain the substring between positions 6 and 8 (inclusive) of the string.

```
#String indexing and slicing
my_str = 'Hello Alain flouflou'
print(my_str[3])
print(my_str[-4])
print(my_str[5:8])
```

PROBLEM 2.6

Check if the substring **Alain** is present in the string **Hello Alain flouflou**.

```
#Substring in string
my_str = 'Hello Alain flouflou'
print('Alain' in my_str)
```

PROBLEM 2.7

Format the output displayed in such a way that if the value of the variable **first_name** is **Alain** and the value of the variable **age** is 12, the output will be: **This guy Alain is 12**

```
#Formatting a string for display using %s and %d
age = 12
first_name = 'Alain'
print('This guy %s is %d' % (first_name, age)) # For Python 2.x
print('This guy {} is {}'.format(first_name, age)) # For Python 3.x
```

2.10 Programming problems

PROBLEM 2.8

Solution provided in the appendix

Ask the user for their name and display the result in the following format:

Hello `user_name`

where `user_name` is the name entered by the user.

- Example: If the user enters **Flouflou**

the output will be:

Hello Flouflou.

PROBLEM 2.9

Solution provided in the appendix

Ask the user for their salary and add 500 to it. Display the result in the following format:

Your new salary is `new_salary`

where `new_salary` is the final value of the salary.

- Example: if the user enters 1200

The output will be: Your new salary is 1700.00

PROBLEM 2.10

Solution provided in the appendix

Enter a student's name, their mid-term and final exam grades, and display the result in the following format:

Student name: `student_name` Average: `student_average`

The average is calculated as follows: `4 * mid_term_exam + 0.6 * final_exam`

Here, `student_name` is the name of the student, `mid_term_exam` and `final_exam` are the grades of the mid-term and final exams, respectively.

- Example: If the user enters **Flouflou**, 65, and 70, the output will be:

Student name: flouflou Average: 68.00

PROBLEM 2.11

Solution provided in the appendix

We want to identify the type of a variable.

- Given the following values: 10, 1000000000000, -10, 10.10, '10', True
- Identify the type of each of these values (by first assigning the value to a variable). We will use the `type()` function to determine the type of the variable.

PROBLEM 2.12

Solution provided in the appendix

Use the `isinstance(your_variable, type)` function to check if the variable **var_1** with the value `48.5` is of the specific type `float`.

You can use `isinstance(var_1, float)`.

PROBLEM 2.13

We want to study the results of division, integer division, and modulo operators.

- We will use the variables **var1** and **var2**, and we will assign the initial values **20** and **8** to them.
- We will use the variables **div**, **remainder**, and **integer_div** to store the results of division, modulo, and integer division.
- Write the code that calculates the division of **var1** by **var2**, the remainder of the division, and the integer division of **var1** by **var2**. Add instructions to display the values of **var1**, **var2**, and the results of division, modulo, and integer division.
- Execute your program. Note the messages you get in the output tab.
- What do you notice?

PROBLEM 2.14

We will use explicit variable conversion during arithmetic calculations.

- Ask the user for two numerical values using the `input()` function.
- To perform the sum of the two values, convert the obtained values using `float()` and display the result obtained.

Chapter 3

Decision Structures

Contents of this chapter

Objectives:

- To learn to use a conditional expression
- To learn to incorporate relational and logical operators into conditional expressions
- To implement selection control using if, if-else and if-elif statements
- To use the conditional operator

3.1 Introduction

Many programming languages, including Python, support two types of execution. The first type allows for simple sequential execution, where the program runs from start to finish in a linear fashion, processing one instruction at a time.

For example, if the first instruction is at line 1 and the last instruction is at line 100, the execution would proceed from instruction 1 to instruction 100 in order.

The second type of execution is based on the concept of selective execution. This introduces the possibility of making choices, in the execution path, that do not necessarily follow a linear sequence from the first instruction to the last. In this case, expressions can be used to conditionally determine whether a series of instructions is executed or if an alternative series is taken.

To continue with the example of instructions from 1 to 100, the execution could follow the path from 1 to 14 and then jump to instructions 53 to 100.

Conditional structures, or tests, allow for making decisions based on pre-established conditions. They can be likened to switching tracks for trains based on traffic conditions.

Although the concept of conditional structures is straightforward, they are widely used in programming because many problems require processes to apply only in certain cases, depending on specific conditions.

In Python, there are several types of conditional structures:

- **if** statement
- **if-else** statement
- **if-elif-else** statement
- Conditional test as a ternary operator

Does Python have the switch structure?

The switch or case structure found in other languages is not available in Python.

3.2 The simple if structure (One-way)

The one-way **if** structure is used when we need to test a condition, which can be a variable or a conditional expression. When the test result evaluates to `True`, a specific set of instructions will be executed. This type of conditional structure is referred to as a simple if statement, and it has the following syntax:

```
if  condition :
  block to execute when the condition is True
```

The **if** structure has the syntax shown in figure 3.1.

In Python, the reserved keyword to initiate a **one-way if** test structure is `if`. The condition provided is a boolean expression used to determine whether the subsequent block of code will be executed or not.

- If the condition evaluates to `True`, the corresponding block of instructions will be executed.
- If the condition evaluates to `False`, the subsequent block of instructions will be skipped.

We use the symbol : to define the scope of the `True` part,

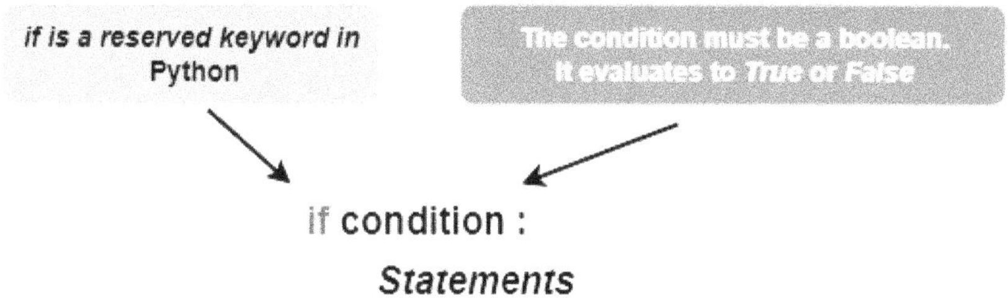

Figure 3.1: If Structure one-way.

The instruction block consists of one or more instructions, each indented the same number of spaces from the left relative to the beginning of the **if** statement.

Typically, the number of spaces used for indentation is 4, although this can be adjusted in your Integrated Development Environment (IDE). It is essential to avoid mixing tabs and spaces in the same code.

3.2.1 Logic of simple or One-way if structure

At the **one-way if** level, the conditional expression is evaluated to determine whether it is `True` or `False`. This expression can be a variable or a logical expression, and in both cases, it will result in either `True` or `False`.

If the expression evaluates to `True`, the series of statements within the **if** block will be executed. On the other hand, if the expression evaluates to `False`, the **if** block will be skipped, and the instructions inside it will not be executed.

In listing 3.1, we test whether the value entered by the user exceeds the value of `MAX`. If it is true, a message is displayed. On the other hand, if it is false, we have not planned to do anything.

Step 1: The condition is evaluated

- If the condition is true, the `print()` function is executed.
- If the condition is false, the `print()` function is not executed.

Listing 3.1: Using the One-way **if** structure

```
MAX = 20
total = int(input('Please enter the total:'))
if total > MAX:
    print('You have exceeded the maximum!')
```

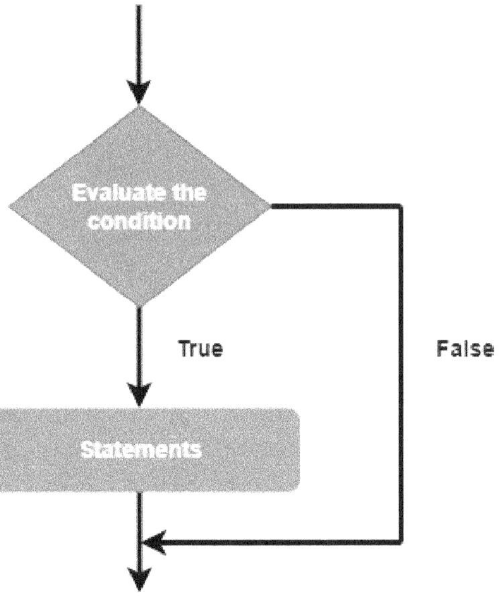

Figure 3.2: Logic of the simple One-way `if` structure.

Output of the program when the total exceeds the maximum

```
Please enter the total: 25
You have exceeded the maximum!
```

3.3 The if-else structure (Two-way)

The one-way **if** structure is sufficient to cover many use cases. However, there are situations where we want to execute instructions if the condition is not fulfilled, or more precisely, if the condition is `False`. In such cases, we can extend the existing **if** structure to include an **else** clause, creating an **if-else** structure.

```
if condition:
    # Statements to be executed when the condition is True
else:
    # Statements to be executed when the condition is False
```

With this **if-else** structure, we have two mutually exclusive paths, and the execution of operations depends on the value of the condition. If the condition is `True`, the statements in the **if** block will be executed; if the condition is `False`, the statements in the **else** block will be executed.

Therefore, only one of the two blocks of instructions is executed, but not both. The keywords reserved for an **if-else** test structure are `if` and `else`.

- The condition is a boolean expression that determines which of the two blocks will be executed.
- If the condition is `True`, the statement block following the `if` is executed.
- If the condition is `False`, the statement block following the `else` will be executed.

The **else** keyword marks the beginning of the second part of the **if**. We use the symbol : to denote the beginning of this scope. The statement block for the **if** or **else** part can contain one or more statements. These statements are indented the same number of spaces from the left, relative to the start of the **if** or **else** statement.

The block must contain at least one valid Python statement. It's important to note that a comment is not considered a valid instruction. If you haven't defined the code yet, you can use the `pass` keyword to keep the block valid as shown in listing 3.2.

Listing 3.2: Using the pass keyword

```
MAX = 20
total = int(input('Please enter the total:'))
if total > MAX:
    pass
else:
    pass
```

3.3.1 Logic of the `if-else` structure

In the **if-else two-way** structure, the conditional expression will be evaluated to compare to `True` or `False`.

As with the **if one-way** structure, the conditional expression can be a variable or a logical expression, both resulting in either `True` or `False`.

If the expression evaluates to `True`, statement series 1 will be executed; otherwise, the statements 2 will be executed.

Instruction Block

The statements block does not necessarily need to contain a single instruction. It can consist of multiple instructions enclosed within indentation.

In listing 3.3, we test whether the value entered by the user exceeds the value of `MAX`. If it is true, a message is displayed. On the other hand, if it is false, two messages are displayed.

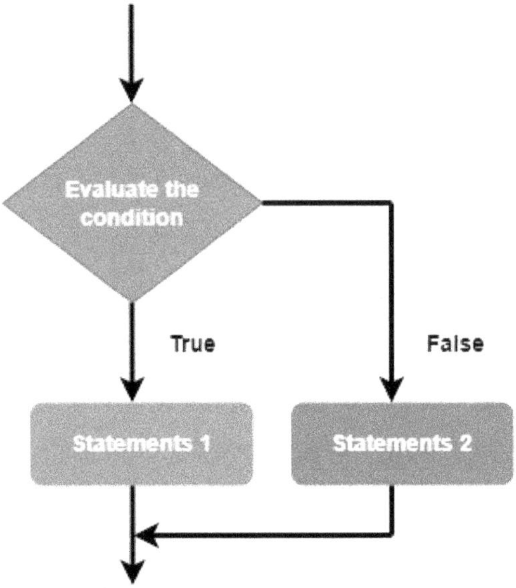

Figure 3.3: Logic of the `if` two-way structure.

Listing 3.3: Using the two-way if structure

```
MAX = 20
total = int(input('Please enter the total:'))
if total > MAX:
    print('You have exceeded the maximum!!')
else:
    print('Total:', total)
    print('You have not exceeded the maximum')
```

Output of the program when the total exceeds the maximum

```
Please enter the total: 25
You have exceeded the maximum!!
```

Output of the program when the total does not exceed the maximum

```
Please enter the total: 14
Total:  14
You have not exceeded the maximum
```

3.4 The complex if-elif-else structure (Multi-way)

When there are several mutually exclusive paths and we want to execute operations based on different conditions, we use the complex structure **if-elif-else**. This structure takes the following form:

```
if condition:
    statements 1
elif condition:
    statements 3
.
.
.
else:
    statements N
```

This structure is useful when we need to choose instructions to be executed from a number of different options. The `if` keyword is mandatory in this structure, while the `else` keyword is optional. You can include as many `elif` statements as needed.

In listing 3.4, we test whether the user is a teenager, an adult or a senior based on their age.

Listing 3.4: Using the multi-way if structure

```
age = int(input('Please enter your age:'))
if age > 55:
    print('You are a senior citizen!!')
elif age > 18:
    print('You are an adult!!')
else:
    print('You are a teenager')
```

Output of the program

```
Please enter your age:25
You are an adult!!
```

3.5 The conditional operator

Python offers a ternary conditional operator that uses a boolean condition to select which of two expressions (`True` or `False` cases) is evaluated and possibly assigned to a variable. For instance, consider the two-way conditional structure with assignment in the following form:

```
if condition:
    val = expr1
else:
    val = expr2
```

A simpler alternative for this scenario is to use a conditional expression with the following structure:

```
val = expr1 if condition else expr2
```

If the condition is `True`, `expr1` is evaluated; if it is `False`, `expr2` is evaluated. The returned value is the value of the selected expression, which will be assigned to the variable `val`.

Example

```
num1 = int(input('enter value for num1:'))
num2 = int(input('enter value for num2:'))
my_var = num1 if num1 > num2 else num2
print(my_var)
```

If `num1` is greater than `num2`, then `num1` is assigned to `my_var`; otherwise, `num2` is assigned to `my_var`.

Best practice

Although it is useful as a replacement for an assignment operation, the ternary conditional operator should be used with care.

3.6 Quick summary

This quick summary highlights the essential concepts of decision structures in Python programming, providing a concise overview of the key elements you have learned:

- Decision structures are based on the concept of execution by selection.
- Condition expressions can include relational and logical operators.
- You can use if, if-else, and if-elif decision structures.
- The conditional test ternary operator is a useful alternative in certain situations to replace an if-else structure.

3.7 Quiz

Please answer the following questions. There may be one or more correct answers.

1. The test structures in Python that can be used are:
   (a) if
   (b) if-elif
   (c) switch

2. A one-way if test structure can contain an else structure:
   (a) True
   (b) False

3. A two-way if test structure contains an else structure:
   (a) True
   (b) False

4. The following two structures give the same result and are therefore equivalent:

```
value = int(input('Enter a value:'))
if value < 20:
    print('The value is less than 20.')
elif value < 30:
    print('The value is greater than or equal to 20 and less than
    ↪ 30.')
else:
    print('The value is greater than or equal to 30.')
```

and

```
value = int(input('Enter a value:'))
if value < 20:
    print('The value is less than 20.')
if value < 30:
    print('The value is less than 30.')
else:
    print('The value is greater than or equal to 30.')
```

   (a) True
   (b) False

5. Execution of the following code gives the result:

```
age = 10
if age > 20:
    print('You are an adult.')
print('Thank you.')
```

(a) You are an adult
(b) You are an adult
Thank you
(c) Thank you

6. To represent a logical OR operation, we use:
(a) OR
(b) or
(c) ||

7. If you want the message "You are ten years old" to appear, you must replace ? by:

```
age = 10
if age ? 10:
    print('You are ten years old.')
```

(a) =
(b) ==
(c) equals

8. What is the result displayed by the following code?

```
age = 10
message = 'adult' if age > 18 else 'child'
print(message)
```

(a) adult
(b) child
(c) error

9. We consider the logical operator `and`. What are the statements that are true?

(a) Result is `True` if both operands are `True`
(b) Result is `True` if either operand is `True`
(c) Result is `False` if either operand is `False`

10. Consider the following code. What is the result obtained?

```
age = 10
if age = 20 :
    print('You are twenty years old.')
```

(a) Error
(b) The variable **age** receives the value 20
(c) The message "You are twenty years old" is displayed.

3.8 Practice problems

PROBLEM 3.1

Ask the user for an integer. Store it in the variable **val_a**. Display whether the number is even.

```
# Check if the number is even
val_a = int(input('Enter an integer:'))
if val_a % 2 == 0:
    print('val_a: {} is even'.format(val_a))
```

Output

```
Enter an integer:12
val_a: 12 is even
```

Note: The code only tells us if the entered value is even. However, it does not indicate if the value is odd.

PROBLEM 3.2

Consider problem 3.1. Develop the code to display whether the number is even or odd.

```
# Check if the number is even or odd
val_a = int(input('Enter an integer:'))
if val_a % 2 == 0:
    print('val_a: {} is even'.format(val_a))
else:
    print('val_a: {} is odd'.format(val_a))
```

Output

For an even number, we will have:

```
Enter an integer:12
val_a: 12 is even
```

Otherwise, in case of an odd number, we will have:

```
Enter an integer:51
val_a: 51 is odd
```

PROBLEM 3.3

Ask the user for an integer. Store it in the variable **val_a**. Display whether the number is less than or equal to 20, greater than 20 but less than or equal to 50, or greater than 50.

```
# Check if the number is within a given range
val_a = int(input('Enter an integer:'))
if val_a <= 20:
    print('Less than or equal to 20')
elif val_a <= 50:
    print('Greater than 20 but less than or equal to 50')
else:
    print('Greater than 50')
```

Output

```
Enter an integer:75
Greater than 50
```

Note: We have shown the output for a value greater than 50. There are several ways to improve the code here, but the main goal is to understand the conditional structure used.

3.9 Programming problems

PROBLEM 3.4

Solution provided in the appendix

Ask the user for three integers. Store them in variables **a**, **b**, and **c**. Find the maximum and minimum.

PROBLEM 3.5

Solution provided in the appendix

In some countries, including Canada, some people measure distances in feet, while officially, measurements should be in meters. To help these individuals, develop a program that converts meters to feet, knowing that one foot is approximately 30.48 centimeters.

Modify your code to perform the reverse conversion as well. Add a prompt at the beginning to ask for the desired conversion type.

PROBLEM 3.6

An international food distribution chain offers its products in kilograms for most of its customers. To assist its customers who use the imperial system, they want to provide them with the same information but in pounds. Develop a program that converts kilograms to pounds, knowing that one kilogram is equivalent to 2.2 pounds.

Modify your code to perform the reverse conversion as well. Add a prompt at the beginning to ask for the desired conversion type.

PROBLEM 3.7

Develop a program that asks the user to enter a number corresponding to a month of the year and then displays the name of the associated month based on the input number. In case the entered number does not correspond to a valid month, an error message will be displayed, and the program will terminate.

PROBLEM 3.8

For taxation purposes, employees are classified into salary categories.

For those earning over `100,000`$, the tax rate is `45`%. For those earning between `70,000`$ and less than `100,000`$, the tax rate is `32`%. For those earning between `40,000`$ and less than `70,000`$, the tax rate is `18`%. Lastly, those earning less than `40,000`$ are taxed at `10`%.

Develop a program that asks the user for their salary and then displays the amount they need to pay in taxes.

PROBLEM 3.9

Develop a program that asks the user for two numbers, stores them in two pre-defined variables, and then displays the sum, product, and difference of the two numbers.

To provide a user-friendly experience, we will present the user with a simple menu as follows:

- Addition
- Subtraction
- Multiplication
- Quit

We will use an appropriate conditional structure:

- If the user chooses options 1, 2, or 3, we will ask for the input of two numbers and perform the corresponding operation. Finally, we will display the result and the exit message.
- If the user chooses option 4, we will display the message **Thank you for using our application** and terminate the program.

PROBLEM 3.10

Develop a program that prepares the monthly statement for the customers of MasterPop International, a bank that issues credit cards across the country.

Data

The program takes as input the previous account balance, the payment made by the customer, and the total amount of additional charges (Purchases) during the month. The current balance is calculated as the previous balance minus the payment made by the customer. The program should calculate the interest due for the month, the new total balance (current balance plus additional charges plus interest), and the minimum payment required. The business rule used by MasterPop International for interest calculation is based on the current balance. If the current balance is 0, then the interest applied for the current month is 0%. However, if the current balance was greater than 0, then the interest applied is 5% on the current total (current balance plus additional charges).

Requirements

The program should calculate the minimum payment required. The business rule for calculating the minimum payment is based on the new balance. If the new balance is less than 50$, then the minimum payment will be the amount of the new balance. If the new balance is between 50$ and 295$, then the minimum payment is 50$. If the new balance exceeds 295$, then the minimum payment is 25% of the new balance.

Display Format

The output of your program should have the following format:

MasterPop International
Monthly Statement of Charges
Previous Balance: XXXX.XX $
Payment: XXXX.XX $
Current Balance: XXXX.XX $
Interest Charges: XXXX.XX $
Purchases: XXXX.XX $
New Balance: XXXX.XX $
Minimum Required: XXXX.XX $

Chapter 4

Repetition Structures

Contents of this chapter

Objectives:

- To understand when to use a repetitive structure
- To write loops using `while` statements
- To write loops using `for` statements
- To implement program control with `break` and `continue`

4.1 Introduction

In the previous chapter, we discussed the two types of program execution, namely the sequential mode and the mode with selection, which allowed us to introduce decision structures. However, there is a third type of execution in which a series of instructions can be defined and repeated under certain conditions.

In this chapter, we will explore repetition structures, also known as loops. These structures play a crucial role as they enable interactivity with the user, such as asking for input, continuing or stopping a process based on the user's response, and performing a series of instructions based on expressions with boolean values.

A loop is a set of actions that repeat in a specific order, a determined number of times based on a condition. It is essential to define the sequence of instructions to be executed and the number of repetitions. In some cases, the number of repetitions may be unknown, so we need to specify the event that will terminate the loop and allow the program to exit.

In Python, we have the following repetition structures:

- **while** loop: This loop uses a condition that evaluates to either `True` or `False` to control the number of repetitions.
- **for** loop: This loop uses a counter or an iterable to repeat a specific number of times.

4.2 The `while` loop

The **while** loop allows you to repeatedly execute a series of instructions as long as a specific condition remains `True`.

Syntax

```
while <condition>:
    # Instruction block
```

If the condition is `True`, the statement block is executed. After each execution of the block, the condition is evaluated again. If the condition is still `True`, the statement block is executed again. This process continues until the condition becomes `False`.

4.2.1 Logic of the `while` Loop

The **while** loop follows the algorithmic structure:

```
Loop ...
    # Instruction block
End Loop
```

To utilize the **while** loop, we need two main components: the condition, which is evaluated as either `True` or `False`, and the series of instructions that are repeated as long as the condition remains `True`. The logic of the **while** loop is illustrated in figure 4.1.

In this diagram, the diamond shape represents the condition, and the rectangle represents the series of instructions. When the loop is executed, the condition is evaluated. If it is `True`, the series of instructions is executed. After the execution of the instruction block, the loop brings us back to the beginning, as shown in figure 4.1. The condition is re-evaluated, and if it is still `True`, the series of instructions is executed again. This process continues until the condition becomes `False`. Note that if the condition is initially `False`, the loop will not execute at all.

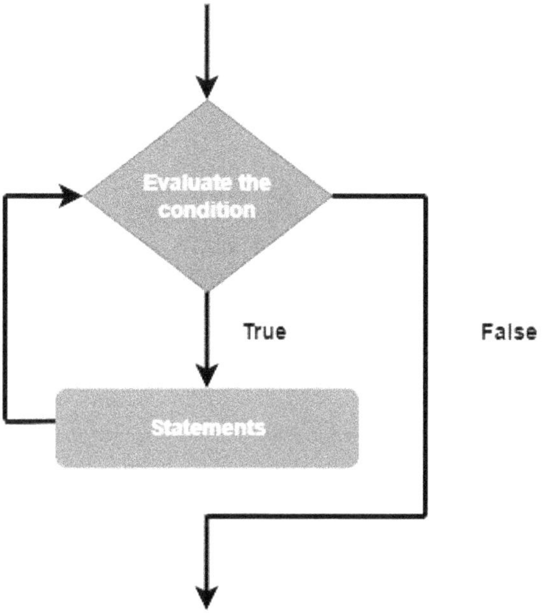

Figure 4.1: Logic of the while loop.

In listing 4.1, we have a simple **while** loop structure. Before entering the loop, we initialize the **counter** variable. Inside the loop, we print the value of **counter**, and then we increment it by 1. The loop will execute as long as the **counter** is less than or equal to 5.

Listing 4.1: Simple Counting Loop

```
counter = 1
while counter <= 5 :
   print(counter)
   counter += 1
```

Output during execution

```
1
2
3
4
5
```

It is crucial to ensure that the loop eventually reaches a condition where it evaluates to

False, or else the loop will execute indefinitely, leading to what is known as an infinite loop. In this example, the loop stops when the **counter** becomes 6, and the condition `counter <= 5` becomes False.

4.3 The for Loop

The **for** loop is used to repeat the execution of a series of statements a specific number of times, iterating through a sequence of elements.

Syntax

```
for tmp in [value1, value2, ..., valueN] :
    # Instructions
```

The **for** loop iterates through a given sequence and assigns each element in the sequence to the variable **tmp** one by one. The series of statements within the loop is then executed using the current value of **tmp**.

This process continues for each element in the sequence until the last element is assigned to **tmp**. The loop will step through the sequence, executing the statements for each element.

Listing 4.2: **for** Loop Using an Iterable

```
for tmp in [0, 1, 2, 3, 4, 5]:
    print(tmp)
```

Listing 4.3: Output in execution mode

```
0
1
2
3
4
5
```

In the above example, we used a sequence of 6 consecutive numbers starting with 0 and ending with 5. However, it is essential to note that the sequence can contain arbitrary values, not necessarily consecutive numbers. The elements can also be non-numeric, as shown in the following example:

Listing 4.4: Arbitrary Iterable Sequence

```
for tmp in ['foo', 'dodo']:
    print(tmp)
```

Output in execution mode

```
foo
dodo
```

In this case, we used a sequence of strings **foo** and **dodo**, demonstrating that the **for** loop can work with a variety of data types.

4.3.1 The range() function

If you wish to create a **for** loop with an iterable containing numeric values, you can utilize the range() function. This function allows you to generate a sequence of values on which you can iterate.

The general form of range() is range(start, end, step), where **start** is the starting value, **end** is the value up to which the sequence will go (excluding this value), and **step** is the value by which the sequence will increment between each element.

The following example generates the iterable of values from 1 to 5 with a step of 2.

Listing 4.5: Using the range() function

```
for tmp in range(1, 6, 2):
    print(tmp)
```

Output in execution mode

```
1
3
5
```

If the **step** is equal to 1, it can be omitted, resulting in the following form.

Listing 4.6: Using the range() function with a step of 1

```
for tmp in range(1, 6):
    print(tmp)
```

Output in execution mode

```
1
2
3
4
5
```

In some situations, if we want to indicate only the last value of the iterable, we can omit the beginning, which will automatically be assigned the value 0.

Listing 4.7: Using the range() function with only the end value

```
for tmp in range(6):
    print(tmp)
```

Output in execution mode

```
0
1
2
3
4
5
```

Finally, if we want the sequence of numbers in the iterable to be from a larger number to a smaller number, we can use a negative **step**, as shown in the following code.

Listing 4.8: Using the range() function with a negative step

```
for tmp in range(5, 0, -1):
    print(tmp)
```

Output in execution mode

```
5
4
3
2
1
```

4.4 Transfer of control

The Python language offers the possibility of introducing an unconditional transfer of the execution flow of our program using either the **break** or **continue** statement.

4.4.1 Break statement

The **break** statement can be used inside a loop to immediately and completely exit from the loop. When the **break** statement is encountered, the execution sequence is transferred out of the loop. As a result, the conditional expression or the variable will no longer be evaluated since we have completely exited the loop's context.

For example, consider listing 4.9. In this case, we want to exit the loop when the number encountered in the iterable is equal to 4.

Listing 4.9: Using break

```
for count in range(1, 6):
    if count == 4:
        break
    print(count)

print('Exit after break')
```

Output in execution mode

```
1
2
3
Exit after break
```

4.4.2 Continue statement

The **continue** statement can be used in a loop to skip the execution of a series of statements immediately following the **continue** statement. When the **continue** statement is reached, the rest of the statements is not executed, and the execution sequence is transferred to the conditional expression or variable for evaluation. If the conditional expression or variable evaluates to `True`, the loop continues to execute.

Listing 4.10: Using continue

```
for count in range(1, 6):
    if count == 4:
        continue
    print(count)
```

We can observe that, at the output, all the numbers have been printed except for the number 4. This is because the **continue** instruction is executed when **count** is equal to 4, and therefore, the rest of the instructions (in this case, the `print()` function) is skipped.

Output in execution mode

```
1
2
3
5
```

It is important to note that the **continue** statement keeps the flow of execution inside the loop, while the **break** statement brings it outside the loop.

4.5 Quick summary

This quick summary highlights the essential concepts of repetition structures in Python programming, providing a concise overview of the key elements you have learned:

- A repetition structure is a series of actions that repeat in a specific order, for a specified number of times depending on a condition.
- The **while** loop structure uses a condition that evaluates to either `True` or `False` to control the number of repetitions.
- The **for** loop structure uses a counter to repeat a specific number of times.

4.6 Quiz

Please answer the following questions. There may be one or more correct answers.

1. Loop structures in Python are:
   (a) while
   (b) do-while
   (c) for

2. A **for** loop can be converted into a **while** loop:
   (a) True
   (b) False

3. In a loop, we can use the **continue** and **break** keywords:
   (a) True
   (b) False

4. The following **for** loop:

```
for counter in range(0, 5):
    print(counter)
```

can be transformed into the following **while** loop:

```
counter = 0
while counter < 5:
    print(counter)
    counter += 1
```

   (a) True
   (b) False

5. Consider the following code:

```
counter = 0
while counter < 5:
    counter += 1
    if counter == 3:
        continue
    print(counter)
```

The output obtained is:
(a) 1 2 3 4
(b) 1 2 4
(c) 1 2 4 5

6. In order to get the following output: 10 20 30
What would be the condition to use instead of ? in the following code:

```
counter = 10
while ? :
    print(counter)
    counter += 10
```

(a) counter < 30
(b) counter < 40
(c) counter < 20

7. Consider the following code:

```
counter = 0
while counter < 0:
    print(counter)
    counter += 10
print(counter)
```

The output obtained is:
(a) 1
(b) 0
(c) error

8. Consider the following nested loops:

```
i = 0
while i < 5:
    j = 0
    while j < 4:
        print("i:{}, j:{}".format(i,j))
        j += 1
    i += 1
```

The number of lines displayed will be:
(a) 19
(b) 5

(c) 25
(d) 20

9. Consider the following nested loops:

```
i = 0
while i < 5:
    j = 0
    while j < i:
        print("i:{}, j:{}".format(i,j))
        j += 1
    i += 1
```

The number of lines displayed will be:
(a) 9
(b) 10
(c) 11
(d) 25

10. We have a **while** loop in which we would like, under a certain condition, to stop the execution of the instructions and to return to the evaluation of the condition of the loop. We must therefore use:
(a) break
(b) continue
(c) goto
(d) return

4.7 Practice problems

PROBLEM 4.1

Using a **while** loop, write code to display numbers from 1 to 7.

```
counter = 1
while counter <= 7:
    print(counter)
    counter += 1
```

Output

```
1
2
3
4
5
6
7
```

PROBLEM 4.2

Using a **for** loop and the `range()` function, write code to display numbers from 1 to 7.

```
for counter in range(1,8):
    print(counter)
```

Output

```
1
2
3
4
5
6
7
```

PROBLEM 4.3

Ask the user to enter a string of characters. Then, display all the characters that are in this string.

```
# Loop with string iterator
phrase = input('Enter a string of characters:')
for character in phrase:
    print(character)
```

Output

```
Enter a string of characters:Fox
F
o
x
```

PROBLEM 4.4

Ask the user to enter the character 0 to continue the execution. If any other character is entered, the script or program will stop.

```
response = '0'
while response == '0':
    response = input("Do you want to continue? Enter '0' to continue:
    ↪  ")

print("Thank you for using our software.")
```

Output

```
Do you want to continue? Enter '0' to continue: 0
Do you want to continue? Enter '0' to continue: N
Thank you for using our software.
```

Note: The code does not produce the expected result if the input is in lowercase.

PROBLEM 4.5

Ask the user to enter the character 0 to continue the execution. If any other character is entered, the script or program will stop. Take into account that the user can enter the characters in uppercase or lowercase.

```
response = 'o'
while response.lower() == 'o':  # Use the lower() method of str
    response = input("Do you want to continue? Enter 'O' to continue:
    ↪  ")

print("Thank you for using our software.")
```

Output

```
Do you want to continue? Enter 'O' to continue: o
Do you want to continue? Enter 'O' to continue: O
Do you want to continue? Enter 'O' to continue: n
Thank you for using our software.
```

Note: The code produces the expected result whether the input is in uppercase or lowercase.

4.8 Programming problems

PROBLEM 4.6

Solution provided in the appendix

Develop a program that allows a user to guess an integer between 1 and 100. This secret number will be generated randomly. We will ensure the following points are met:

- We will display a message to the user asking them to enter a number.
- We will indicate to the user whether their number is greater or smaller than the secret number.
- If the user correctly guesses the secret number, we will display **Congratulations** and the number of attempts they made.

PROBLEM 4.7

Given the iterable [10, 12, 14, 16, 18, 20], use a **for** loop to display the sequence of numbers as 13 15 17 19 21 23.

Modify your code to obtain the same result but this time using the `range` function instead of the sequence.

PROBLEM 4.8

Solution provided in the appendix

Ask the user for an integer. Develop a program that gives us the total of even numbers (starting from 2) that need to be used to make their sum equal to or greater than the given number. Display these numbers.

Example: If the sum is 8, we would need to use 2, 4, 6, making it a total of 3 numbers. We cannot use only 2 and 4 because their sum is 6, which is less than 8.

PROBLEM 4.9

Develop a program that allows the user to enter an indeterminate number of integers. The input should stop when the user enters the number 999. Then, the program will display the sum and the average of the numbers entered.

Modify the code to also display the total of positive numbers and the number of times the number zero has been entered.

PROBLEM 4.10

Develop a program that asks the user for 2 numbers, stores them in 2 pre-defined variables, and then displays the sum, product, and difference of the two numbers.

- Addition
- Subtraction
- Multiplication
- Quit

The following rules should be implemented.

- If the user does not enter an option from the menu, the menu will be displayed again.
- If the user chooses option 1, 2, or 3, the program will ask for the input of 2 numbers and perform the corresponding operation. Finally, it will display the result.
- If the user chooses option 4, the message **Thank you for using our application** will be displayed, and the application will end.

PROBLEM 4.11

Develop a program that asks the user for a sentence and then gives the number of characters it contains. For example, if the user enters **I want to go to Andromeda**, the program should display **Number of characters: 27**. The program will ask the user for the sentence to manipulate.

Modify the program to also give the number of times the letter 'a' appears in the sentence. For example, in the case of the previous example sentence, it will display **The letter -a- is used 1 time**. Note that only lowercase 'a' is considered.

Modify your program to take into account both uppercase and lowercase letters. For example, in the previous case, it will display **The letter -a or A- is used 2 times**.

PROBLEM 4.12

Develop a program that informs us of possible activities based on the weather. We will ask the user for the temperature and then propose the most appropriate activity based on the business rule.

- If the temperature is 25°C or higher, the proposed activity is swimming. However, if the temperature is 18°C or higher but less than 25°C, we will suggest playing tennis. If the temperature is lower than 18°C but 2°C or higher, we will advise a hike in the woods. Finally, if the temperature is lower than 2°C, the proposed activity will be skiing.

PROBLEM 4.13

A university student pays 2500$ as tuition fees for the first year. The registrar's office has informed him that due to inflation, the fees will increase by 3.5% each year.

Develop the code that will allow him to obtain the total amount paid at the end of his studies, assuming that his studies may last for 4 years.

PROBLEM 4.14

Develop a program that calculates the change to give to customers during their purchases.

Cashiers will enter the total amount to be paid and the amount given by the customer (cash). The system should display the change to be given to the customers.

We will make the following assumptions:

- The total amount is always an integer.
- The available denominations are 1$, 5$, 10$, and 20$ only.

PROBLEM 4.15

Develop the code that asks the user to enter an integer. This value will be stored in a variable called **repetition**.

The program will output the following figure (the case shown is for a value of **repetition** equal to 4):

repetition =1

*#

repetition =2

*#**#

repetition =3

*#**#***#

repetition =4

*#**#***#****#

PROBLEM 4.16

Develop a program that generates an arbitrary number of random integers with values between 0 and 100. The user will be asked for the desired number of values, and the program will output the following statistics:

- The number of generated odd values
- The minimum and maximum generated values
- The range, which is defined by the difference between the maximum and minimum values

Chapter 5

Functions

Contents of this chapter

Objectives:

- To understand the importance of functions
- To define a function
- To understand how to use function parameters
- To invoke a function
- To understand how to use keywords in a function signature
- To determine the scope of variables
- To write reusable code

5.1 Introduction

When designing an algorithm to solve a problem, it is necessary to break down the problem into less complex sub-problems.

This approach leads us to isolate different processes required to solve the problem and try to implement separate program units, each performing a specific task.

In general, this results in the creation of blocks of instructions known as procedures or functions. We are already familiar with this concept, which can be found, for example, in pocket calculators. When you press the **SIN** key, you are actually calling a function that calculates the sine.

In Python, these units are defined as functions or methods, depending on the declaration case.

Designing a function involves defining the function's code and parameters, which represent the data that the function will use.

On the other hand, when using the function, real values will be associated with these parameters through the passing of data to the function. These values are called arguments. Figure 5.1 shows the passage of the values present in **a** and **b** towards the parameters **A** and **B** of the function.

This exchange of data gives significance to the modular breakdown that we mentioned in the introduction.

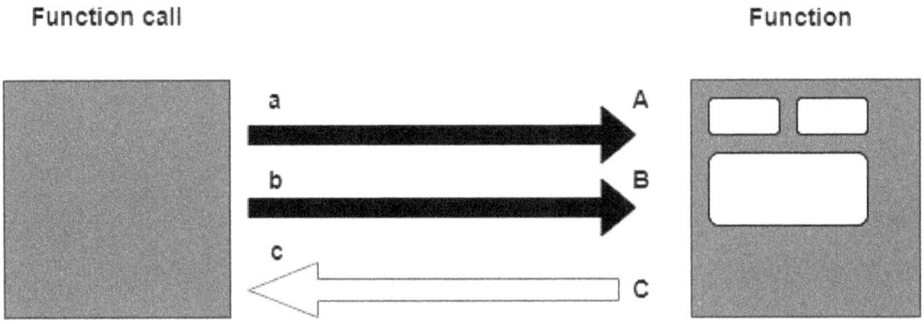

Figure 5.1: Function call with value return.

5.1.1 Why should we use functions?

Using functions in our scripts and programs offers several advantages. Firstly, it allows us to reuse code, minimizing redundancy or repetition throughout the script. This reusability promotes efficiency and maintainability. Additionally, functions help reduce the potential for bugs, as the code surface is reduced due to less redundancy. Lastly, functions enable us to break down complex problems into smaller, more manageable sub-problems.

5.1.2 Definition

A function is a reusable sequence of instructions designed for a specific process. It can be utilized as many times as needed and returns a value whose type is specified in the function declaration.

In Python, a function can return one or more values.

Input and Output

A function:

- Receives input data.
- Produces output data.

Qualities of a Function

A function must be consistent, focusing on a single task. It should be concise, with code or instructions that are easy to understand and not overly lengthy.

5.1.3 Syntax

The definition of a function begins with the keyword `def` in the function header. It is advisable to name the function according to the task it will perform. Generally, a verb is used followed by a descriptor. The function parameters are enclosed within parentheses `()`. Functions can have parameters, or they can have no parameters.

The function body, where the statements are written, starts with a colon : indicating the beginning of the function's scope. Unlike some other languages like Java or C++, Python does not use curly braces `{}` for the scope; instead, indentation is used to define the scope. The indentation is typically four spaces, but it can be adjusted according to the development editor's settings.

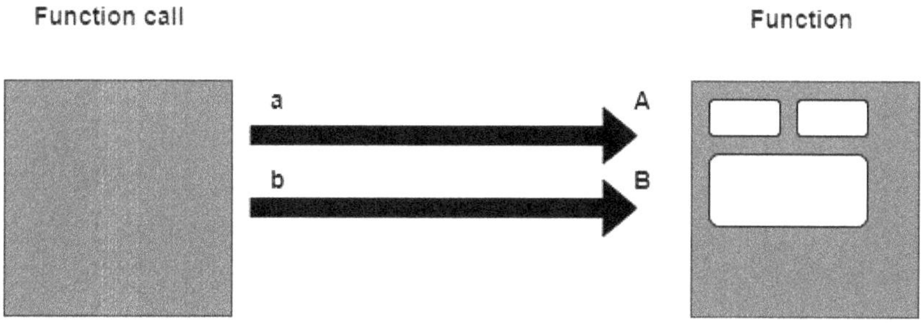

Figure 5.2: Function call without returning values.

The `return` keyword is used to specify the value that the function will return. If `return` is omitted, the function returns `None`, effectively behaving like a procedure. Figure 5.2 demonstrates a function call without returning values.

The code in listing 5.1 provides examples of three different functions:

Listing 5.1: Defining functions

```
def print_line():
    print('='*50)

def compute_tax(amount, tax_rate):
    return amount * tax_rate

def return_activity(temperature):
    if temperature < 10:
        activite = 'Ski'
    else:
        activity = 'Walking'

    return activity
```

- **print_line()**: This function has no parameters and displays the symbol = fifty times. It returns `None`. In some other programming languages, **print_line()** is considered as a procedure.
- **compute_tax(amount, tax_rate)**: This function uses the parameters **amount** and **tax_rate**. It consists of a single statement and returns a value.
- **return_activity(temperature)**: This function uses a single parameter, **temperature**, and contains several instructions. It uses a local variable **activity** for intermediate calculations, and the final value in this variable is returned.

5.1.4 Docstrings

Listing 5.1 lacks comments. As such, it is essential to include some information related to what the function is all about. These descriptions are called **docstrings**. To add a **docstring** to a function in PyCharm, follow these steps:

- Position the cursor after the colon :
- Press the Enter key to create a new line.
- Type three single quotes `'''` on the new line.
- Press the Enter key again.

You can then fill in the information necessary for the function description within the **docstring**. Listing 5.2 provides an example of a **docstring** for the **compute_tax()** function.

Listing 5.2: Including docstrings for a function

```
def compute_tax(amount, tax_rate):
    '''
    Calculation of the purchase tax according to the paid amount
    :amount: total amount of the purchase
    :param tax_rate: applicable tax
    :return: amount of tax to pay
    '''
    return amount * tax_rate
```

With the **docstrings** included, you can display help when calling this function by pressing the **CTRL** + **Q** keys in PyCharm while holding the cursor over the function name.

5.1.5 Calling a function

To use a function, you simply need to specify the function's name followed by parentheses. If the function requires parameters, you include the corresponding values inside the parentheses, following the order of the parameters as defined in the function. In later sections, we will explore techniques that allow us to bypass the strict ordering of parameters during function calls.

Parameters vs Arguments.

A parameter is a variable defined between the parentheses of a function. An argument is the value sent to a function parameter at call time.

It is important to note that the variables used during the function call and the function's parameters do not necessarily have to be named in the same way.

Let's take the functions from listing 5.1 as examples and make the calls as shown in listing 5.3.

Listing 5.3: Function calls

```
def print_line():
    print('='*50)

def compute_tax(amount, tax_rate):
    return amount * tax_rate
```

```
def return_activity(temperature):
    if temperature < 10:
        activite = 'Ski'
    else:
        activity = 'Walking'

    return activity

# Function Calls
print_line()
total = 89.5
tax_r = 0.07
tax_to_pay = compute_tax(total, tax_r)
print('Amount of tax to pay: {0:5.2f}'.format(tax_to_pay))
activity = return_activity(14)
print('Activity to do: {0:20s}'.format(activity))
print_line()
```

The output obtained will be:

Output in execution mode

```
==================================================
Amount of tax to pay: 6.27
Activity to do: Walking
==================================================
```

The function call to **print_line()** is made without passing any values since it was defined without parameters. Additionally, as it does not return any value, we do not assign it to any variable.

For the **compute_tax()** function, we passed the values 89.5 and 0.07 as arguments. The variables used here, **total** and **tax_r**, do not have the same names as the function parameters. As this function returns a value (the tax to be paid), we assign this returned value to the variable **tax_to_pay**.

Finally, for the **return_activity()** function, we passed a single value since the function only accepts one parameter. At the same time, we assign the returned value, which is the activity to do, to the variable **activity**.

5.2 Scope of a variable

5.2.1 Local variables

To perform its task, a function will need data storage variables. These variables can be local to the function or global, i.e., defined outside the function.

A local variable is defined inside a function. Function parameters are also considered local variables.

It is important to note that local variables exist only during the execution of the function.

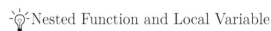

Nested Function and Local Variable

In Python, a function can enclose another function, and the inner function retrieves all the variables of the enclosing function.

Consider the code in listing 5.4.

Listing 5.4: Local variables

```
def calculate_exponent(oper1, oper2):
    result = oper1 ** oper2
    return result
```

The variables used in the function, i.e., **result**, **oper1**, and **oper2**, are local variables. Once the function returns, these variables will no longer be available.

Expression and Return

In listing 5.4, we don't really need to use `result`. The method body can be reduced to `return oper1 ** oper2`.

5.2.2 Global variables

In Python, we have the possibility to use variables defined outside of functions or classes. They are available to all the functions present in the module. In general, we should avoid them if we have the choice!

In listing 5.5, **bias** is considered a global variable because it is defined outside the function.

Listing 5.5: Global variables

```
bias = 5
def calculate_exponent(oper1, oper2):
    return oper1 ** oper2 + bias
```

Note that the **calculate_exponent()** function itself is a global variable. Indeed, functions are considered objects in Python. On the other hand, **oper1** and **oper2** are local variables.

5.3 Using parameters

5.3.1 Using keywords

When passing values or arguments to a function, the order of parameters in the header determines their assignment. However, this may not always be intuitive, especially when some parameters have default values, making it unnecessary to provide values for them explicitly.

In listing 5.6, we proceed with two calls to the **calculate_exponent()** function. The first call utilizes ordered parameter passing, while the second one explicitly specifies the parameter names.

Listing 5.6: Using parameter names

```
def calculate_exponent(oper1, oper2):
    return oper1 ** oper2

# Call with ordered parameter passing
print(calculate_exponent(2,3))
# Approach using keyword arguments
print(calculate_exponent(oper2=2, oper1=55))
print(calculate_exponent(oper1=55, oper2=2))
```

This demonstrates that we can change the order of parameter passing as long as we use the parameter names. This flexibility, combined with the utilization of default values (which we will explore in the next section), showcases the strength of Python.

5.3.2 Default values

In the **calculate_exponent()** function, we can assume that it calculates the square of **oper1**. Consequently, the value 2 passed to **oper2** could be considered as the default value for this parameter. As a result, we can simply pass the value of **oper1** during the function call.

Listing 5.7 illustrates the **calculate_exponent()** function with the default value of **oper2**.

Listing 5.7: Default value

```
def calculate_exponent(oper1, oper2=2):
    return oper1 ** oper2

print(calculate_exponent(2, 3))
print(calculate_exponent(5))
```

In the first call, the function calculates the cube of 2, while in the second call, it calculates the square of 5.

Up to this point, we have covered normal parameter settings and default settings. In Python, the order of parameters in a function is as follows:

- Normal parameters
- Parameters with default values
- *Parameter (tuple)
- **Parameter (dictionary)

Although we have not yet discussed tuples and dictionaries until now, it is sufficient to know that they are data structures that can contain data in a specific format. We will introduce them in Chapter 6.

5.3.3 Using * in the header

The * notation allows us to gather a certain number of values into a tuple during a function call. This approach proves to be valuable when the number of values or arguments that the function will receive is uncertain during development.

Listing 5.8: Using * as a parameter

```
def calculate_series_sum(*oper):
    result = 0
    for index in oper:
        result += index
    return result
```

Function call

Listing 5.9: Calling with a tuple parameter

```
print(calculate_series_sum(1, 5, 6, 9))
```

5.3.4 Using ** in the header

The ** notation is used to collect a certain number of key-value pairs in a dictionary during a function call. This strategy resembles the one used for passing a tuple, but in this case, the function receives a dictionary of arguments.

Docstrings

*In Python documentation, and especially in docstrings, it is common to use *args and **kwargs for tuple and dictionary parameters, respectively.*

In the code shown in listing 5.10, the function takes a dictionary as a parameter. During the function call, we pass two key-value pairs to create the dictionary.

Listing 5.10: Using ** as a parameter

```
def display_details(**oper):
    for key, value in oper.items():
        print(key, value)
```

Function call

Listing 5.11: Calling with a dictionary parameter

```
display_details(last_name='flouflou', first_name='Alain')
```

5.4 Parameter typing

Python does not mandate explicit typing for functions and variables. However, developers can utilize explicit annotations to provide contextual help and information to aid in development.

In listing 5.12, we present an example where optional typing is introduced in the definitions of three functions.

Listing 5.12: Function definition with parameter typing

```
def display_line() -> None:
    '''
    Display a line of 50 asterisks
    :return: None
    '''
    print('=' * 50)

def compute_tax(amount: float, tax_rate: float) -> float:
    '''
    Calculate the amount of tax to pay
    :param amount: total amount
    :param tax_rate: tax percentage
    :return: amount of tax to pay
    '''
    return amount * tax_rate

def determine_activity(temperature: int) -> str:
    '''
    Determine the activity to do based on the temperature
    :param temperature: temperature value
    :return: activity to do
    '''
    if temperature < 10:
        activity = 'Skiing'
    else:
        activity = 'Walking'

    return activity
```

The function calls remain the same and are repeated in listing 5.13.

Listing 5.13: Function calls

```
# Function calls
display_line()
total = 89.5
tax_r = 0.07
tax_to_pay = compute_tax(total, tax_r)
print('Amount of tax to pay: {0:5.2f}'.format(tax_to_pay))
activity = determine_activity(14)
print('Activity to do: {0:20s}'.format(activity))
display_line()
```

The output obtained will be:

Output in execution mode

```
=======================================================
Amount of tax to pay: 6.27
Activity to do: Walking
=======================================================
```

If we position ourselves on one of the functions, for example **compute_tax()**, and press **Ctrl** and **Q**, the complete docstring will appear.

```
mod_ex
def compute_tax(amount: float,
                tax_rate: float) -> float
Calculate the amount of tax to pay
```

```
Params: amount - total amount
        tax_rate - tax percentage
Returns: amount of tax to pay
```

5.5 Quick summary

This quick summary highlights the essential concepts in defining and calling functions in Python, providing a concise overview of the key elements you have learned:

- A function is a program unit that contains a set of instructions.
- Each function should focus on performing only one specific task.
- The definition of a function starts with the keyword `def`.
- A function may or may not return values.
- Functions can have parameters or no parameters at all.
- When calling a function, values can be passed to its parameters using the parameter names.
- Default values can be assigned to the parameters of a function.
- The `global` keyword is used inside a function to indicate that a variable has a global scope.
- Functions can utilize `tuple` and `dict` type parameters.

5.6 Quiz

Please answer the following questions. There may be one or more correct answers.

1. We use functions to:
   (a) Minimize code redundancy
   (b) Increase the number of lines of code
   (c) Decompose a problem into sub-problems

2. The definition of a function begins with the keyword:
   (a) function
   (b) def
   (c) func

3. A function must have parameters:
   (a) True
   (b) False

4. To indicate that a parameter **param** of a function can have a default value equal to 3, we use the notation:
   (a) param=3
   (b) param:3
   (c) param->3

5. If we call the following function:

```
def simple_calculation(a):
    return a ** 3
```

   with the value 5, we obtain:
   (a) 15
   (b) 125
   (c) 225

6. When you define a function, you must add a `return` statement:
   (a) True
   (b) False

7. Consider the following code:

```
def simple_calculation(a, b=12):
    return a + b

result = simple_calculation(5)
print(result)
```

Once the function is called, the displayed value is:
(a) 5
(b) 12
(c) 17
(d) error

8. Consider the following code:

```
var_a = 10

def simple_calculation(a):
    global var_a
    var_a = 20
    return a ** 3 + var_a

result = simple_calculation(5)
print(result)
print(var_a)
```

Once the function is called, the displayed values will be:
(a) 145 and 20
(b) 145 and 10
(c) 135 and 20
(d) 135 and 10

9. Consider the following code:

```
var_a = 10

def simple_calculation(a):
    var_a = 20
    return a ** 3 + var_a

result = simple_calculation(5)
print(result)
print(var_a)
```

Once the function is called, the displayed values will be:
(a) 145 and 20
(b) 145 and 10
(c) 135 and 20
(d) 135 and 10

10. Consider the following code:

```
def simple_calculation(b, *a):
    return a[0] + b

result = simple_calculation(7, 5, 2)
print(result)
```

Once the function is called, the displayed value is:
(a) 5
(b) 12
(c) 14
(d) error

5.7 Practice problems

5.7.1 Function declaration and call

PROBLEM 5.1

Develop the function to calculate the square of a number. Make a function call, passing the value 12.

```
def calculate_square(x):
    return x*x

#Function call
val_x = calculate_square(12)
print(val_x)
```

PROBLEM 5.2

Define a variable outside the function with the name **x** and assign it the value 0. Use the square calculation function developed in Exercise 5.1, but make sure the parameter name is **x**. Make a function call, passing the value 12. Display the value of **x** before and after the function call. What do you observe?

```
# Variable outside the function
x = 0

def calculate_square(x):
    # x is local here
    return x*x

# Function call
print('Before the call, x =', x)
val_y = 12
val_x = calculate_square(val_y)
print('After the call, x =', x)
print('The square of:', val_y, ' is:', val_x)
```

Output

```
Before the call, x = 0
After the call, x = 0
The square of: 12 is: 144
# The value of x does not change
```

5.7.2 Modifying a global variable inside a function, using the global keyword

PROBLEM 5.3

Let us consider problem 5.2 and define a variable outside the function with the name **y** and assign it the value 10. Use the square calculation function developed in this problem, but declare **y** as global inside the **calculate_square()** function. Add an expression to add the value 3 to **y**. Make a function call, passing the value 12. Display the values of **x** and **y** before and after the function call. What do you observe?

```
# Global variables
x = 0
y = 10

def calculate_square(x):
    # x is local here
    x = 20
    global y
    y += 3
    return x*x

# Function call
print('Before the call, x =', x)
print('Before the call, y =', y)
val_y = 12
val_x = calculate_square(val_y)
print('After the call, x =', x)
print('After the call, y =', y)
print('The square of:', val_y, ' is:', val_x)
```

Output

```
Before the call, x = 0
Before the call, y = 10
After the call, x = 0
After the call, y = 13
The square of: 12 is: 400
# The value of x does not change
# The value of y changes
```

PROBLEM 5.4

Develop the function to calculate the power of a number, taking the parameter **x** as the base and **y** as the exponent. Make a function call, passing the values 2 and 3 for **x** and **y**, respectively. Execute this function call.

Output of the Base Call

```
def calculate_power(x, y):
    return x**y

# Function call
val_x = 2
val_y = 3
result = calculate_power(val_x, val_y)
print(val_x, ' raised to the power of ', val_y, ' is:', result)
```

PROBLEM 5.5

Let us consider problem 5.4, but this time, use keyword arguments. Try making a function call without following the order of the parameters.

```
def calculate_power(x, y):
    return x**y

# Function call
val_x = 2
val_y = 3
result = calculate_power(x=val_x, y=val_y)
print(val_x, ' raised to the power of ', val_y, ' is:', result)
```

Version 2

```
def calculate_power(x, y):
    return x**y

# Function call
val_x = 2
val_y = 3
result = calculate_power(val_x, y=val_y)
print(val_x, ' raised to the power of ', val_y, ' is:', result)
```

Version 3: Without following the order of the parameters

```
def calculate_power(x, y):
    return x**y

# Function call
val_x = 2
val_y = 3
result = calculate_power(y=val_y, x=val_x)
print(val_x, ' raised to the power of ', val_y, ' is:', result)
```

PROBLEM 5.6

Let's consider problem 5.5, but this time, provide a default value of 2 for the parameter **y**. Make a function call without providing a value for **y**.

```
def calculate_power(x, y=2):
    return x**y

# Function call
val_x = 2
result = calculate_power(x=val_x)
print(val_x, ' raised to the power of 2 is:', result)
```

5.8 Programming problems

PROBLEM 5.7

Solution provided in the appendix

Develop a function that displays a message and then reads the value entered by the user. The value will be returned to the calling method.

PROBLEM 5.8

Solution provided in the appendix

Develop a function that converts a number of seconds into its equivalent hours, minutes, and seconds. Make a call to this function and display the result in the format `Hours: 2, Minutes: 32, Seconds: 11` for example.

PROBLEM 5.9

Develop a function that returns the change to be given to customers during their purchases. Cashiers will enter the total amount to be paid and the amount given by the customer (cash). Make a call to this function and display the change to be given to the customers.

We will make the following assumptions:

- The total amount to be paid is always an integer.
- The amount given by the customer is always greater than or equal to the total amount to be paid.
- The available bills are 1$, 5$, 10$, and 20$ only.

PROBLEM 5.10

Develop a function that calculates the factorial of a value entered by the user.

We must first verify that the value is strictly positive.

PROBLEM 5.11

Develop a program that calculates either the square, cube, or factorial of a value entered by the user.

We will ask the user for their choice and verify if the value is strictly positive.

We will use functions to organize our program.

PROBLEM 5.12

The postage rates for letters and other items by Canada Post are given in table 5.1.

Weight	Canada Rate	USA Rate
Up to 30g	1.07$ for one stamp or 0.92 $/stamp in a booklet	2.71$
More than 30g and up to 50g	1.30$	3.88$

Table 5.1: Postage rates for letter, postcards, and standard cards.

Develop the function that calculates the postage rate based on the destination and weight of the letter. If the weight is outside the given range, an appropriate message should be displayed. However, if the destination country is not provided, Canada will be assumed by default. For simplicity, we assume that stamps are sold individually and booklets are not available.

Test your code with a letter weighing 47 grams to be sent to the USA. Repeat the test, but this time for a letter weighing 18 grams with no destination provided.

PROBLEM 5.13

The Fibonacci numbers are obtained using the equation:

$$U_n = \begin{cases} u_{n-1} + u_{n-2} & if \quad n > 2 \\ u_1 = 0 \\ u_2 = 1 \end{cases} \tag{5.1}$$

Develop the function that calculates the Fibonacci numbers for a given value **n**. Generate the numbers for n=10.

PROBLEM 5.14

Develop a program that calculates the amount to be paid for a mortgage based on an interest rate.

The basic functionalities are as follows:

- Ask the user for the value representing the annual interest rate.
- Ask the user for the number of years for this mortgage (usually 5, 10, 15, 20, 30 years).

- Ask the user for the amount borrowed for this mortgage.

The amount to be calculated is based on the formula:

$$monthly\_payment = \frac{monthly\_interest * mortgage\_amount}{1 - (\frac{1}{1+monthly\_interest})^{(12*number\_of\_years)}}$$

DIn this formula, we define the following parameters:

- **monthly_payment**: amount to be paid monthly
- **monthly_interest**: monthly interest rate
- **number_of_years**: number of years chosen for this mortgage
- **mortgage_amount**: amount of the mortgage

You should output the following information on the console:

- The annual interest rate in percentage
- The amount of the mortgage in dollars
- The amount to be paid each month in dollars with 2 decimal places
- The total amount that will be paid at the end of the mortgage
- The difference between the amount borrowed and the total amount paid.

PROBLEM 5.15

The delivery department of ACME Inc needs to generate a random code for every product to be shipped. This code should consist of three letters followed by 4 numbers. Develop a function that generates this random code. We will call this function to obtain the code and then display the result.

The letters will be generated randomly, but the numeric part will start from 0000 and will be incremented with each generation. If it reaches 9999, the numeric part will be reset. The allowed letters are those found in the ASCII table between 65 and 90, which are uppercase letters only. We will use the `chr` function to generate the letters. Additionally, there is no need to check if the generated code has already been generated before.

As an example of generated code, we may have: APP0009, DZA1987, etc...

PROBLEM 5.16

We propose to develop a simple application that allows an insured person to enter their reimbursement request. For the purpose of this problem, we have used only a few fields for illustration.

The most important field is the one where the insured person enters the estimated amount of the work. Additionally, they must indicate their contribution. An example of input is:

```
Name: Flouflou
First Name: Alain
Email: alain.flouflou@site.com
Amount to be paid for the work: 1250
Your contribution: 150
```

Once submitted, we will calculate the reimbursement amount for the requested work. This is based on the simple formula:

$$Reimbursement = Amount \times 0.85 - contribution$$

The confirmation for the insured person will then display:

```
Here are the details of the reimbursement request for your expenses.
Here are the amounts that concern you.
Amount of necessary work: 1250.0
Your declared contribution: 150.0
Reimbursement you are entitled to: 912.5
```

It should be noted that the names, first names, email, contribution, and amount are not hard-coded in the confirmation and will be taken from the insured person's information.

PROBLEM 5.17

In many cases, we need to generate a random password. Once the password is generated, we need to check for example the following rules:

- The length is at least 12 characters.
- At least one letter must be uppercase.
- At least one letter must be lowercase.
- There must be at least one digit.
- At least one of the following characters: `#`, `!`, `&`, or `?`, must be included.

Develop the function that checks a string representing the password. The function should return `True` if the password meets the conditions. Otherwise, it should return `False`.

We will call this function to check a password and then display the result obtained.

Chapter 6

Sequences and Collections

Contents of this chapter

Objectives:

- To understand the need for a collection
- To identify the collections `list`, `tuple`, `set` and `dict`
- To use collections as storage structures
- To manipulate collections using their methods

6.1 Introduction

In the previous chapters, we introduced the concept of variables, allowing us to refer to memory locations where we can store values. Once these variables are created, they can be manipulated as needed.

This approach is very useful, for example, when entering the name and grade of a student, as shown in the following code:

Listing 6.1: Variables

```
name = input("Enter the student's name: ")
grade = float(input("Enter the student's grade: "))
print('The name is: {0:20s} and the grade is: {1:5.2f}'.format(name,
↪  grade))
```

Output in execution mode

```
Enter the student's name: Alain Flouflou
Enter the student's grade: 85
The name is: Alain Flouflou       and the grade is: 85.00
```

Now, let's imagine that we want to enter the names and grades of a group of 25 students. Additionally, we need to calculate the average grade of these students and display it.

An easy solution would be to use variables like **name_1**, **name_2**, ..., **name_25** to store the names and **grade_1**, **grade_2**, ..., **grade_25** to store the grades. However, this approach would result in 50 variables cluttering the program. Moreover, calculating the average of the grades would require us to write a cumbersome expression like:

$$\frac{\text{grade\_1} + \text{grade\_2} + \ldots + \text{grade\_25}}{25} \tag{6.1}$$

This approach is not practical. An alternative is to find a way to store all the student grade values in a single variable, which would provide us with a way to access each individual grade.

In Python, collections serve as such variables, grouping multiple values and allowing access to individual elements. Collections offer a wide range of possibilities that would be difficult to achieve using separate variables.

The fundamental collections in Python are `list`, `tuple`, `set`, and `dict`. Additional collections are available in the **collections** module.

Before delving into each collection in detail, it's worth noting that each collection provides various methods and properties for manipulating the data it contains.

6.2 Lists

Lists are fundamental sequences in Python, known for their versatility and ease of use. They can contain elements of the same type, such as integers, or a mix of different types, like integers and floats.

The `list` collection is mutable, meaning it can change in size by adding or removing elements, and its elements can also change values.

By default, a list is sorted. When adding an item to a list using the `append()` method, the element is placed at the end of the list.

There are several ways to create a Python list. The easiest approach is to use square brackets `[]` or the `list()` function.

The following code demonstrates different ways to create an empty list:

Listing 6.2: Creating lists

```
liste1 = []
liste2 = list()
# Display the lists
print(liste1)
print(liste2)
```

Output in execution mode

```
[]
[]
```

List Initialization

You can initialize a list by providing a sequence of values, which can be of the same type or different types.

Listing 6.3: Creating and initializing lists

```
products = ['candy', 'tv', 'notebook']
data = ['Top', True, 42.5]
# Display the lists
print(products)
print(data)
```

Output in execution mode

```
['candy', 'tv', 'notebook']
['Top', True, 42.5]
```

List Packing and Unpacking

You can assign a set of values to a variable of type `list`, which is known as **packing**. The reverse operation, where you extract these values into separate variables, is called **unpacking**.

Listing 6.4: List packing and unpacking

```
# Packing
person = ['Flouflou', 'Alain', 25]
# Unpacking
last_name, first_name, age = person
```

```
# Display
print(person)
print(last_name)
print(first_name)
print(age)
```

Output in execution mode

```
['Flouflou', 'Alain', 25]
Flouflou
Alain
25
```

List slicing

We can retrieve specific elements from a list using the slicing technique. To do this, we need to indicate the start index, end index, and the slicing increment. The code in listing 6.5 shows some variations of slicing.

Listing 6.5: List slicing

```
# List
details = ['Mr', 'Alain','Flouflou','Quebec', 'Canada']
# Slicing
sub1 = details[1:3]
sub2 = details[1:4:2]
sub3 = details[-2:-4:-1]
# Display
print(sub1)
print(sub2)
print(sub3)
```

Output in execution mode

```
['Alain', 'Flouflou']
['Alain', 'Quebec']
['Quebec', 'Flouflou']
```

Note that when slicing a `list`, we can start from the first element with the first index being 0. Similarly, we can start from the last element with the start index being -1. Furthermore, the last index when slicing is not included in the result.

The slicing increment defaults to 1 and can be omitted. If the increment is different from 1, you indicate it after the end index of the slicing.

Useful Methods for Lists

Below are some useful operations for manipulating `list` collections:

- `sort()`: sorts the elements of the list
- `reverse()`: sorts the list in reverse order
- `count()`: counts the number of occurrences of an element in the list
- `append()`: adds an element to the end of the list
- `insert()`: inserts an element at a specific position in the list
- `remove()`: removes a specific element from the list
- `extend()`: appends elements from one list to another list
- `pop()`: removes and returns an element from the list
- `index()`: searches for the index of an element in the list

The code in listing 6.6 demonstrates some examples of applying the previously mentioned methods.

Listing 6.6: List manipulations

```
# List
details = ['Mr', 'Alain', 'Flouflou', 'Quebec', 'Canada', 'Mr']
# Operations
details.sort() # Sorts the elements of the list
print('List sorted in alphabetical order:', details)
details.reverse() # Reverses the list
print('Reversed list:', details)
total = details.count('Mr') # Counts the occurrences of 'Mr' in the
↪   list
print('Number of occurrences:', total)
details.append('final') # Appends 'final' to the end of the list
print('List after append:', details)
details.insert(2, 'part') # Inserts 'partie' at position 3
print('List after insert:', details)
details.remove('Alain') # Removes 'Alain' from the list
print('List after removal:', details)
details.extend(['detail', 'plus']) # Appends a list to the list
print('List after extending with another list:', details)
elem = details.pop(2) # Removes and returns the element at position 3
print('Element after pop:', elem)
print('List after pop:', details)
index = details.index('Quebec') # Searches for the index of 'Quebec'
print('Index of an element in the list:', index)
```

Output in execution mode

```
List sorted in alphabetical order: ['Alain', 'Canada', 'Flouflou',
↪ 'Mr', 'Mr', 'Quebec']
Reversed list: ['Quebec', 'Mr', 'Mr', 'Flouflou', 'Canada', 'Alain']
Number of occurrences: 2
List after append: ['Quebec', 'Mr', 'Mr', 'Flouflou', 'Canada',
↪ 'Alain', 'final']
List after insert: ['Quebec', 'Mr', 'part', 'Mr', 'Flouflou', 'Canada',
↪ 'Alain', 'final']
List after removal: ['Quebec', 'Mr', 'part', 'Mr', 'Flouflou',
↪ 'Canada', 'final']
List after extending with another list: ['Quebec', 'Mr', 'part', 'Mr',
↪ 'Flouflou', 'Canada', 'final', 'detail', 'plus']
Element after pop: part
List after pop: ['Quebec', 'Mr', 'Mr', 'Flouflou', 'Canada', 'final',
↪ 'detail', 'plus']
Index of an element in the list: 0
```

6.3 Tuples

Tuples are similar to lists, but with immutable elements, meaning that once they are created, their elements cannot be changed. They can contain elements of the same type, such as integers, or elements of different types, such as strings, integers, and floats.

The `tuple` collection is also immutable, which means that its size cannot be changed after creation. This immutability property is important in many situations, such as passing values to a function through a tuple or returning values from a function through a tuple.

There are several ways to create a tuple in Python. The simplest way is to use parentheses `()` or the `tuple()` function. This is especially useful when you want to create a tuple from an iterable.

The code in listing 6.7 demonstrates the different ways to create a tuple. We can observe that **tup3** was created based on a string of characters.

Listing 6.7: Tuple creation

```
tup1 = ()
tup2 = tuple()
tup3 = tuple('Python')
```

```
# Display the tuples
print(tup1)
print(tup2)
print(tup3)
```

Output in execution mode

```
()
()
('P', 'y', 't', 'h', 'o', 'n')
```

Tuple Initialization

You can initialize a tuple in the same way as a list, by using a collection of values. These values can be of the same type or of different types.

Listing 6.8: Tuple creation and initialization

```
products = ('candy', 'tv', 'notebook')
data = ('Top', True, 42.5)
articles = True, False, True
# Display the tuples
print(products)
print(data)
print(articles)
```

Output in execution mode

```
('candy', 'tv', 'notebook')
('Top', True, 42.5)
(True, False, True)
```

Are parentheses mandatory for a tuple?

We can even omit the parentheses when initializing tuples.

Tuple Packing and Unpacking

Similar to a `list` variable, you can assign a set of values to a `tuple` variable. The packing/unpacking property of tuples, along with their immutable nature, makes `tuple` type parameters highly valuable in functions.

Listing 6.9: Tuple packing and unpacking

```
# Packing
person = ('Flouflou', 'Alain', 25, 3550.25)
# Unpacking
last_name, first_name, age, salary = person
# Display
print(person)
print(last_name)
print(first_name)
print(age)
print(salary)
```

Output in execution mode

```
('Flouflou', 'Alain', 25, 3550.25)
Flouflou
Alain
25
3550.25
```

To simplify unpacking and avoid identifying the types of values, it is preferable to store identical types in the tuple whenever possible.

Tuple Slicing

We can retrieve elements from a tuple using the same slicing technique as for lists.

Listing 6.10: Tuple slicing

```
# Tuple
details = ('Mr', 'Alain','Flouflou','Quebec', 'Canada')
# Slicing
sub1 = details[1:3]
sub2 = details[1:4:2]
sub3 = details[-2:-4:-1]
# Display
print(sub1)
print(sub2)
print(sub3)
```

Output in execution mode

```
('Alain', 'Flouflou')
('Alain', 'Quebec')
('Quebec', 'Flouflou')
```

Useful Methods and Functions for `tuple` Collection

Here are two methods that are useful for manipulating `tuple` collections:

- `count()`: returns the number of occurrences of a specific element in the tuple.
- `index()`: searches for the index of a particular element in the tuple.

Additionally, there are some other useful functions for the `tuple` collection:

- `len()`: returns the number of elements in the tuple.
- `max()`: returns the maximum value in the tuple.
- `min()`: returns the minimum value in the tuple.

Listing 6.11: Tuple manipulation

```
# Tuple
details = ('Mr', 'Alain','Flouflou','Quebec', 'Canada', 'Mr')
# Operations
total = details.count('Mr') # Count the number of occurrences of 'Mr'
↪ in the tuple
print("Number of occurrences:", total)
index = details.index('Quebec') # Find the index of the element
↪ 'Quebec'
print("Index of an element in the tuple:", index)
```

Output in execution mode

```
Number of occurrences: 2
Index of an element in the tuple: 3
```

6.4 Sets

In certain situations, we require a collection where each element is unique. The `set` type collection provides this property of uniqueness.

A `set` type object is not sorted by default. When adding an element to a `set` using the add() method, the element is first checked for uniqueness before being placed in the collection. Consequently, the order of the elements is not guaranteed.

Sets can contain elements of identical types, such as integers, or different types, such as strings, integers, and floats.

The set collection is mutable, meaning it can change size. However, the elements of a set must be of an immutable type.

To represent objects of type set, we use braces {}. It is important to note that dictionaries (dict type) also use braces {}. Therefore, to create a set object, we use the set() function.

The code in listing 6.12 demonstrates different ways to create a set().

Listing 6.12: Creating a set

```
sop = set()
sop.add(1)
print(sop)
products = {'candy', 'bread', 'carrot', 'candy', 'flour'}
# Display the contents of the set
print(products)
```

Output in execution mode

```
{1}
{'flour', 'bread', 'carrot', 'candy'}
```

Notice that the duplicate element **candy** was represented only once in the **products** set during initialization. The set **sop** is initially empty, and we used the add() method to add an element to it.

Set initialization

You can initialize a set using a list of values. These values can be of the same type or of different types.

Listing 6.13: Creating and initializing a set

```
products = {'candy', 'tv', 'notebook'}
data = {'Top', True, 42.5}
# Display the sets
print(products)
print(data)
```

Output in execution mode

```
{'candy', 'notebook', 'tv'}
{True, 42.5, 'Top'}
```

Immutability of elements

The elements themselves must be immutable. Therefore, you cannot use `list` and `dict` as part of a `set`. However, you can use a `tuple` since it is immutable.

Listing 6.14: Set immutability

```
# Using a set
details = {'Mr', 'Alain', 'Flouflou', ('Quebec', 'Canada')}
# Display
print(details)
# Using a list
products = {'candy', 'notebook', ['tv', 'radio']}
# Display
print(products)
```

Output in execution mode

```
{('Quebec', 'Canada'), 'Alain', 'Mr', 'Flouflou'}
Traceback (most recent call last):
  File "C:/temp/PycharmProjects/modo/mod_set3.py", line 6, in <module>
    products = {'candy', 'notebook', ['tv', 'radio']}
TypeError: unhashable type: 'list'
```

Useful methods for a `set`

By their nature, objects of type `set` are neither indexable nor suitable for slicing.

We have the `add()` method, which allows you to add elements to a `set` object, as shown in the code in listing 6.15.

Listing 6.15: Using add()

```
details = {'candy', 'bread'}
details.add('carrot')
# Display
print(details)
```

Output in execution mode

```
{'bread', 'carrot', 'candy'}
```

Another method that can be useful in some cases is pop(). This method randomly removes an item from a set object and returns it for assignment.

Listing 6.16: Using pop()

```
# Using pop()
details = {'candy', 'bread', 'carrot', 'apple'}
item = details.pop()
# Display
print(details)
print(item)
```

Output in execution mode

```
{'carrot', 'candy', 'apple'}
bread
```

6.5 Dictionaries

The sequences or collections we have seen so far have interesting properties from a storage and manipulation point of view. For example, lists are mutable, support indexing, and maintain the order of elements, making them popular as a storage structure.

A collection that provides similar properties is the dictionary. It plays a central role due to its storage structure of key-value pairs, thus offering unique properties. Instead of indexing with numerical indices, dictionaries use keys to access their elements. Dictionaries maintain uniqueness with respect to the keys during insertion. Therefore, dictionaries are mutable but not sorted like lists.

Is the key always a string?

The key in a dictionary is usually a string, but it can be any immutable type.

There are several ways to create a dictionary in Python. The easiest way is to use braces {} or the dict() function.

Listing 6.17 shows the different ways to create an empty dictionary.

Listing 6.17: Creating dictionaries

```
dict1 = {}
dict2 = dict()
#Display the dictionaries
print(dict1)
print(dict2)
```

Output in execution mode

```
{}
{}
```

Dictionary initialization

You can initialize a dictionary in the same way as a list, using key-value pairs. We separate the key from the value using the symbol : and the pairs of the dictionary will be separated by the symbol , just like we do with the other collections.

Listing 6.18: Dictionary initialization

```
person = {'last_name': 'Flouflou', 'first_name': 'Alain', 'age': 25}
print(person)
```

Output in execution mode

```
{'last_name': 'Flouflou', 'first_name': 'Alain', 'age': 25}
```

Important properties of the `dict` type

Consider the following dictionary:

```
{'last_name': 'Flouflou', 'first_name': 'Alain', 5: ['val1','val2']}
```

Table 6.1 summarizes some properties associated with this dictionary.

Property	Description
The dictionary is an unordered collection of elements	The order of the three elements is not guaranteed to remain the same
Each value in the dictionary is indexed by a key	We have the keys **last_name**, **first_name**, and 5
The key in a dictionary is immutable	There cannot be another key that can have the value **last_name**, **first_name**, or 5
The key is usually of type `str` but can be of another type	Two keys are of type `str`, and another is of type `int`
The value can be any type	We see that the value for key 5 is of type `list`

Table 6.1: Dictionary properties.

Operating on dictionaries

Once you have created a dictionary, you can add key-value pairs to it, modify values, and delete pairs. Several approaches can be used to perform these operations.

We consider the dictionary described in listing 6.19, that is:

Listing 6.19: Dictionary manipulation

```
person = {'last_name': 'Flouflou', 'first_name': 'Alain', 'age': 25,
↪   'children': ['annie', 'sonia']}
# Display the dictionary
print(person)
```

If we want to see the value corresponding to a key, we will use indexing with respect to that key. For example, to get the name, we use the key **last_name** as shown:

```
person_last_name = person['last_name']
print(person_last_name)
```

This gives the result:

Output in execution mode

```
Flouflou
```

Now, it's possible that we try to index against a key that doesn't exist in the dictionary like **address**:

Listing 6.20: Dictionary manipulation

```
person_address = person['address']
print(person_address)
```

The code attempts to retrieve the value associated with the key **address** from the dictionary **person**. However, there is no such key **address** in the **person** dictionary. As a result, the code will raise a **KeyError**.

This gives the result:

Output in execution mode

```
person_address = person['address']
KeyError: 'address'
```

To avoid this error, one can check the existence of the key in the dictionary before using it. Keys can be obtained using the `keys()` method. Note that this will be invoked by default on a dictionary.

We will then use the `in` operator to check if the key exists among the keys of this dictionary, i.e.:

Listing 6.21: Checking keys in a dictionary

```
if 'address' in person.keys():
    person_address = person['address']
    print(person_address)
else:
    print('Sorry, there is no key with this description!')
```

This gives the result:

Output in execution mode

```
Sorry, no key with this description!
```

Another interesting approach is to use the `get()` method, which allows returning the value corresponding to the key if it exists, otherwise returning a default value.

Listing 6.22: Checking keys with get()

```
person_address = person.get('address', 'Address not declared!')
print(person_address)
person_last_name = person.get('last_name', 'Name is not declared!')
print(person_last_name)
```

This gives the result:

Output in execution mode

```
Address not declared!
Flouflou
```

Keys are case-sensitive!

Yes, the case is important for keys. Because of this, the key 'name' is not the same as 'Name'.

Now, what happens if we want to modify the value corresponding to a key that does not exist in the dictionary? In this case, a new pair is added, as shown in the code in listing 6.23.

Listing 6.23: Adding a new pair to a dictionary

```
# Adding a new key-value pair
person['address'] = '14 Park Street'
# Modifying the value of an existing key
person['last_name'] = 'Claiclair'
# Displaying the updated dictionary
print(person)
```

This gives the result:

Output in execution mode

```
{'last_name': 'Claiclair', 'first_name': 'Alain', 'age': 25,
↪ 'children': ['annie', 'sonia'], 'address': '14 Park Street'}
```

If you can add pairs, you can also remove them by using the `pop()` and `clear` methods as well as `del`.

Imagine that we want to delete the pair with the key `'children'`. The code in listing 6.24 first checks if the key exists before deleting.

Listing 6.24: Removing a pair with Validation

```
# Deletion with del
if 'children' in person:
    del person['children']
else:
    print("Sorry, the key does not exist!")

# Displaying the updated dictionary
print(person)
```

This gives the result:

Output in execution mode

```
{'last_name': 'Flouflou', 'first_name': 'Alain', 'age': 25}
```

If we wish to retrieve the value corresponding to the key before deleting the pair, we can utilize the code shown in listing 6.25.

Listing 6.25: Using the pop() method

```
# Deletion with pop
children_list = person.pop('children', [])
person_address = person.pop('address', "Key does not exist!")
# Display
print(person)
print(children_list)
print(person_address)
```

Executing this code produces the following output:

Output during execution

```
{'last_name': 'Flouflou', 'first_name': 'Alain', 'age': 25}
['annie', 'sonia']
Sorry, the key does not exist!
```

Please note that the `pop()` method not only allows you to delete the key-value pair but also enables you to retrieve the value associated with the key. Additionally, you can set a default value to be returned in case the specified key does not exist in the dictionary.

Useful methods for dictionaries in Python

In addition to the `get()` and `pop()` methods, there are three other useful methods for iterating through dictionaries. Each of these methods returns an object of type `iterator`.

Method	Description
`items()`	The iterator consists of `tuple` elements in the form of a pair (key, value).
`keys()`	The iterator consists of the keys present in the dictionary.
`values()`	The iterator consists of the values present in the dictionary.

Table 6.2: Dictionary methods.

Listing 6.26 demonstrates how to retrieve key-value pairs from the dictionary.

Listing 6.26: Using the items() method

```
person = {'last_name': 'Flouflou', 'first_name': 'Alain', 'age': 25}
# Displaying the key-value pairs
for k, v in person.items():
    print(k, ':', v)
```

Output during execution

```
last_name : Flouflou
first_name : Alain
age : 25
```

Should we use specific letters k and v for the key and the value respectively?

While we can use any letters, it is a common convention to use `k` for `key` and `v` for `value`.

In many practical cases involving communication between web clients and servers, it is often necessary to identify the keys used in the data format. Therefore, knowing how to iterate through a dictionary to obtain this information is important.

The code in listing 6.27 shows how to retrieve the keys using a default recovery technique, which implicitly calls the `keys()` method since the iterator itself contains the keys.

Listing 6.27: Using the keys() method

```
person = {'last_name':'Flouflou', 'first_name':'Alain', 'age':25}
# Display the keys
print("Using the keys() method:")
for k in person.keys():
    print(k)
```

```
print("Without using the keys() method:")
for key in person:
    print(key)
```

Output in execution mode

```
Using the keys() method:
last_name
first_name
age
Without using the keys()method:
last_name
first_name
age
```

Finally, if you want to retrieve the values from the dictionary, you can use the code in listing 6.28.

Listing 6.28: Using the values() method

```
person = {'last_name':'Flouflou', 'first_name':'Alain', 'age':25}
# Display the values
print("Values of the dictionary:")
for v in person.values():
    print(v)
```

Output in execution mode

```
Values of the dictionary:
Flouflou
Alain
25
```

6.6 Quick summary

This quick summary highlights the essential concepts in using collections and sequences in Python, providing a concise overview of the key elements you have learned:

- Collections like `list`, `tuple`, `set`, and `dict` serve as valuable memory structures for storing multiple elements efficiently.
- Each collection type has its unique properties and methods, making them suitable for specific use cases.
- The `list` collection is particularly versatile and advantageous due to its mutability and ability to accommodate duplicate elements.

- On the other hand, the `tuple` collection is immutable, providing protection to its elements against unauthorized modifications when required.
- For operations involving sets, the `set` collection proves to be highly beneficial, allowing us to perform actions like **UNION**.
- Lastly, the `dict` collection stands as one of the most popular choices due to its capability to store items using key-value pairs.

6.7 Quiz

Please answer the following questions. There may be one or more correct answers.

1. The data structures provided in Python are:
   (a) `list`
   (b) `tuple`
   (c) `array`
   (d) `dict`
   (e) `set`

2. One of the most interesting data structures in Python is the `list`. It is mutable and can accept duplicates.
   (a) True
   (b) False

3. The `dict` data structure uses key-value pairs to represent data.
   (a) True
   (b) False

4. A collection of type `dict` or `tuple` cannot be used as a parameter of a function.
   (a) True
   (b) False

5. Consider the list `my_list=[14, 45, 58, 45]`. To retrieve the element `58`, we use:
   (a) `my_list[3]`
   (b) `my_list[2]`
   (c) `my_list['2']`

6. The `tuple` data structure is immutable.
   (a) True
   (b) False

7. Consider the dictionary `info={'name':'flouflou'}`. To retrieve the value `flouflou`, we use:
   (a) `info[name]`
   (b) `info['name']`

(c) `info["name"]`

8. The parentheses used to indicate a `tuple` are optional and therefore could be omitted.
   (a) True
   (b) False

9. You can add and remove elements from a `set`. However, its elements are immutable.
   (a) True
   (b) False

10. To find the length or number of elements in a collection, for example, a `list`, we can use the function:
    (a) length()
    (b) len()
    (c) Length()

6.8 Practice problems

6.8.1 Practice: Manipulating Lists

PROBLEM 6.1

Create and display the contents of a list containing the integers 43, 11, 23, and 4.

```
tab_int = [43, 11, 23, 4]
print(tab_int)
```

Output

```
[43, 11, 23, 4]
```

PROBLEM 6.2

Create and display the content of a list containing the strings **Hello**, **alain**, and **flouflou**.

```
tab_str = ['Hello', 'alain', 'flouflou']
print(tab_str)
```

Output

```
['Hello', 'alain', 'flouflou']
```

PROBLEM 6.3

Create and display the content of a list containing the elements **Hello**, 23, **flouflou**, and 34.5.

```
tab_mul = ['Hello', 23, 'flouflou', 34.5]
print(tab_mul)
```

Output

```
['Hello', 23, 'flouflou', 34.5]
```

PROBLEM 6.4

Create and display the content of a list containing the elements **Hello**, **alain**, **flouflou**, and the list [34, 4, 56].

```
tab_mel = ['Hello', 'alain', 'flouflou', [34, 4, 56]]
print(tab_mel)
```

Output

```
['Hello', 'alain', 'flouflou', [34, 4, 56]]
```

PROBLEM 6.5

Consider the list from problem 6.2 and display the values of the second and third elements.

```
tab_str = ['Hello', 'alain', 'flouflou']
print(tab_str[1], tab_str[2])
```

Output

```
alain flouflou
```

PROBLEM 6.6

Using a negative index from the end of the list from problem 6.2, display the values of the last and second-to-last elements.

```
tab_str = ['Hello', 'alain', 'flouflou']
print(tab_str[-1], tab_str[-2])
```

Output

```
flouflou alain
```

PROBLEM 6.7

Using the slicing technique, retrieve the list that contains the second and third elements from problem 6.2.

```
tab_str = ['Hello', 'alain', 'flouflou']
print(tab_str[1:3])
```

Output

```
['alain', 'flouflou']
```

PROBLEM 6.8

Using the slicing technique with a negative index, reverse the list from problem 6.2.

```
tab_str = ['Hello', 'alain', 'flouflou']
print(tab_str[::-1])
```

Output

```
['flouflou', 'alain', 'Hello']
```

PROBLEM 6.9

Using the function `len()`, find and display the number of elements in the list from problem 6.1.

```
# List with len()
tab_int = [43, 11, 23, 4]
#print(tab_int)
print('Size of tab_int:', len(tab_int))
```

Output

```
4
```

PROBLEM 6.10

Using the functions `list()` and `range()`, generate the list that contains the integers from 4 to 11.

```
# List with range() and list()
tab_mel = list(range(4, 12))
print(tab_mel)
```

Output

```
[4, 5, 6, 7, 8, 9, 10, 11]
```

PROBLEM 6.11

Using the + operator, perform the concatenation of the lists [1,2,3] and [8,9,10].

```
tab_1 = [1, 2, 3]
tab_2 = [8, 9, 10]
print(tab_1)
print(tab_2)
tab_f = tab_1 + tab_2
print(tab_f)
```

Output

```
[1, 2, 3]
[8, 9, 10]
[1, 2, 3, 8, 9, 10]
```

PROBLEM 6.12

Using the * operator, perform the concatenation of the list [1,2,3] three times.

```
# List with * operator
tab_1 = [1, 2, 3]
print(tab_1 * 3)
```

Output

```
[1, 2, 3, 1, 2, 3, 1, 2, 3]
```

PROBLEM 6.13

Using a **for** loop, display each of the elements from problem 6.2.

```
# Looping through list with for
tab_str = ['Hello', 'alain', 'flouflou']
for i in tab_str:
    print(i)
```

Output

```
Hello
alain
flouflou
```

PROBLEM 6.14

Using the append() method, add the element 'tel:(514-555-9876)' to the list from problem 6.2.

```
tab_str = ['Hello', 'alain', 'flouflou']
tab_str.append('tel:(514-555-9876)')
print(tab_str)
```

Output

```
['Hello', 'alain', 'flouflou', 'tel:(514-555-9876)']
```

PROBLEM 6.15

Given the list containing the elements **'bAllo'**, **'alain'**, **'flouflou'**, **'damo'**, sort it using the sort() method.

```
tab_str = ['bAllo', 'alain', 'flouflou', 'damo']
tab_str.sort()
print(tab_str)
```

Output

```
['alain', 'bAllo', 'damo', 'flouflou']
```

PROBLEM 6.16

Given the list containing the elements **'bAllo'**, **'alain'**, **'flouflou'**, **'damo'**, sort it and assign the sorted result to a variable using the sorted() function.

Note: If you want to avoid modifying the original list, you can use the sorted() function.

```
tab_str = ['bAllo', 'alain', 'flouflou', 'damo']
res = sorted(tab_str)
print(tab_str)
print(res)
```

Output

```
['bAllo', 'alain', 'flouflou', 'damo']
['alain', 'bAllo', 'damo', 'flouflou']
```

6.8.2 Practice: Manipulating Tuples

PROBLEM 6.17

Create and display the tuples with the following elements: **tuple 1**: integers 1, 2, and 3, **tuple 2**: strings **'Hello'**, **'Alain'**, and **'flouflou'**, and **tuple 3**: elements **'Hello'**, **'Alain'**, **'flouflou'**, 11, and 45.6.

```
# Tuple of integers
tup_int = (1, 2, 3)
print(tup_int)
# Tuple of strings
tup_str = ('Hello', 'Alain', 'flouflou')
print(tup_str)
# Mixed-type tuple
tup_mel = ('Hello', 'Alain', 'flouflou', 11, 45.6)
print(tup_mel)
```

Output

```
(1, 2, 3)
('Hello', 'Alain', 'flouflou')
('Hello', 'Alain', 'flouflou', 11, 45.6)
```

Note: We can use slicing and indexing on tuples.

PROBLEM 6.18

Using the tuple that contains the strings **'Hello'**, **'Alain'**, and **'flouflou'**, try to modify the element at index 1.

```
tup_str = ('Hello', 'Alain', 'flouflou')
print(tup_str)
tup_str[1] = 'Annie'
print(tup_str)
```

Output

```
tup_str[1] = 'Annie'
TypeError: 'tuple' object does not support item assignment
```

6.8.3 Practice: Manipulating Sets

PROBLEM 6.19

Using the notation {}, create the set that contains the strings **'Hello'**, **'Alain'**, **'flouflou'**, and **'Alain'**. Similarly, create the set that contains the values 1, 4, 5, 3, and 1 using the set() function. Display the contents of each set.

```
# Set using curly braces
set_str = {'Hello', 'Alain', 'flouflou', 'Alain'}
print(set_str)
# Set using set() function
set_int = set([1, 4, 5, 3, 1])
print(set_int)
```

Output

```
{'flouflou', 'Alain', 'Hello'}
{1, 3, 4, 5}
```

PROBLEM 6.20

Using the notation {}, create the set that contains the strings **'Hello'**, **'Alain'**, **'flouflou'**, and **'Alain'**. Now, add the string **'babel'** using the add() method. Display the contents of the set. What do you notice?

```
# Set using curly braces and adding an element
set_str = {'Hello', 'Alain', 'flouflou', 'Alain'}
print(set_str)
set_str.add('babel')
print(set_str)
```

Output

```
{'flouflou', 'Alain', 'Hello'}
{'flouflou', 'Alain', 'babel', 'Hello'}
```

Note: The order of elements in the output is not necessarily sorted.

6.8.4 Practice: Manipulating Dictionaries

PROBLEM 6.21

Consider the dictionary **{'first_name':'Alain','last_name':'flouflou','age':'10'}**. Display its content.

```
# Basic dictionary
person_dict = {'first_name': 'Alain', 'last_name': 'Flouflou', 'age':
↪  '10'}
print(person_dict)
```

Output

```
{'first_name': 'Alain', 'last_name': 'Flouflou', 'age': '10'}
```

PROBLEM 6.22

Consider the dictionary from Exercise 6.21. Modify the value corresponding to the key **first_name** to be **'Annie'**. Then, display the updated dictionary.

```
# Basic dictionary with indexing
person_dict = {'first_name': 'Alain', 'last_name': 'Flouflou', 'age':
↪  '10'}
print(person_dict)

# Modifying the value associated with the 'first_name' key
person_dict['first_name'] = 'Annie'
print(person_dict)
```

Output

```
{'first_name': 'Alain', 'last_name': 'Flouflou', 'age': '10'}
{'first_name': 'Annie', 'last_name': 'Flouflou', 'age': '10'}
```

PROBLEM 6.23

Consider the dictionary from problem 6.21. Delete the key-value pair where the key is **first_name**. Then, display the updated dictionary.

```
# Basic dictionary with deletion
person_dict = {'first_name': 'Alain', 'last_name': 'Flouflou', 'age':
↪   '10'}
print(person_dict)

# Deleting the 'first_name' key-value pair
del person_dict['first_name']
print(person_dict)
```

Output

```
{'first_name': 'Alain', 'last_name': 'Flouflou', 'age': '10'}
{'last_name': 'Flouflou', 'age': '10'}
```

PROBLEM 6.24

Consider the dictionary from problem 6.21. Perform the following operations:

- Display the keys of this dictionary.
- Display the values of this dictionary.
- Display the key-value pairs of this dictionary.

```
# Basic dictionary with display methods
person_dict = {'first_name': 'Alain', 'last_name': 'Flouflou', 'age':
↪   '10'}
print(person_dict.keys())
print(person_dict.values())
print(person_dict.items())
```

Output

```
dict_keys(['age', 'last_name', 'first_name'])
dict_values(['10', 'Flouflou', 'Alain'])
dict_items([('age', '10'), ('last_name', 'Flouflou'), ('first_name',
↪   'Alain')])
```

PROBLEM 6.25

Consider the dictionary from problem 6.21. Traverse the dictionary and display each key.

```
# Basic dictionary traversal
person_dict = {'first_name': 'Alain', 'last_name': 'Flouflou', 'age':
↪ '10'}
# Traversing the keys
for key in person_dict:
    print(key)
```

Output

```
age
last_name
first_name
```

PROBLEM 6.26

Consider the dictionary from problem 6.21. Traverse the dictionary and display each value.

```
# Basic dictionary traversal
person_dict = {'first_name': 'Alain', 'last_name': 'Flouflou', 'age':
↪ '10'}
for v in person_dict.values():
    print(v)
```

Output

```
10
flouflou
Alain
```

PROBLEM 6.27

Consider the dictionary from problem 6.21. Traverse the dictionary and display each key-value pair.

```
# Basic dictionary traversal
person_dict = {'first_name': 'Alain', 'last_name': 'Flouflou', 'age':
↪ '10'}
for k,v in person_dict.items():
    print(k,v)
```

Output

```
age 10
last_name flouflou
first_name Alain
```

PROBLEM 6.28

Consider the dictionary from problem 6.21. Add the following key-value pairs:

- **'address': '14 Park street'**
- **'age': 14**

Use key indexing and the `update()` method.

```
person_dict = {'first_name': 'Alain', 'last_name': 'flouflou', 'age':
↪  '10'}
person_dict['address'] = '14 Park Street'
person_dict.update({'age': 14})
print(person_dict)
```

Output

```
{
'first_name': 'Alain',
'last_name': 'Flouflou',
'age': 14,
'address': '14 Park Street'
}
```

6.9 Programming problems

PROBLEM 6.29

Solution provided in the appendix

Write a program that allows the user to enter 10 real values into a list. Once the input is complete, calculate the average of the entered values and display the result.

Important: Before displaying the average, print the values stored in the list.

We will use two functions for this program: one for inputting the values and another for calculating the average.

PROBLEM 6.30

Solution provided in the appendix

We ask the user to enter 2 sets of values into 2 different lists. Each list should have 5 elements.

Once these 2 lists are created, we will construct 2 other lists. The first list will have each element as the sum of the elements from each corresponding index in the two lists, and the second list will have each element as the product of the elements from each corresponding index in the two lists.

PROBLEM 6.31

Ask the user to enter a fixed number of values (for example 7 values). These values will be placed one by one into a list. Once the entry is complete, we must indicate whether the elements of the list are all consecutive or not.

For example, if the values, once entered into the list, are:

```
[8 9 10 11 12 13 14]
```

then we display that its elements are all consecutive.

However, if the list is, for example:

```
[7 9 13 16 17 18 19]
```

we display that its elements are not all consecutive.

PROBLEM 6.32

We want to evaluate the efficiency of players in a team. For this, we need the number of goals scored by each player and the number of assists made. An assist is a decisive pass made by the player that results in a goal scored by their team.

We need to enter the number of goals and assists for each player on this team. We assume that the team has 12 players, and each player has a name and a code.

Once these values are entered, we want to display the average number of goals scored by the players, the average number of assists made by the players, the number of players whose number of goals scored is below the average, and the number of players whose number of assists is greater than or equal to the average.

The general manager uses the previous results when choosing which players to let go at the end of the season. For this, he uses the following formula:

Player Efficiency = (0.6 * goals scored by the player / total team goals) + (0.4 * assists by the player / total team assists)

Thus, the rule to be used by the general manager is that any player whose efficiency is greater than 0.3000 will be kept by the team for the next season.

PROBLEM 6.33

The lottery is a very popular game of chance in many countries. For example, in Canada, with Lotto 649, six numbers are drawn from a set of 49 numbers. If a ticket contains the six winning numbers, the player wins the jackpot.

In order to help our players, develop a program that generates numbers for the Lotto 649.

Hint: to generate a random selection of 6 numbers from 1 to 49 without any duplicates, we can use the `random` module and a `set` in Python.

PROBLEM 6.34

A palindrome is a word or phrase that reads the same forwards and backwards. For example, the word **ABBA** is a palindrome.

To determine if a word is a palindrome, we can compare the word with its reverse. If they are the same, then the word is a palindrome.

Develop a program that checks if a word or a sentence is a palindrome.

PROBLEM 6.35

Two words are considered anagrams if they contain the same letters, possibly in different orders. For example, the two words **AMINÉ** and **ANIMÉ** are anagrams.

Develop the necessary code to determine if two words are anagrams. You can use the `enumerate()` function and dictionaries to solve this problem.

PROBLEM 6.36

Develop the code that determines if a Canadian postal code is valid. The code consists of six characters and must contain a letter in the first, third, and fifth positions.

Positions two, four, and six are numbers. The first letter must not be part of the following set: `D, F, I, O, Q, U, W, Z`.

Examples of Canadian postal codes are:

- E4V 3C3 Saint-Antoine, NB
- V1N 1K6 Castlegar, BC
- G7A 2Z0 Saint-Nicolas, QC
- L4P 1E2 Keswick, ON

Chapter 7

Classes and Objects

Contents of this chapter

Objectives:

- To understand the notion of class
- To describe objects and classes
- To define attributes
- To define methods
- To use UML graphical notation to describe classes
- To learn to define a constructor-initializer
- To create objects using a constructor
- To use objects in a program

7.1 Introduction

In the preceding chapters, we explored the fundamental syntax of the Python language, along with an introduction to procedural programming. Essentially, we identified the requirements and then proceeded with the development of the necessary operations to be applied to the data in order to achieve the desired outcomes.

Various programming approaches are utilized in software development. One of the most significant and foundational paradigms, upon which Python is built, is the object-oriented approach.

In Chapter 1, we provided a brief introduction to the core concept of a **class**, which, in turn, enables us to create **instances** or **objects**. In the forthcoming sections, we will delve deeper into these concepts and illustrate specific examples of integrating the object-oriented approach into our scripts and programs.

7.2 Structure of a class

Programming languages like Java, C++, and Python offer developers pre-defined types to declare variables and store data. For instance, the type `str` is used to define character strings.

However, despite the range of available types provided by the language, there will always be a need to define our custom types. These custom types not only serve as containers for data but also possess operations that can manipulate the data.

This is where the concept of a **class** comes into play. For us, a class serves as a blueprint for creating a new **type**. It allows data and the operations using that data to be encapsulated together. Consequently, this new type enables the creation of objects based on this specific blueprint.

In essence, a class acts as a model for the objects to be instantiated. For instance, a **Book** class encompasses all functionalities and data essential for processing a **book** instance or object.

What is the difference between the procedural and object-oriented approaches?

In the procedural approach, our focus lies in developing processing procedures. On the other hand, in the object-oriented approach, we direct our attention towards creating objects that collaborate to fulfill the requirements.

7.2.1 Terminology

To effectively utilize the object-oriented paradigm, one must grasp the specific terms used, whether in Python or other languages like Java. The most common terms are the following:

- **Class**: This term designates the container that groups the data and the operations applicable to this data. The class can be likened to a building mold.
- **Object** or **Instance**: An object is the result of instantiating an entity using the class blueprint. Here, we refer to instances or objects derived from the class that share the same attributes. However, it's essential to note that the objects might not necessarily contain the same data.
- **Attribute**: An attribute is a member that holds a particular piece of data. An object can have multiple attributes, each corresponding to a specific data type.

- **State**: The state of an object refers to the values present in its attributes. This state is subject to change over time.
- **Method**: A method is an operation defined for an object, enabling it to modify its data. Objects can have multiple methods.

7.2.2 Classes in Python

In an application, numerous objects collaborate. Often, we can identify types of objects with nearly identical structures and very similar, if not identical, behavior.

Roles of a Class

A class represents a new type that encompasses both a structure (state variables) and behaviors (methods). Additionally, it plays a vital role in breaking down the application into smaller entities. Through constructors, a class becomes a generator or factory for creating objects.

When you create a class, you define the type of data contained within the class, as well as the code responsible for manipulating this data. The keyword used for declaring a class is `class`. The general form of a class in Python is as follows:

```
# Class declaration
class <Class_Name>:
    # Class-level variables / attributes
    var_1 = value1
    var_2 = value2

    # Initializer
    def __init__(self, param_1, ..., param_n):
        # Instance variable or attribute
        self.param_1 = param_1
        ...
        self.param_n = param_n
        ...

    # Functions or methods
    def func_1(self, ..., param_n):
        ...

    def func_n(self, ..., param_2):
        ...
    ...
```

What naming convention should be adopted for the class name?

We will follow the PascalCase convention for naming classes. According to this convention, every word in the class name should start with a capital letter.

The class model presented above incorporates the initializer, which is a special method used to initialize the attributes of an object from the class. In this case, the `__init__()` method takes `self` and the parameters **param_1** to **param_n**.

The usage of `self` serves as a reference to the object itself. The other parameters **self.param_1** to **self.param_n** represent the attributes of the objects that can be instantiated or created from this class.

Do we have to use `self`?

As a convention, each method in a class, including the initializer, will have `self` as its first parameter. While it is technically possible to use a different word for this parameter, it is uncommon to see other developers use anything other than `self`.

The class model also includes the functions **func_1** to **func_n**. The first parameter for these functions is `self`. In this context, these functions are referred to as **methods**, as they require an object to be executed.

Furthermore, there are the variables **var_1** and **var_2**. These variables are class attributes and are associated with the class itself. Since they have the same values for all instances, they are not specific to any particular object.

Listing 7.1: A basic class

```
from math import *

class Point:
    def __init__(self, x, y):
        self.x = x
        self.y = y

    def distance_origin(self):
        return sqrt(self.x * self.x + self.y * self.y)
```

In the preceding example, we defined the **Point** class with two instance variables, **x** and **y**, along with a **distance_origin()** method.

Do we have to have such a complicated class definition?

Basically, a class can be created using the following definition:

```
class Point:
    pass
```

Here, we have the bare minimum structure for a class. The `pass` *keyword is utilized to prevent a runtime error, as we haven't yet provided valid Python code within this context.*

7.2.3 Class members

Class Variables

Class variables are designed to store data that is common to all instances of the class.

Instance Variables

Instance variables or attributes are intended to hold the data specific to an object instantiated from the class.

Initializer

The initializer is responsible for setting the initial state of an object created through the constructor.

Methods

Methods define the behavior of instances of the class when they receive a message or are invoked.

7.3 Objects in Python

7.3.1 What is an object?

An object can be any identifiable entity, either concrete or abstract.

When an object receives messages from external sources, it responds in a manner that defines its behavior. However, its reaction to the same message may vary based on its current state. An object will hold data and has access to operations or methods.

7.3.2 Notion of object in Python

An object possesses the following characteristics:

- An address in memory, which identifies the object.
- A behavior (or interface) defined by functions or procedures, referred to as methods in Python.
- An internal state determined by the values of variables within the object. These variables are known as attributes, which define the specific characteristics of the object.

Now, we may wonder how an object is represented in Python code. To address this, we revisit the fundamental concept of a **variable**, which we have previously discussed in earlier chapters. Essentially, a variable serves as a means of representing data in memory. For example, if we wish to represent a person's age as the value 25 in Python code, we would use a scalar variable, as demonstrated in listing 7.2.

Listing 7.2: Scalar variable

```
age = 25
```

However, if we aim to represent both the age and the name of a person within the same variable, it becomes more convenient to consider an object. This object will contain both the age value and the name value, providing simultaneous access to both attributes.

For instance, consider the object **point2D** which will hold two values, 5 and 4, as attributes **x** and **y** respectively. It remains to define the means of creating this variable, which brings us to the concept of instantiation or object creation.

7.3.3 Constructors and initializers

An instance of a class is formed using a constructor of that class. Once created, the instance possesses its internal state (the values in instance variables) and shares the code that determines its behavior (the methods) with other instances of the class.

Each class has a constructor, which is responsible for creating the object, and an initializer, denoted by `__init__`, whose role is to initialize the object created by the constructor. The initializer is never called directly for the creation of the object.

Hence, we utilize the constructor for object creation, and it typically takes the same number of parameters as the initializer. In the example shown in 7.3, we have a class with an initializer where we define two attributes.

The resulting object, named **point2D**, will have the values 5 and 4 for its attributes **x** and **y**, respectively.

Listing 7.3: Constructor and initializer

```
from math import *

class Point:
    def __init__(self, x, y):
        self.x = x
        self.y = y


point2D = Point(5,4)
print(point2D)
```

Running the code in listing 7.3 gives the following output:

```
<__main__.Point object at 0x0000022607E24290>
```

What we see here is the exact type of object **point2D** followed by its address in memory.

7.4 Methods

Methods define the actions or treatments to be applied. The types of methods that can exist in a class are:

- Service methods
- Utility methods

There is no specific keyword to differentiate a utility method from a service method. It is the responsibility of the developer to design the class with a well-organized set of methods, particularly by utilizing the concept of visibility.

7.4.1 Encapsulation – Visibility

To protect certain methods and attributes, the concept of **private** visibility is employed. In Python, we indicate this level of visibility by adding `__` in front of a member. While some languages like Java enforce strict visibility rules, Python keeps things relatively simple and does not have strict rules for accessing data in attributes.

7.4.2 Service methods

Service methods allow instances of the class to offer more complex services to other instances. For instance, they can provide operations related to:

- Business rules
- User interface
- And more...

7.4.3 Utility methods

Utility methods serve as supporting "subroutines" to other methods of the class. They are typically set to **private** visibility. For example, consider the **Student** class, which includes the **do_homework()** method. This method is considered a service method, but it may, in turn, call the **search_google()** method. The latter will not be directly called by the object but only via **do_homework()**. In this scenario, we consider it as a utility method.

7.4.4 Parameters of a method

Methods or initializers require initial data to be passed in the form of parameters.

```
def set_author(self, author):
    pass

def calculate_rate(self, year, premium):
    pass
```

In the method or constructor that has no parameters, we only include the `self` parameter.

Is it necessary to include `self` during the method call as well?

No, the `self` parameter is only used when declaring the method. It is not required to include it at the time of the method call.

7.4.5 Returning values from a method

Unlike the separate notion of functions and procedures that we discussed in the chapter on functions, the Python language does not distinguish between them based on return types. In Python, the difference is made by whether the method returns a value or not. When a method returns a value, we include the keyword `return` as the last instruction in the method:

```
def calculate_rate(self, year, premium):
  # instructions
  ...
  return something
```

Listing 7.4 showcases the various methods available in a typical Python class.

Listing 7.4: Class with methods

```
from math import sqrt

class Point:
    def __init__(self, x, y):
        self.x = x
        self.y = y

    def distance_origin(self):
        return sqrt(self.x * self.x + self.y * self.y)

    def move(self, x0, y0):
        self.x += x0
        self.y += y0

# Creating an object
point2D = Point(5, 4)
# Displaying its state after creation
print(point2D)
```

Output in execution mode

```
<__main__.Point object at 0x000001E6071D47D0>
```

We observe that to obtain the **point2D** object, we utilize the **Point()** constructor, which automatically calls the initializer, ensuring that the object now possesses a state represented by the values **5** and **4**, found in the attributes **x** and **y**.

Additionally, we notice that the **distance_origin()** method performs a task and then returns a result. On the other hand, the second method **move()** performs a task but does not return any value.

It is important to note that when an instance (object) is created, its state is stored in the attributes. In the example provided, the display does not directly reveal the values of the attributes **x** and **y**.

In reality, the displayed output shows the type of the object, along with its memory location. If you wish to display the state of the object, which is represented by the values in attributes **x** and **y**, you can achieve this by introducing the `__str__()` method. Listing 7.4 can be modified to include this method:

Listing 7.5: Using the str() method

```
from math import sqrt

class Point:
    def __init__(self, x, y):
        self.x = x
        self.y = y

    def distance_origin(self):
        return sqrt(self.x * self.x + self.y * self.y)

    def move(self, x0, y0):
        self.x += x0
        self.y += y0

    def __str__(self):
        return 'x={}, y={}'.format(self.x, self.y)
```

The code for object creation and method calls is as follows:

```
# Creating an object
point2D = Point(5, 4)
# Displaying its state after creation
print('Initial state of the object:')
print(point2D)
# Calling the move() method
point2D.move(3, 5)
# Displaying its state after the method call
print('After method call:')
print(point2D)
```

Output in execution mode

```
Initial state of the object:
x=5, y=4
After method call:
x=8, y=9
```

As seen in the output, the state is now correctly displayed after implementing the `str()` method.

7.5 Case study

Let's examine the scenario of a soccer coach tasked with training a beginner player. They both have a 3-hour training session, during which the player's performance will be evaluated, and the coach's ability to train soccer players will be assessed.

Before delving into the code, we must first go through the steps of identifying the needs and entities involved in the task, as well as their modeling.

To start, let's consider the needs of the individuals involved in this problem. The soccer player's primary objective for attending training is to acquire and improve their soccer skills. Simultaneously, the coach aims to effectively impart their expertise in soccer to the players.

We may also explore other needs in this problem, such as the coach's motivation for participating in training to earn money or a salary.

In the context of object-oriented programming, it is crucial to clearly identify the specific need(s) to be addressed. In this study's case, the acquisition and transmission of soccer skills are recognized as the primary needs.

Moving on to the next stage, we identify the entities implicated in fulfilling these needs. While we discussed things in the previous step, now we must determine the nature of these entities. Considering that we have a player and a coach, it seems appropriate to identify these two entities as the **Player** and **Coach** classes. However, it is also necessary to assess whether other entities play a role in meeting these needs. For instance, is the ball, field, or water bottle essential for fulfilling these needs? In a real-world scenario, it would be vital to conduct a rigorous identification process. For the present case, we consider that the base classes **Player** and **Coach** suffice to represent the entities involved.

UML diagram

UML is a notation language useful for representing classes in a project, among other things. In our case, we specifically use the domain class diagram.

Once this step is completed, we obtain the class diagram representing the entities tied to the domain. Figure 7.1 presents the fundamental diagram for this case study. The essential element in this diagram is the name of each class. The other elements, which we will explore later, are optional.

In the third step, we must identify the attributes and methods that the objects, based on the **Player** and **Coach** classes, will possess.

For the **Player** class, it is evident that the **first_name** and **last_name** attributes of the player are crucial. We may explore other relevant attributes such as weight,

Figure 7.1: Basic classes.

height, and other factors related to the context of soccer. However, to simplify this case study, we will consider the most essential attribute directly linked to the player's needs. Therefore, to assess whether the player has acquired the basic soccer skills, we will include the **performance** attribute in addition to the **first_name** and **last_name** attributes.

Similarly, for each **Coach** type object, we should have the **first_name** and **last_name** attributes. Additionally, we will add the **expertise** attribute to indicate the coaching expertise associated with a coach.

Figure 7.2 illustrates the modified class diagram, incorporating the identified attributes.

Figure 7.2: Basic classes with attributes.

Finally, we need to identify the operations or methods that each object can perform. In this case, we will incorporate the methods depicted in diagram 7.3.

It is important to note that while the method **go_gym()** is present in both classes, there is no obligation that the operation or code in each class is the same.

We can now start the collaboration between objects. This will involve the creation of **Player** and **Coach** type objects, followed by calling methods in a well-defined sequence.

To demonstrate the impact of method execution on an object's state, we have established the following rules as constraints:

Figure 7.3: Basic classes with attributes and methods.

- A **Player** object will experience a 5-point increase in performance when executing the **go_gym()** method, a 10-point increase when executing **listen()**, and a 20-point increase when executing **practice()**.

- A **Coach** object will have their expertise augmented by 10 points when executing the **train()** method and 30 points when executing **examine()**.

In listing 7.6, we have defined attributes and methods specific to objects of type **Coach**. Particular attention has been given to incorporating the rules for modifying the expertise based on the performed method.

Listing 7.6: Coach class

```
class Coach:
    def __init__(self, last_name, first_name, expertise):
        self.last_name = last_name
        self.first_name = first_name
        self.expertise = expertise

    def __str__(self):
        return "Last Name: {}, First Name: {}, Expertise:
        ↪ {}".format(self.last_name,
                                self.first_name, self.expertise)

    def go_gym(self, msg):
        print("Presence in the gym as: " + msg)
```

```
    def train(self):
        print("Coach conducts a training session")
        self.expertise += 10

    def examine(self):
        print("Coach gives an exam")
        self.expertise += 30
```

For objects of the class **Player**, as shown in listing 7.7, we have defined specific attributes and methods. Particular attention has been given to incorporating rules for modifying performance depending on the executed method.

Listing 7.7: Player class

```
class Player:
    def __init__(self, last_name, first_name, performance):
        self.last_name = last_name
        self.first_name = first_name
        self.performance = performance

    def __str__(self):
        return "Last Name: {}, First Name: {}, Performance:
        ↪  {}".format(self.last_name,
                                    self.first_name, self.performance)

    def go_gym(self, msg):
        print("Presence in the gym as:" + msg)
        self.performance += 5

    def listen(self):
        print("Player listens")
        self.performance += 10

    def practice(self):
        print("Player takes an exam")
        self.performance += 20
```

In terms of organization, it is recommended to create the two classes in a separate module. The code for utilizing these classes should be placed in another module to maintain a clear division of functionalities.

The code demonstrating the usage of these classes is presented in listing 7.8. Here, we created the objects and called various methods while carefully adhering to the correct order of execution.

For better understanding, we have included the visualization of each object's state both before and after the collaboration to observe the state changes.

Listing 7.8: Calling sequence of methods

```
# Calling sequence of methods
# Creating objects
objJ = Player("flouflou", "alain", 0)
objE = Coach('flouclair', 'Annie', 0.0)

# Display initial state
print("Before collaboration")
print(objJ)
print(objE)

# Invoking methods
objJ.go_gym("Player")
objE.go_gym("Coach")
objE.train()
objJ.listen()
objE.examine()
objJ.practice()

print("=" * 50)
# Display state after collaboration
print("After collaboration")
print(objJ)
print(objE)
```

We get the following result:

```
Before collaboration
Last Name: flouflou, First Name: alain, Performance: 0
Last Name: flouclair, First Name: Annie, Expertise: 0.0
Presence in the gym as:Player
Presence in the gym as: Coach
Coach conducts a training session
Player listens
Coach gives an exam
```

```
Player takes an exam
==================================================
After collaboration
Last Name: flouflou, First Name: alain, Performance: 35
Last Name: flouclair, First Name: Annie, Expertise: 40.0
```

7.6 Quick summary

This quick summary highlights the essential concepts of object-oriented programming in Python, including class structure, attributes, methods, and their practical application in a case study involving soccer players and coaches:

- Explanation of how classes define custom types in programming.
- Introduction of terms like class, object, attribute, state, and method.
- Overview of class declaration, instance variables, and methods.
- Description of an object's characteristics: memory address, behavior, and internal state.
- Explanation of method parameters and returning values from methods

7.7 Quiz

Please answer the following questions. There may be one or more correct answers.

1. A class contains:
   (a) Attributes
   (b) Methods
   (c) Files

2. Class is a model for grouping data and operations:
   (a) True
   (b) False

3. The method `init()` is called:
   (a) Initializer
   (b) Constructor

4. The method `str()` returns:
   (a) A string representation of the state of an object
   (b) The result of the call to the `init()` method

5. An instance method must have `self` as its first parameter:
   (a) True
   (b) False

6. The keyword `self` indicates:
   (a) A reference to an instance of the current object
   (b) A reference to an instance of the parent object

7. The constructor of a class must have the same name as the class:
   (a) True
   (b) False

8. When a call to the constructor is made, the initializer is called implicitly:
   (a) True
   (b) False

9. An object is an instance of:
   (a) A method
   (b) A set of attributes
   (c) a class

10. Consider the following code:

```
class Car:
    def move(self):
        print('The car is in motion')

v = Car()
v.move()
```

Executing the code leads to the following result:
   (a) Error because `init()` was not set
   (b) Display of: The car is in motion
   (c) Error because `move()` has no parameters

7.8 Practice problems

PROBLEM 7.1

Create a base class **BankAccount** that represents a bank account. For now, create the skeleton of the class with the keyword pass. Then, create an object of type **BankAccount** and display its state.

```
# Creating a base class
class BankAccount:
    pass


# Creating an object of type BankAccount
account = BankAccount()
print(account)
```

Output

```
<__main__.BankAccount object at 0x000001C17C72FE10>
```

Note: The memory address 0x000001C17C72FE10 of the object will most likely be different on your machine.

PROBLEM 7.2

Revisit problem 7.1 by adding an initializer for the attributes **holder**, **code**, and **amount**. Create and display the object with the data as follows: **'flouflou'**, **'ABC123'**, and 5000.

```
class BankAccount:
    def __init__(self, holder, code, amount):
        self.holder = holder
        self.code = code
        self.amount = amount


# Creating an object of type BankAccount
account = BankAccount("Flouflou", "ABC123", 5000)
print(account)
```

Output

```
<__main__.BankAccount object at 0x0000020E6BEA4250>
```

Note: The memory address 0x0000020E6BEA4250 of the object will most likely be different on your machine. Also, we can observe that even though the object has been initialized with specific values for the attributes, the output does not show the object's state.

PROBLEM 7.3

Revisit problem 7.2 by adding the method `__str__()`. Create and display the object with the data as follows: **'flouflou'**, **'ABC123'**, and 5000.

```
#Adding the str method
class BankAccount:
    def __init__(self, holder, code, amount):
        self.holder = holder
        self.code = code
        self.amount = amount

    def __str__(self):
        return 'Holder:{}, code:{}, amount:{}'.format(self.holder,
                                                      self.code, self.amount)

#Creating an object of type BankAccount
account = BankAccount("Flouflou", "ABC123", 5000)
print(account)
```

Output

```
Holder:Flouflou, code:ABC123, amount:5000
```

Note: Now, we can observe that we obtain the object's state in the output.

PROBLEM 7.4

Revisit problem 7.3 by adding the methods **withdraw_money()** to subtract a certain amount and **deposit_money()** to add a certain amount. Create and display the object with the data as follows: **'flouflou'**, **'ABC123'**, and 5000$. Deposit 2000$ into the account, then withdraw 1000$ from the account. Display the account's state after each operation.

```
# Adding methods or operations
class BankAccount:
    def __init__(self, holder, code, amount):
        self.holder = holder
        self.code = code
        self.amount = amount

    def __str__(self):
        return 'Holder:{}, code:{}, amount:{}'.format(self.holder,
                                self.code, self.amount)

    def withdraw_money(self, amount):
        self.amount -= amount

    def deposit_money(self, amount):
        self.amount += amount


# Creating an object of type BankAccount
account = BankAccount("Flouflou", "ABC123", 5000)
print('Initial state')
print(account)
account.deposit_money(2000)
print('State after deposit')
print(account)
account.withdraw_money(1000)
print('State after withdrawal')
print(account)
```

Output

```
Initial state
Holder:Flouflou, code:ABC123, amount:5000
State after deposit
Holder:Flouflou, code:ABC123, amount:7000
State after withdrawal
Holder:Flouflou, code:ABC123, amount:6000
```

7.9 Programming problems

PROBLEM 7.5

Solution provided in the appendix

In this problem, we are developing a Python program consisting of a class with a basic constructor. We will create objects for collaboration.

- Create your Python file and name it **student.py**. A student has the attributes **last_name (str)**, **first_name (str)**, **gender (str)**, **address (str)**, and **student_code (str)**, along with the **final_grade (float)**.
- Now, we want to use this class to create an object representing a student. We have the following student information:

  Obj1: Alain Flouflou, M, 14 Park street, 118907, 78

- In the same module, add the function **main()** that will allow you to instantiate and create an object of type **Student**. Note that we will need a constructor with parameters for the creation of the object.
- Next, we will display a description (state) of the student in the following format:

```
Student  last name: Flouflou first name: Alain gender: M  address: 14
↪  Park Street        code: 118907 final grade: 78
```

In this specific case, we will use the method `__str__()` which will allow us to display the state of the object.

- Add, at the level of the **Student** class, a method **do_homework()**. This method does not take any arguments for now. The body of this method should contain only the following instruction:

```
print('I am a diligent student')
```

- Call this method from the object related to **Flouflou**.

PROBLEM 7.6

Solution provided in the appendix

Develop a class called **Stock** that contains:

- A field named **symbol** for the action symbol.

- A field named **title** for the action name.
- A field named **closing_price** to store the action's value from the previous day.
- A field named **current_price** to store the current value of the action.
- A constructor that establishes an action with the specified name and symbol, along with the closing and current prices for the action.
- A method named **get_percentage_change()** that calculates and returns the percentage change from **closing_price** to **current_price**.

1. Draw the UML class diagram for the **Stock** class.

2. Create an object of type **Stock** named **obj_stock**, with the symbol **MSFT** and the title name **Microsoft**. The previous day's or closing stock price was `123.24` USD, and the current stock price is `127.04` USD. Display the percentage change.

PROBLEM 7.7

Develop a **Fan** class that represents a fan. This class contains:

- Three constants named **LOW**, **MEDIUM**, and **HIGH** with values 1, 2, and 3 to represent possible fan speeds.
- A field named **speed** that indicates the fan speed (default is **LOW**).
- A boolean field named **is_running** that indicates whether the fan is operating (default is **False**).
- A field named **radius** that indicates the fan's radius (default is 5).
- A field named **color** that indicates the fan's color (default is blue).
- A constructor with parameters that allows the creation of a fan.
- The method `__str__()` that returns a description of the fan. If the fan is running, the method returns a single sentence containing the speed, color, and state. If the fan is not running, the method returns a sentence containing the color, speed, and the phrase **fan stopped**.

1. Draw the UML diagram for this **Fan** class.

2. Using the **main()** method, create 2 fan objects. For the first fan, set the speed, color, and radius to maximum speed, yellow, and 10, respectively. For the second fan, set the speed, color, and radius to medium speed, blue, and 5, respectively. The first fan will be turned on, while the second will be turned off. Display the states of each fan using the `__str__()` method.

PROBLEM 7.8

Develop a program that calculates the net salary of an employee, knowing that there are two types of employees: full-time and part-time.

We need to enter the type of employee to calculate the appropriate net salary. Each employee has a first name, last name, and an employee code.

If the employee is full-time, we must enter the salary amount.

If the employee is part-time, we must enter the hourly rate and the number of hours worked. Full-time employees are not allowed to work overtime. However, overtime hours are paid at a rate of 1.5 for any hours exceeding 35 hours for part-time employees.

Consider the following employees as examples:

Obj1: Alain Flouflou, code = 10, full-time, salary = 3750
Obj2: Annie Clairclair, code = 20, part-time, rate = 12.5, hours = 40

PROBLEM 7.9

Solution provided in the appendix

Develop a program that calculates the cost of a trip made by car.

For this, you will develop a class that includes the distance traveled, the unit cost (per liter) of gasoline, and the number of liters consumed.

As an example, we will consider cars with a consumption of 7 liters per 100 km or a consumption of 10 liters per 100 km.

Chapter 8

Inheritance

Contents of this chapter

Objectives:

- To understand the notion of inheritance
- To define a parent class or superclass
- To define a subclass from a superclass through inheritance
- To understand the notion of redefinition
- To invoke the superclass's constructor and methods using the super keyword
- To understand multiple inheritance

8.1 Introduction

In this chapter, we will introduce the concept of inheritance, a fundamental object-oriented technique that plays a crucial role in organizing and creating classes.

In object-oriented applications, we work with various objects that collaborate through messages to solve problems. An object, in this context, represents an instance created from a class that has been designed to encapsulate the attributes and methods needed to solve a specific problem.

Thinking of a class as an abstract notion, similar to a mold or architectural plan, allows us to produce explicit representations of objects based on that class.

In everyday life, we encounter similar representations. For instance, an architect prepares an architectural plan for a house, and a contractor builds houses based on that plan.

Similarly, an automaker designs a master plan for a production car, such as the X200 series. This plan defines all the attributes of the car, like weight, length, and height, as well as its standard functionalities or behaviors, such as forward and reverse movements and door opening.

While the master plan provides an overall structure for the X200 series, the manufacturer recognizes that different target customers will have diverse needs. To accommodate this, the manufacturer develops derivative plans by modifying the master plan according to specific customer requirements.

Each derivative plan caters to a different category of customers, resulting in series like the X200F (family), X200S (sport), and X200T (all-terrain).

In these derived plans, specific attributes and methods are incorporated to meet the needs of each customer category. For instance, the X200S series might include a **zero_acceleration()** method for a unique acceleration feature, while the X200T series could have an **all wheel drive** attribute.

By starting with a single master plan and creating derivative plans, the manufacturer simplifies the process of bringing the new X200 series to market. Otherwise, designing each series from scratch with specific specifications would be much more time-consuming.

At the class level, we will apply a similar concept called **inheritance**, which is a fundamental aspect of object-oriented programming. It enables the frequent reuse of classes in developing new applications, making the development process more efficient and maintainable. It's important to note that inheritance applies to both attributes and methods in a class.

Derived or Child Classes

The foundation of inheritance lies in the need to reuse existing programs to minimize the effort required for creating new ones.

Inheritance is the process through which a new class, known as a child class, is derived from one or multiple existing classes, which we refer to as parent classes.

This concept of inheritance applies to class members, including attributes and methods. Consequently, the new child class automatically inherits all the members from its parent class or classes.

The essence of code reuse in inheritance lies in the ability to provide general properties defined in the parent class to child classes without the need to declare them separately within each child class.

For illustration, consider the **Publication** class presented in listing 8.1, which serves as a representation for any entity containing information.

It is important to note that, for now, the visibility modifiers for the attribute members (**author**, **no_page**, and **editor**) are set to public. In object-oriented programming, it is essential to keep attributes **private** to maintain encapsulation principles. However, for explanatory purposes, we are using **public** visibility here to explain the concept of inheritance.

Listing 8.1: Parent class

```
class Publication :
    def __init__(self, author, no_page, editor):
        self.author = author
        self.no_page = no_page
        self.editor = editor

    def __str__(self):
        return 'Author: {0:20s}, Number of Pages: {1:4d}, Editor:
        ↪  {2:20s}'.format(
            self.author, self.no_page, self.editor)
```

Now, let's consider creating the **Book** class derived from the **Publication** class. In Python, we use parentheses ( ) to indicate that a class is derived from another class.

For instance, from the parent class **Publication**, we will have:

```
class Book(Publication):
    pass
```

Please note that the **Book** class, being derived from the **Publication** class, will inherit all the members present in **Publication**. It is crucial to understand that these classes are developed as abstract representations. Thus, when we state that **Book** has the same members as **Publication**, it simply means that the description plan of **Book** includes the same members as those found in **Publication**, as well as members specific to **Book**.

Inheritance in the context of class hierarchies refers to the child class's ability to inherit the general properties of the parent classes in the chain of inheritance.

Once we obtain the new class resulting from inheritance, we can proceed with the following transformations according to our requirements:

- Adding new variables or attributes to the new class
- Adding new methods to the new class

- Modifying inherited methods

It is important to note that these operations can be performed separately or together, depending on the specific needs of the program.

In object-oriented terminology, the original class is referred to as the parent class, super class, or base class. The class derived from this parent class is known as the child or subclass.

8.1.1 Declaration syntax

For simple inheritance, the syntax for the derived class is as follows:

```
class <derived_class_name>(base_class_name):
        instructions
        ...
```

Here, we indicate the parent class between the parentheses.

Let's consider the **Participant** parent class as an example. This class represents a participant in a training activity. Any object created from this class will have attributes **last_name** and **first_name**. Additionally, we have added the **go_college()** method, which allows the participant to go to the college where the training takes place.

The UML diagram for this class is shown in figure 8.1.

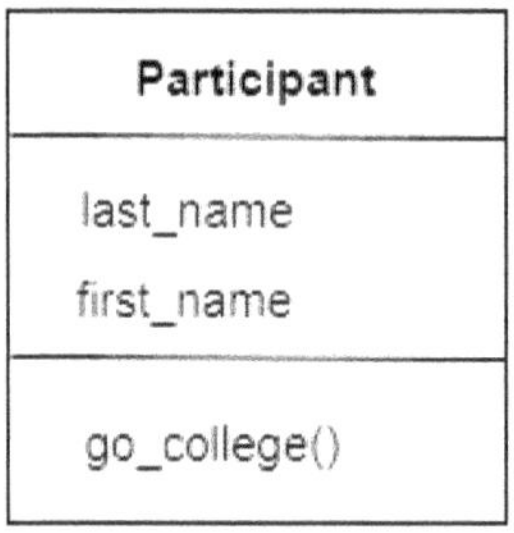

Figure 8.1: Parent class.

Listing 8.2 provides the code for this class, which is standard and includes the initializer and the method that returns the state of the object.

The method **go_college()** will likely be redefined in some or all of the child classes.

Parent Class

Listing 8.2: Parent class

```
class Participant:
    def __init__(self, last_name, first_name):
        self.last_name = last_name
        self.first_name = first_name

    def go_college(self):
        print('The participant goes to college.')

    def __str__(self):
        return 'Last Name={0:15s}, First
        ↪  Name={1:10s}'.format(self.last_name, self.first_name)
```

The code in 8.3 allows us to create a participant object and apply the available method to it, which is **go_college()**. We display the state of the object before the move.

Listing 8.3: Object Creation

```
participant = Participant('Flouflou','Alain')
print(participant)
participant.go_college()
```

Upon execution, we get the following output:

Output during execution

```
Last Name=Flouflou       , First Name=Alain
The participant goes to college.
```

Now, let's consider the relationship between the **Participant** parent class and the **Student** child class.

This relationship is shown in the UML diagram in figure 8.2.

The arrow used is empty in the case of the **is-a** relationship, and it points from the child class to the parent class.

In the diagram, we only include the specific members of the **Student** child class. The methods of the **Participant** parent class are implicitly available in **Student**.

This relation can be expressed as shown in listing 8.4.

We have introduced the use of `super()` in the code of the **Student** class to call the methods of the parent class **Participant**.

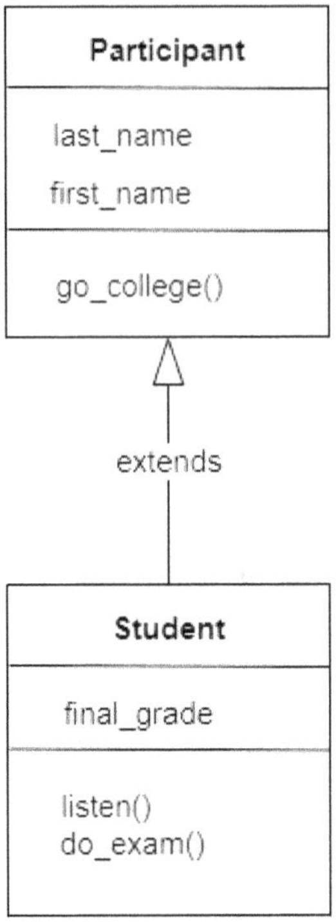

Figure 8.2: Inheritance - Parent and Child.

The `super()` function returns an object of the type of the parent class, which in our case is **Participant**. The object returned by `super()` can be used to call methods from this parent class.

For instance, we used the methods:

- `super().__init__(last_name, first_name)`
- `super().__str__()`

to call the parent class methods. This concept of calling parent methods through `super()` is important because a child object can augment or modify the behavior of a parent method in this manner.

Child class

Listing 8.4: Child class

```
class Student(Participant):
    def __init__(self, last_name, first_name, final_grade):
        super().__init__(last_name, first_name)
        self.final_grade = final_grade

    def listen(self):
        print('Student listens and participates.')

    def do_exam(self):
        print('Student takes the exam.')

    def __str__(self):
        return super().__str__() +',
        ↪  final_grade={0:4.2f}'.format(self.final_grade)
```

There is another use of the super() method that involves using two parameters. Code 8.5 shows the general form.

Listing 8.5: Using super()

```
super(Child_Type, child_type_object)
```

The first parameter is the child type, while the second parameter is an object of the child type.

Note that this form of super() is not very common.

Inheritance establishes a type relationship **is-a** between the parent class and the child class. Referring to the previous example, we can say that the child class is a more specific version or a specialization of the parent class.

In the case of specialization, the **Student** child class has its own methods, **listen()** and **do_exam()**, but it also inherits the **go_college()** method from its parent, the **Participant** class.

Moreover, it has its specific attribute **final_grade**, in addition to the **last_name** and **first_name** attributes that it inherits from **Participant**.

Listing 8.6 allows us to create both the **participant** and the **student** objects and apply the methods of interest to them, which are **go_college()** and **listen()** respectively. We display the state of the objects before and after the operations.

Listing 8.6: Creating parent and child objects

```
# Object Participant
participant = Participant('Flouflou','Alain')
print(participant)
participant.go_college()
print('=' * 50)
# Object Student
student = Student('Flouclair', 'Annie', 86)
print(student)
student.go_college()
student.listen()
```

Upon execution, we get the following output:

Output during execution

```
Last Name=Flouflou    , First Name=Alain
The participant goes to college.
==================================================
Last Name=Flouclair   , First Name=Annie     , final_grade=86.00
The participant goes to college.
Student listens and participates.
```

In summary, with the **Student** class, we were able to:

- Add an attribute and two methods that were not present in the parent class **Participant**.
- Use `super()` to call the parent's `__init__()` and `__str__()` methods.

Next, we will introduce method redefinition at the level of the child class. For this, let's consider the **Professor** class, as shown in the UML diagram in figure 8.3.

In this class, we have the specific attribute **salary** and three methods: **go_college()**, **teach()**, and **give_exam()**. The last two methods mentioned are specific to the child class.

If we explicitly added the **go_college()** method, it means that we intend to redefine the body of the method. It is important to understand that the redefinition does not change the signature of the method. By signature, we mean the number and type of method parameters.

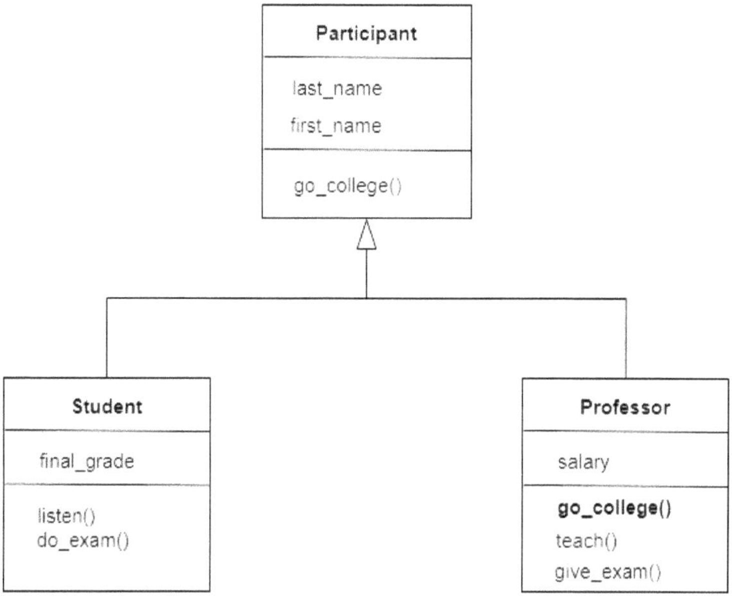

Figure 8.3: Inheritance hierarchy.

When should methods be included in the UML class diagram?

Methods should be included in the UML class diagram when they contribute to the overall understanding of the class's behavior and interactions.If the method is not redefined in the child class, it does not need to be included in the diagram.

The code for the **Professor** class is provided in listing 8.7.

Similar to the **Student** class, we have used `super()` at the code level of the **Professor** class to call the methods of the parent class **Participant**.

Child Class

Listing 8.7: Child class

```
class Professor(Participant):
    def __init__(self, last_name, first_name, salary):
        super().__init__(last_name, first_name)
        self.salary = salary
```

```
    def go_college(self):
        print('The professor goes to college in a Ferrari.')

    def teach(self):
        print('The professor is teaching.')

    def give_exam(self):
        print('The professor gives an exam.')

    def __str__(self):
        return super().__str__() + ',
        ↪   salary={0:7.2f}'.format(self.salary)
```

In this case, we observe that in the **Professor** child class, we have modified the code of the **go_college()** method, which is inherited from its parent, the **Participant** class.

Furthermore, the **Professor** class has its specific **salary** attribute, in addition to the **last_name** and **first_name** attributes inherited from the **Participant** class.

Listing 8.8 demonstrates the creation of objects based on the **Participant**, **Student**, and **Professor** classes and apply their respective methods, such as **go_college()**, **listen()**, and **teach()**. We display the state of each object before the actions.

Listing 8.8: Using parent and child classes

```
# Participant Object
participant = Participant('Flouflou', 'Alain')
print(participant)
participant.go_college()
print('=' * 50)
# Student Object
student = Student('Flouclair', 'Annie', 86)
print(student)
student.go_college()
student.listen()
print('=' * 50)
# Professor Object
professor = Professor('Clairclair', 'Smith', 4000)
print(professor)
professor.go_college()
professor.teach()
```

Upon execution, the output will be as follows:

Output

```
Last Name=Flouflou       , First Name=Alain
The participant goes to college.
==================================================
Last Name=Flouclair      , First Name=Annie      , final_grade=86.00
The participant goes to college.
Student listens and participates.
==================================================
Last Name=Clairclair     , First Name=Smith      , salary=4000.00
The professor goes to college in a Ferrari.
The professor is teaching.
```

In practice, the order of method calls should be adjusted to ensure that the **student** object executes the **listen()** method after the **professor** object has executed the **teach()** method. The updated calling code is provided in listing 8.9.

Listing 8.9: Method call sequence

```python
# Participant Object
participant = Participant('Flouflou', 'Alain')
print(participant)
participant.go_college()
print('=' * 50)
# Student Object
student = Student('Flouclair', 'Annie', 86)
print(student)
student.go_college()
print('=' * 50)
# Professor Object
professor = Professor('Clairclair', 'Smith', 4000)
print(professor)
professor.go_college()
print('=' * 50)
professor.teach()
student.listen()
```

The updated output now better reflects a realistic scenario.

Output

```
Last Name=Flouflou       , First Name=Alain
The participant goes to college.
=====================================================
Last Name=Flouclair      , First Name=Annie      , final_grade=86.00
The participant goes to college.
=====================================================
Last Name=Clairclair     , First Name=Smith      , salary=4000.00
The professor goes to college in a Ferrari.
=====================================================
The professor is teaching.
Student listens and participates.
```

In summary, with the **Professor** class, we have accomplished the following:

- Added an attribute and two methods that were not present in the parent class **Participant**.
- Utilized `super()` to invoke the parent's `__init__()` and `__str__()` methods.
- Redefined a method inherited from the **Participant** parent class.

Polymorphism

To observe polymorphism in action, let's introduce a variable **registry** of type `list` in which we will store the **participant**, **student**, and **professor** objects. By iterating through this list and calling the **go_college()** method on each object, we can avoid separate calls for each of the objects.

The updated code is shown in listing 8.10.

Listing 8.10: Polymorphism in action

```python
participant = Participant('Flouflou', 'Alain')
student = Student('Flouclair', 'Annie', 86)
professor = Professor('Clairclair', 'Smith', 4000)
# List
registry = [participant, student, professor]
# Iteration
for entry in registry:
    entry.go_college()
```

The output is identical to that obtained for separate calls through the objects.

Output in execution mode

```
The participant goes to college.
The participant goes to college.
The professor goes to college in a Ferrari.
```

We can observe polymorphism through the **registry** object. All objects, despite being of different types, are treated as if they were of the same type, which, in our case, is the parent class, **Participant**.

The calling code used, i.e.:

```
# Iteration
for entry in registry:
    entry.go_college()
```

was initially designed for the parent class rather than the child classes. However, at runtime, polymorphism is used to call the specific method based on the inheritance hierarchy.

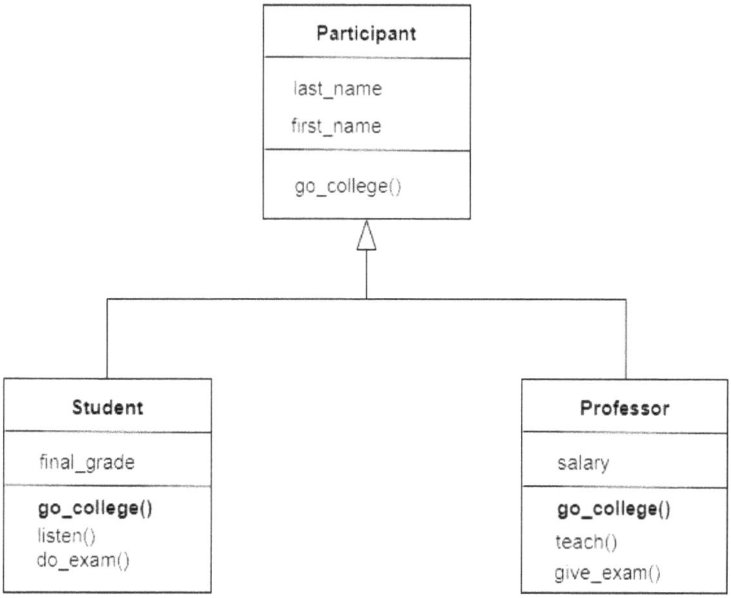

Figure 8.4: Method redefinition in subclasses.

When traversing the **registry** list, the **participant** object sees that it has its own definition of **go_college()**. The second object, **student**, realizes that it hasn't set **go_college()**, so it will inherit the implementation of its parent, meaning the original code of the **go_college()** method in **Participant** will be used.

Moving on, the last object in the list, **professor**, finds that the **go_college()** method is redefined at its level. This redefined version will be used.

Now, let's consider that to reward a **student** object, we want to give them an additional five points on their final grade when they come to college. This new requirement implies that we have to modify the **go_college()** method inherited by the **Student** class. Thus, we need to redefine it and update the UML class diagram accordingly. The new version of the diagram is shown in figure 8.4.

The updated code for the **Student** class is now as shown in listing 8.11.

Listing 8.11: Class with a overridden method

```
class Student(Participant):
    def __init__(self, name, surname, final_grade):
        super().__init__(name, surname)
        self.final_grade = final_grade

    def listen(self):
        print('Student listens and participates.')

    def do_exam(self):
        print('Student takes the exam.')

    def go_college(self):
        self.final_grade += 5
        print('The student goes to college.')

    def __str__(self):
        return super().__str__() + ',
        ↪  final_grade={0:4.2f}'.format(self.final_grade)
```

The **go_college()** method is now available in three versions. Firstly, the one in the **Participant** class. Secondly, the overridden versions in each of the child classes, **Student** and **Professor**.

The code for calling these methods by each of the objects is shown in listing 8.10. The output matches the expected result.

Execution output

```
The participant goes to college.
The student goes to college.
The professor comes to college in a Ferrari.
```

We observe that the **student** object has used its own implementation of **go_college()** since we have redefined the parent method.

Furthermore, we can display the state of the object, and we will see that its final grade has increased by five points:

```
Last name=Flouclair, First name=Annie, final_grade=91.00
```

Multiple inheritance

In Python, we have the flexibility to implement not only simple or single inheritance, but also multiple inheritance. This approach allows a child class to inherit from one or more parent classes.

The syntax for declaring a class derived from multiple base classes is as follows:

```
class <derived_class>(base_class1, base_class2, ..., base_classn):
    instructions
    ...
```

The methods from the various base classes will be inherited by the child class, similar to single inheritance.

However, a challenge arises when two or more parent classes have methods with the same name. This creates ambiguity in determining which method to use in the child class.

To address this issue, Python utilizes the **MRO** (Method Resolution Order) technique to find the appropriate method. The resolution process begins with the leftmost class in the declaration, i.e., **base_class1**, and continues to the rightmost class, **base_classn**. If the method is still not found, Python proceeds to the **Object** class.

To simplify method resolution, it is recommended to rename methods differently at the class level if there is a risk of ambiguity.

Below is an example of another parent class.

Listing 8.12: Another parent class

```
class Athlete:
    def __init__(self, speed):
        self.speed = speed

    def run(self):
        print('Athlete runs with a speed of {}'.format(self.speed))

    def __str__(self):
        return 'speed={0:4.2f}'.format(self.speed)
```

To illustrate multiple inheritance, let's consider the example from the previous section, where a student enjoys playing sports while a professor does not. We will modify the inheritance hierarchy shown in figure 8.4 to include these changes, resulting in the new hierarchy shown in figure 8.5.

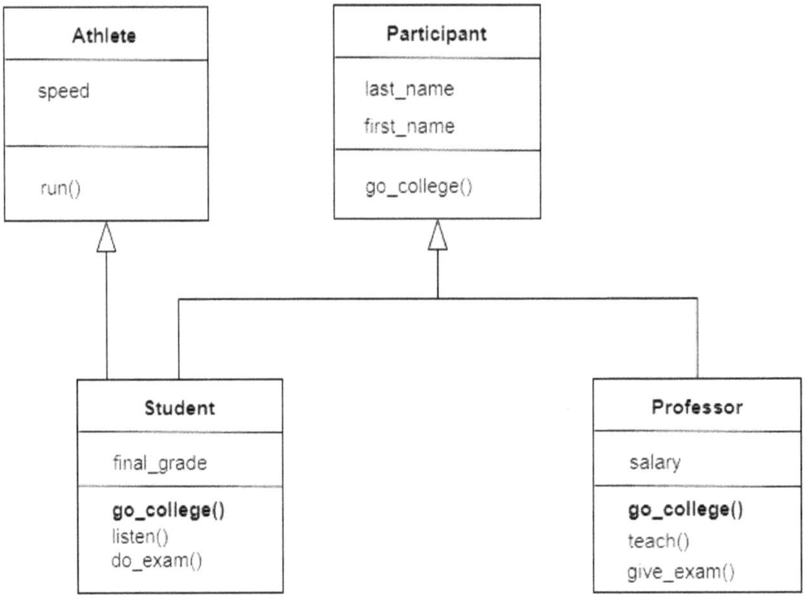

Figure 8.5: Multiple inheritance hierarchy.

Upon inspecting the **Athlete** class, we observe that it includes the **speed** attribute and the **run()** method as members, thereby defining an object of the **Athlete** type. The corresponding code is provided in listing 8.12.

With the introduction of inheritance from the **Athlete** class, the definition of the **Student** class is expanded as depicted in listing 8.13.

Listing 8.13: Inheritance through two parents classes

```
class Student(Participant, Athlete):
    def __init__(self, last_name, first_name, final_grade, speed):
        Participant.__init__(self, last_name, first_name)
        Athlete.__init__(self, speed)
        self.final_grade = final_grade

    def listen(self):
        print('Student listens and participates.')

    def do_exam(self):
        print('Student takes the exam.')

    def come_to_college(self):
        self.final_grade += 5
        print('The student goes to college.')

    def __str__(self):
        return Participant.__str__(self) + ',
        ↪ final_grade={0:4.2f}'.format(self.final_grade) + ', ' +
        ↪ Athlete.__str__(self)
```

To bypass the use of the **MRO** technique, we have opted to make direct calls to the methods of the parent classes `init()` and `str`.

The creation of the **student** object is achieved with the following code:.

```
student = Student('Flouclair', 'Annie', 86, 4)
```

Do we have to use multiple inheritance?

In certain situations, the use of multiple inheritance may become necessary. However, it is crucial to approach this design choice with care and diligence to ensure proper class structures.

In most cases, though, it is possible to avoid the complexities of multiple inheritance by utilizing alternative techniques like class composition. These approaches can provide more straightforward and manageable solutions to the design requirements.

8.1.2 How to determine the type or parent of an object?

When working with instances or objects in an inheritance hierarchy, it becomes necessary to ascertain the actual type of an object. Python provides two methods that enable us to identify both the precise type of an object and whether it belongs to a parent class.

The two available methods are `isinstance()` and `issubclass()`.

The `isinstance()` Method

The `isinstance()` method allows you to test whether an object belongs to a specific type. The syntax is as follows:

```
isinstance(object, target_type)
```

This method returns `True` if the **object** is of the same type as the **target_type** parameter.

To illustrate the usage of `isinstance()`, let's consider the **student** object example from the previous section. We can expand upon the code presented in listing 8.14, which verifies whether the **student** object belongs to a particular type. By utilizing the **status** variable, we can further utilize it as a condition in a test structure.

Listing 8.14: Discovering the type of an object

```
# Check if student is of type Participant
status = isinstance(student, Participant)
print(status)

# Check if student is of type Athlete
status = isinstance(student, Athlete)
print(status)

# Check if student is of type Professor
status = isinstance(student, Professor)
print(status)
```

Upon execution, we receive the confirmation that the **student** object is of the **Participant** type and also of the **Athlete** type. However, it is not of the **Professor** type.

Execution output

```
True
True
False
```

This result can be utilized to implement specific processing, for instance, in situations where the object belongs to a particular type.

The issubclass() Method

The issubclass() method is used to test if a class inherits from another class. The syntax is as follows:

```
issubclass(child_class, search_class)
```

This method returns True if the **child_class** inherits from the **search_class**.

Continuing with the example of the **Student** class, we can further develop the code presented in listing 8.15, which checks whether **Student** inherits from the **Participant** class.

The resulting output can be utilized to implement specific treatment, for instance, in situations where the class indeed inherits from **Participant**.

Listing 8.15: Discovering inheritance relationships

```
# Check if Student inherits from Participant
status = issubclass(Student, Participant)
print(status)

# Check if Student inherits from Athlete
status = issubclass(Student, Athlete)
print(status)

# Check if Student inherits from Professor
status = issubclass(Student, Professor)
print(status)
```

Upon execution, we receive confirmation that **Student** inherits from **Participant** and **Athlete**, but it has no relationship with **Professor**.

Execution output

```
True
True
False
```

8.2 Case study

In this section, we will continue with the case study we initiated in the previous chapter.

Figure 8.6 illustrates the class diagram, including the **Player** and **Coach** classes.

Figure 8.6: Base classes with attributes and methods.

We notice that certain attributes and methods have the same names in both classes. Hence, we will proceed with extracting these common members into a parent class, which we shall refer to as **Athlete**. The resulting hierarchy structure is depicted in figure 8.7. It is important to note that the **go_gym()** method will be retained (redefined) in the **Player** class, as it serves a distinct purpose from the **go_gym()** method present in the **Athlete** class.

Listing 8.16: Parent class Athlete

```
class Athlete:
    def __init__(self, last_name, first_name):
        self.last_name = last_name
        self.first_name = first_name

    def __str__(self):
        return "Last Name: {}, First Name: {}".format(self.last_name,
        ↪  self.first_name)

    def go_gym(self, msg):
        print("Presence in the gym as: " + msg)
```

Listings 8.16, 8.17, and 8.18 provide an overview of the relationships between the various classes.

In listing 8.16, you can find the attributes and methods specific to **Athlete** objects.

Listing 8.17 presents the attributes and methods that are specific to **Coach** objects.

It's important to note that we did not redefine the **go_gym()** method for **Coach**

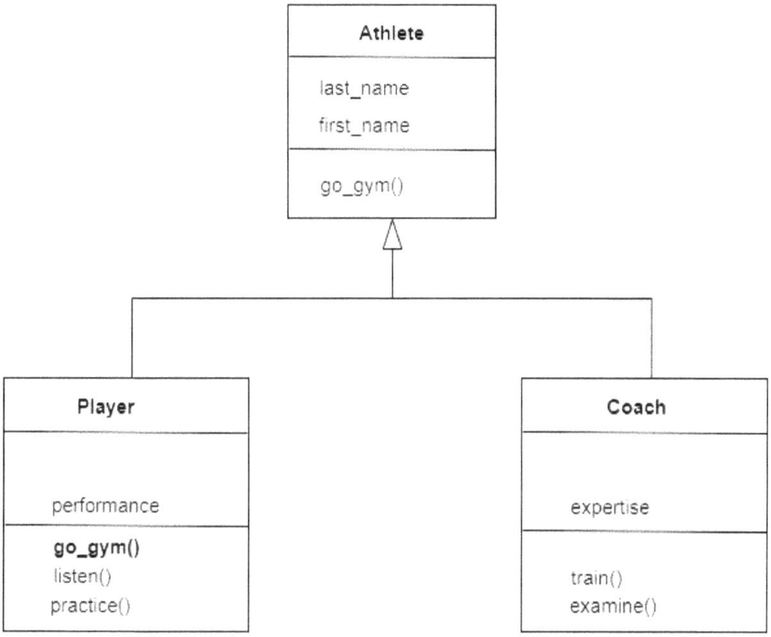

Figure 8.7: Basic classes with attributes and methods.

objects because it has the same code as the method found in the parent class **Athlete**.

We used `super()` within the `__str__()` method and the initializer to access the parent type object.

Furthermore, we passed the values **last_name** and **first_name** to the parent's initializer.

Listing 8.17: Parent class Coach

```
class Coach(Athlete):
    def __init__(self, last_name, first_name, expertise):
        super().__init__(last_name, first_name)
        self.expertise = expertise

    def __str__(self):
        return super().__str__() + ",
        ↪ expertise:{}".format(self.expertise)
```

```
    def train(self):
        print("Coach conducts a training session")
        self.expertise += 10

    def examine(self):
        print("Coach administers an exam")
        self.expertise += 30
```

Listing 8.18 presents the attributes and methods specific to **Player** objects. It is important to note that we have overridden the **go_gym()** method because it performs additional actions beyond those in the parent method of **Athlete**.

Listing 8.18: Class Player

```
class Player(Athlete):
    def __init__(self, last_name, first_name, performance):
        super().__init__(last_name, first_name)
        self.performance = performance

    def __str__(self):
        return super().__str__() + ", performance:
        ↪  {}".format(self.performance)

    def go_gym(self, msg):
        super().go_gym(msg)
        self.performance += 5

    def listen(self):
        print("Player is listening")
        self.performance += 10

    def practice(self):
        print("Player practices for an exam")
        self.performance += 20
```

In listing 8.19, we proceed with the creation of objects and the invocation of various methods, ensuring that the correct order of calls is maintained.

Upon comparing this listing with the one from the previous chapter, we observe that nothing has changed, which is entirely expected since we have merely restructured the code of the classes.

Listing 8.19: Sequence of object creation and method calls

```
# Object creation
objJ = Player("flouflou", "alain", 0)
objE = Coach('flouclair', 'Annie', 0.0)

print("Before Collaboration")
print(objJ)
print(objE)

objJ.go_gym("Player")
objE.go_gym("Coach")
objE.train()
objJ.listen()
objE.examine()
objJ.practice()

print("=" * 50)
print("After Collaboration")
print(objJ)
print(objE)
```

Output

```
Before Collaboration
Last Name: flouflou, First Name: alain, performance: 0
Last Name: flouclair, First Name: Annie, expertise:0.0
Presence in the gym as: Player
Presence in the gym as: Coach
Coach conducts a training session
Player is listening
Coach administers an exam
Player practices for an exam
==================================================
After Collaboration
Last Name: flouflou, First Name: alain, performance: 35
Last Name: flouclair, First Name: Annie, expertise:40.0
```

We can now proceed with the creation of objects for the three classes and validate the concept of polymorphism.

Let's consider the code presented in listing 8.20.

Listing 8.20: Polymorphism

```
# Creating Objects
objJ = Player('flouflou', 'Alain', 0)
objE = Coach('flouclair', 'Annie', 0.0)
objS = Athlete("clairclair", 'Abdel')

registry = [objE, objJ, objS]

# Executing the go_gym() method
for item in registry:
    item.go_gym(type(item).__name__)
```

The output provides us with the messages corresponding to the execution of **go_gym()** method by each object in the list, i.e.:

Output

```
Coach present as: Coach
Player present as: Player
Participant present as: Athlete
```

Please note that we used `type(tmp).__name__` to obtain the name of the class corresponding to the object and then passed it as a parameter to the method.

8.3 Quick summary

This quick summary highlights the essential concepts in using inheritance in Python programming, providing a concise overview of the key elements you have learned:

- Inheritance is a fundamental object-oriented technique used for organizing and creating classes.
- It allows for the reuse of classes in the development of new applications, promoting code reusability.
- Python supports multiple inheritance, enabling a class to inherit from multiple parent classes.
- The `super()` keyword provides a way to access members of the parent class, facilitating method overriding and extension.

8.4 Quiz

Please answer the following questions. There may be one or more correct answers.

1. We use inheritance to:
   (a) Minimize code redundancy
   (b) Reuse code
   (c) Increase the number of lines of code

2. Inheritance in Python can be:
   (a) Single
   (b) Multiple

3. Inheritance is a basic object-oriented concept:
   (a) True
   (b) False

4. The `super()` function returns:
   (a) A reference to an instance of the parent object
   (b) A reference to an instance of the child object

5. A method inherited by a child class can be redefined:
   (a) True
   (b) False

6. Consider the following code:

```
class Car:
    def move(self):
        print('The car is moving')

class SportCar(Car):
    def move(self):
        print('My ferrari is at full speed')

v = SportCar()
v.move()
```

Running the code leads to the following result:
(a) Error because `__init__()` was not defined in the `SportCar` class
(b) Display of: My ferrari is at full speed
(c) Display of: The car is moving

7. Consider the following code:

```
class Car:
    def move(self):
        print('The car is moving')

class SportCar(Car):
    def move(self):
        print('My ferrari is at full speed')

s = SportCar()
print(type(s))
```

Executing the code leads to the following result:
(a) <class '__main__.Car'>
(b) <class '__main__.SportCar'>

8. An object of a child class can call a method of the parent class using:
(a) `base()`
(b) `super()`
(c) `__init__()`

9. A redefined method in a child class must keep the same parameters than the method defined in the parent class:
(a) True
(b) False

10. Consider the following code:

```
class Car:
    def move(self):
        print('The car is moving')

class SportCar(Car):
    def move(self):
        print('My ferrari is at full speed')

v = Car()
s =SportCar()

print(isinstance(v, Car))
print(isinstance(s, Car))
print(isinstance(s, SportCar))
```

Running the code leads to the following result:

(a) `True False True`
(b) `True True True`
(c) `True False False`

8.5 Practice problems

PROBLEM 8.1

Create a base class **Employee** to represent an employee of a company. Consider that an employee has a name and a code. Then proceed to create an object of type **Employee** and display its state. In a second step, add the method **perform_task()** in which the instruction to print the string **Task accomplished** is included.

```
# Inheritance parent class
class Employee:
    def __init__(self, code, name):
        self.code = code
        self.name = name

    def __str__(self):
        return 'Code:{}, name:{}'.format(self.code, self.name)

    def perform_task(self):
        print('Task accomplished')


# Creating an object of type Employee
emp = Employee(12, "Flouflou")
print(emp)
emp.perform_task()
```

Output

```
Code:12, name:Flouflou
Task accomplished
```

PROBLEM 8.2

Building on problem 8.1, create a child class **PartTimeEmployee** to represent an employee working part-time. This employee has a name, a code, and a maximum number of hours per week. Proceed to create an object of type **PartTimeEmployee** and display its state.

```
# Inheritance parent class
class Employee:
    def __init__(self, code, name):
        self.code = code
        self.name = name

    def __str__(self):
        return 'Code:{}, name:{}'.format(self.code, self.name)

    def perform_task(self):
        print('Task accomplished')

class PartTimeEmployee(Employee):
    def __init__(self, code, name, max_hours):
        super().__init__(code, name)
        self.max_hours = max_hours

    def __str__(self):
        return super().__str__()+', hours:{}'.format(self.max_hours)

# Creating an object of type PartTimeEmployee
empP = PartTimeEmployee(15, "Flouclair", 20)
print(empP)
```

Output

```
Code:15, name:Flouclair, hours:20
```

PROBLEM 8.3

Building on problem 8.2, modify the **perform_task()** method in the **PartTimeEmployee** class to indicate that the part-time employee must not exceed the maximum allowed hours.

```python
# Inheritance parent class
class Employee:
    def __init__(self, code, name):
        self.code = code
        self.name = name

    def __str__(self):
        return 'Code:{}, name:{}'.format(self.code, self.name)

    def perform_task(self):
        print('Task accomplished')

class PartTimeEmployee(Employee):
    def __init__(self, code, name, max_hours):
        super().__init__(code, name)
        self.max_hours = max_hours

    def __str__(self):
        return super().__str__()+', hours:{}'.format(self.max_hours)

    def perform_task(self):
        super().perform_task()
        print("You must not exceed the maximum allowed hours")

# Creating an object of type PartTimeEmployee
empP = PartTimeEmployee(15, "Flouclair", 20)
print(empP)
empP.perform_task()
```

Output

```
Code:15, name:Flouclair, hours:20
Task accomplished
You must not exceed the maximum allowed hours
```

8.6 Programming problems

PROBLEM 8.4

Solution provided in the appendix

Let us consider an email list where we define a contact with a name and an email address.

- Create the base class **Contact**.
- Based on this information, create a contact with the name **Alain Flouflou** and the email address **a.flouflou@monsite.com**.
- Display the state of the contact object.

Now, consider that we can have a contact who is also a supplier. In this case, a supplier has an additional attribute called **supplier_code** and a method called **place_order()**.

- Develop the class **Supplier**.
- Create a supplier object with the values **1234**, **a.clairclair@monsite.com** and **Annie ClairClair**.
- Display the state of the supplier object.

PROBLEM 8.5

Solution provided in the appendix

Now, we want to save the contacts from problem 8.4 in a memory structure. For this purpose, we will use a `list` as the memory structure.

- Develop the class **ContactRegister** which has an attribute of type `list` and a title for the collection of contacts called **contact list**. You will add the contacts from problem 8.4 to the register.
- Now, we will add the functionality to display the contents of the list once they have been added.
- The contact register should now provide us with a way to search for a contact by its name. Develop the method **search_contact()** which takes the name of a contact as input and searches if it already exists in the register.

PROBLEM 8.6

Develop a program that calculates the net salary of an employee, knowing that there are two types of employees: full-time and part-time. An employee has a last name, first name, and a code. A full-time employee has a monthly salary.

If the employee is part-time, they have an hourly rate and the number of hours worked, and they may also work overtime. Full-time employees are not allowed to work overtime. However, for part-time employees, overtime hours are paid at a rate of 1.5 for any hours beyond 35 hours.

All employees are subject to a 20% income tax on their salary.

Chapter 9

Files

Contents of this chapter

Objectives:

- To read data from a file
- To write data to a file
- To perform string splitting
- To manipulate `csv` files using the `csv` module

9.1 Input and output files

Until now, all the data we manipulated was lost as soon as the program ended. However, in many cases, we need to save this data on a permanent storage medium.

Since the advent of computing in the last century, we have had access to storage systems such as files and database systems. For now, we are focusing on the use of files, which can be stored on the user's machine or a remote server. This ensures that even after the program terminates, the data remains accessible within the file(s).

This means we can reuse the data stored in these files during a subsequent execution of the same program or even a different one.

9.1.1 File types

When preparing data for storage in files, we use the appropriate encoding for the format of the data. This gives us the option to use **text** and **binary** file types.

Both types enable data storage, but they differ in the nature of the data they hold. A **text** file contains data that has been encoded as plain text in a suitable format. On the other hand, a **binary** file contains data encoded as a sequence of bits (zeros and ones) and is not easily readable as plain text.

The main difference between these two file types is that a **text** file can be manipulated by other software such as **notepad++**, whereas a **binary** file is intended to be manipulated only by the program that created it or understands the sequence of binary data contained within the file.

What is an encoding?

When we manipulate data, we often apply specific encodings to it. In Chapter 9, we will explore the concept of files and how data representation can be altered through these encodings. Some commonly used encodings include ASCII, UTF-8, UTF-16, and more.

9.1.2 Types of access

Data in a file is meant to be written and read repeatedly. The method of accessing the data depends on the physical medium used, such as cylinder hard disks or SSDs, and can have an impact on data retrieval. There are two main ways to access data from a file:

- **Sequential Access**: To access specific data, you must read all the data from the beginning of the file up to the desired data. This process can be time-consuming, especially if the desired data is located far from the beginning of the file.
- **Direct or Random Access**: This method allows you to directly access the desired data without the need to read all the data from the beginning of the file. It enables quicker access to specific data, making it more efficient for certain applications.

The choice of access method depends on the nature of the data and the specific requirements of the application. Understanding these different access types is essential when working with files for effective data management.

9.2 File manipulation

All computer systems follow a similar approach when handling files. This involves a three-step process: opening the file, manipulating its data, and finally closing the file.

9.2.1 Opening a file

Initially, all file manipulations are performed using an object of type `file`. This grants access to various file manipulation methods. The file is opened using the `open()` method, which returns an object of type `file`.

The `open()` function is used in the following format:

```
obj = open(file_name, mode)
```

Where:

- **file_name**: represents the name of the file to be used.
- **mode**: specifies the opening mode of the file, which can be either read or write.

Choosing the appropriate mode depends on the purpose of file manipulation, whether it is reading data from the file or writing data into it.

The available modes, which indicate the type of file, whether **text** or **binary**, are listed in table 9.1.

Mode	Description	Example
t	Opens the file in text mode. This is the default mode.	`obj = open('foo.txt', 't')`
b	Opens the file in binary mode.	`obj = open('foo.txt', 'b')`
x	Creates a new file. If the file exists, the operation ends in failure.	`obj = open('foo.txt', 'x')`

Table 9.1: File opening modes according to type.

In table 9.1, the different modes for opening files are specified along with their respective descriptions and examples of usage. These modes determine how the file will be accessed and manipulated.

The most common modes for reading and writing files are described in table 9.2.

Table 9.2 provides an overview of the different modes used for opening files in Python, along with their corresponding descriptions and examples of usage. These modes determine how the file is accessed and whether it is read, written, or appended.

Mode	Description	Example
`r`	Opens the file in read mode. This is the default mode.	`obj = open('foo.txt', 'r')`
`w`	Opens the file in write mode. If the file does not exist, a new file is created. If the file already exists, its contents are overwritten.	`obj = open('foo.txt', 'w')`
`a`	Opens the file in append mode. If the file does not exist, a new file is created.	`obj = open('foo.txt', 'a')`

Table 9.2: File opening modes for reading and writing.

How to specify read and write mode at the same time?

The symbol + is used to indicate that the file is open in both ***read*** *and* ***write*** *mode simultaneously.*

By using the + character along with the desired modes, such as r+ or w+, you can perform both read and write operations on the file. This combination grants you the ability to read the existing content and write new data to the file, making it a convenient option when you need to perform both types of operations within the same file.

9.2.2 Reading from a file

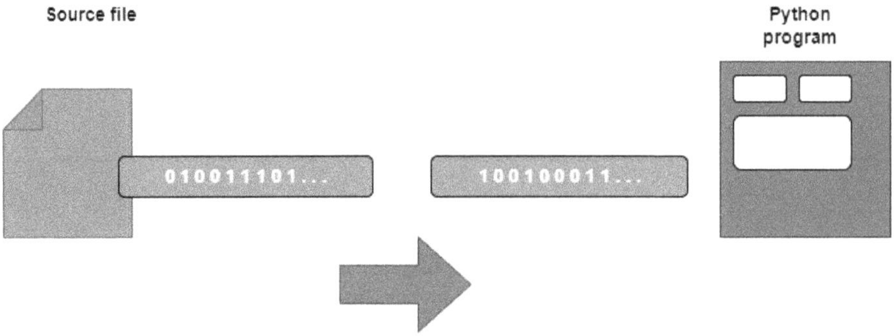

Figure 9.1: Stream in read mode.

Figure 9.1 illustrates the flow of data from the file to the program during the read operation.

In read mode, we have three methods available for reading data from the file. These methods are summarized in table 9.3.

Method	Description	Example
`read()`	Reads the contents of the file as a string.	`text = obj.read()`
`readline()`	Reads a line from the file as a string.	`text = obj.readline()`
`readlines()`	Reads the contents of the file as a list of lines.	`text = obj.readlines()`

Table 9.3: File reading methods.

In table 9.3, we summarize the three different methods that can be used to read data from a file in Python. These methods provide different ways to read the content of the file based on the requirements of the program.

The following examples demonstrate the usage of each of these methods.

9.2.3 The `read()` method

This method reads the contents of the file as a character string. Let's consider the **foo.txt** file with the following content:

```
The fox jumps the barrier.
The sheep saw nothing.
The shepherd will lose his sheep.
```

This file can be created in Pycharm using the right button mouse by first selecting the project then **New-file**.

The code to read the file using the `read()` method is shown in listing 9.1.

Listing 9.1: Reading a file using `read()`

```python
# Open the file
obj = open('foo.txt')
# Read the content of the file
content = obj.read()
# Display the content of the file
print(content)
# Close the file
obj.close()
```

The output will be:

Output in execution mode

```
The fox jumps the barrier
The sheep saw nothing
The shepherd will lose his sheep
```

It is important to note that we followed the three fundamental steps for handling files: opening, processing, and closing the file.

9.2.4 The `readline()` method

This method allows you to read a line from the file as a character string. It reads the content until it finds the first newline character, which is **\n**. If there are no more lines in the file, it returns an empty string.

The code to read the file using the **`readline()`** method is shown in listing 9.2.

Listing 9.2: Reading a file using `readline()`

```
# Open the file
obj = open('foo.txt')
# Read the content of the file, one line at a time
content1 = obj.readline()
content2 = obj.readline()
content3 = obj.readline()
# Display the content of each line
print(content1)
print(content2)
print(content3)
# Close the file
obj.close()
```

The output will be:

Output in execution mode

```
The fox jumps the barrier

The sheep saw nothing

The shepherd will lose his sheep
```

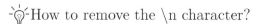

How to remove the \n character?

We can observe that each line is displayed with an additional empty line. This is because of the presence of the **\n** *character at the end of each line. To prevent the additional blank line, we can use* ***obj.readline().rstrip('\n')*** *for each of the variables at the code level. The* `rstrip()` *method removes a specified string from the right side of the variable.*

9.2.5 The `readlines()` method

This method reads the contents of the file as a list of lines. Each line of characters in the file will be read until the newline character **\n** is encountered. The entire content will be read completely once all the lines of the file are read.

The code for reading using the `readlines()` method is shown in listing 9.3.

Listing 9.3: Reading file using readlines()

```
# Opening the file
obj = open('foo.txt')
# Reading the content of the file line by line
content = obj.readlines()
#Iterating and displaying each line
for line in content:
    print(line.rstrip('\n'))
#Closing the file
obj.close()
```

Output during execution

```
The fox jumps the barrier
The sheep saw nothing
The shepherd will lose his sheep
```

Note that we used the `rstrip()` method to remove the **\n** character from each line before displaying.

9.2.6 Writing to a file

Figure 9.2 illustrates the flow of data from the program to the file.

It should be noted that unlike the read mode, the file must be opened for the desired mode before writing.

- Opening the file in `'w'` mode causes the write operation to overwrite the old content.

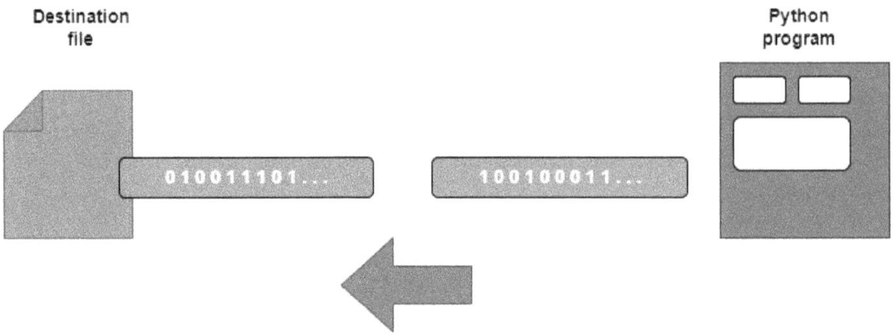

Figure 9.2: Stream in write mode.

```
obj = open('filename', 'w') # write
```

- Opening the file in 'a' mode causes the new data to be appended after the old content.

```
obj = open('filename', 'a') # append
```

Once the file has been opened, we can proceed to write using the `write()` method, like this:

```
line = 'Any string of characters'
obj.write(line)
```

Example: Writing

```
# Opening the file in 'w' mode
obj = open('output.txt', 'w')
# Writing 2 strings of characters
obj.write('Welcome world!\n')
obj.write('Goodbye World!')
# Closing the file
obj.close()
```

9.2.7 Closing a file

After manipulating the file, it is essential to close the object representing the file to free up system resources and allow other programs to manipulate the file. We can do this using the `close()` method.

```
obj.close()
```

9.3 String slicing

In many situations, we need to split a string into its constituent words. A common case is with **csv** files, where lines have a specific structure.

Example

```
'alain;25;2350.0'
```

This contains 3 strings separated by the symbol or separator `;`.

In such cases, we can use the `split()` method of the `str` class. This method splits a string into tokens and returns the tokens themselves as a list of strings (`str`).

By default, the `split()` method uses a white space as a delimiter, but any other character can be specified as a separator.

```
line.split() # split by whitespace
line.split(delimiter) # split by specified delimiter
```

In the following example, the character string is decomposed into four strings using whitespace as a separator.

Listing 9.4: String Slicing

```
string = 'I am standing up'
result = string.split()
print(result)
```

Output

```
['I', 'am', 'standing','up']
```

The `join()` method performs the opposite of `split()`. It uses an appropriate delimiter or separator and reconstructs the original character string.

Listing 9.5: Using join()

```
# Separator
separator = ' '
result = separator.join(['I', 'am', 'standing','up'])
print(result)
```

Output

```
I am standing up
```

9.3.1 Splitting a string into tokens

If we know the number of tokens, we can split the string directly into variables.

```
var1, var2, ..., varN = line.split()
```

Note that the variables are of type `str`. Therefore, it may be useful to convert them to the appropriate type, such as:

Listing 9.6: String splitting

```
line = 'alain 25 2350.0'
name, age, salary = line.split()
print(name)
print(int(age))
print(float(salary))
```

The output values can then be used according to their corresponding type.

Output

```
alain
25
2350.0
```

9.4 Using the `csv` module

When dealing with structured files in **csv** format, it is more convenient to use the **csv** module available natively in Python.

Once imported, we have access to the module's read and write methods, which can be used through the `writer` and `reader` classes of the module.

9.4.1 Reading from a file

Two classes are available for reading from **csv** files. The `reader` class allows reading the values of a line, while the `DictReader` class returns a dictionary corresponding to the column names and the corresponding values present at the line level.

Using the reader class

Consider the file **grades.csv**, which contains the **ID**, **name**, and **average** grade of the students. The data is described in table 9.4.

ID	Name	Average
20	"Flouflou"	84
98	"Flouclair"	87
23	"ClairClair"	98
11	"Sinclair"	92

Table 9.4: Student grades File.

The structure of the file is as follows:

Contents of csv file

```
ID,Name,Average
20,"Flouflou",84
98,"Flouclair",87
23,"ClairClair",98
11,"Sinclair",92
```

With the `reader` class, we can iterate through the file as a list of lines, each consisting of cells of type `str`.

Listing 9.7 demonstrates how to read and display all the lines present in the **grades.csv** file, without taking into account the header, for example. We can observe that the **reader** object has been instantiated with the default parameters of `reader`. Additionally, we have used the `with` statement to simplify the opening and closing of the file.

Listing 9.7: Reading a csv file

```
import csv
with open('grades.csv') as file_object:
    reader = csv.reader(file_object)
    for line in reader:
        print(line)
```

The output will be as follows:

Execution output

```
['ID', 'Name', 'Average']
['20', 'Flouflou', '84']
['98', 'Flouclair', '87']
['23', 'ClairClair', '98']
['11', 'Sinclair', '92']
```

To avoid taking the header into account when reading the **grades.csv** file, we can use the `Sniffer` class, as shown in listing 9.8.

Listing 9.8: Using the Sniffer class

```
import csv
with open('grades.csv') as file_object:
    # CSV reader object
    reader = csv.reader(file_object)
    # Determine if there is a header
    header = csv.Sniffer().has_header(file_object.read(1024))
    # Return to the beginning of the file
    file_object.seek(0)
    # Skip the header
    if header:
        next(reader)

    # Display each line
    for line in reader:
        print(line)
```

Running this code produces the following result:

Execution output

```
['20', 'Flouflou', '84']
['98', 'Flouclair', '87']
['23', 'ClairClair', '98']
['11', 'Sinclair', '92']
```

With this implementation, we can read the file without including the header in the output. The `Sniffer` class helps us determine the presence of a header, and by using `next(reader)`, we can skip it if necessary.

Each line from the **grades.csv** file is represented as a list of strings. We can access and convert each element as needed. The code in listing 9.9 calculates the average of the grades and displays it.

Listing 9.9: Calculating the average

```
import csv
with open('grades.csv') as file_object:
    # CSV reader object
    reader = csv.reader(file_object)
    # Determine if there is a header
    header = csv.Sniffer().has_header(file_object.read(1024))
    # Return to the beginning of the file
    file_object.seek(0)
    # Skip the header
    if header:
        next(reader)

    # Calculate the average
    total = 0
    num_grades = 0
    for line in reader:
        total += float(line[2])
        num_grades += 1

    print('The average is: {}'.format(total/num_grades))
```

Execution output

```
The average is: 90.25
```

With this code, we calculate the average of the grades present in the **grades.csv** file and display it. The program correctly skips the header row when calculating the average.

9.4.2 Using `DictReader`

Next, we explore the usage of the `DictReader` class. This class returns each row of the **csv** file as a dictionary, where each key-value pair represents a column name and its corresponding value. In listing 9.10, we create the **reader** object based on the `DictReader` class.

Listing 9.10: Using DictReader

```
import csv
with open('grades.csv') as file_object:
    # CSV DictReader object
    reader = csv.DictReader(file_object)
    # Displaying the rows
    for row in reader:
        print(row)
```

Execution output

```
{'ID': '20', 'Name': 'Flouflou', 'Average': '84'}
{'ID': '98', 'Name': 'Flouclair', 'Average': '87'}
{'ID': '23', 'Name': 'ClairClair', 'Average': '98'}
{'ID': '11', 'Name': 'Sinclair', 'Average': '92'}
```

As a result, each row of the **grades.csv** file is represented as an `OrderedDict`, where the column names serve as the keys and the corresponding values are the values. This makes it easier to work with structured data from **csv** files, especially when we have headers with meaningful column names.

The `DictReader` provides us with useful methods to process data from the **csv** file.

For instance, listing 9.11 demonstrates how to calculate the average by accessing the **Average** column.

Listing 9.11: Reading csv with DictReader

```
import csv
with open('grades.csv') as file_object:
    # CSV DictReader object
    reader = csv.DictReader(file_object)
    # Displaying the column names
    print(reader.fieldnames)
    # Calculate the average
    sum = 0
    num_lines = 0
    for row in reader:
        sum += float(row['Average'])
        num_lines += 1

    print('The average is:{}'.format(sum / num_lines))
```

Additionally, we have displayed the list of column names, which can be accessed using the public attribute `fieldnames`.

Execution output

```
['ID', 'Name', 'Average']
The average is:90.25
```

Using the `DictReader`, we are able to process data from the **csv** file more conveniently, accessing the columns directly by their names. This approach is especially beneficial when dealing with files that have headers containing meaningful column names.

9.4.3 Writing to a file

There are two classes available for writing to a **csv** file: the `writer` class, which allows writing values of a line, and the `DictWriter` class, which uses a dictionary to specify the column names and their corresponding values for each line.

Using the `writer` class

Let's consider the list of student data shown in the following listing:

```
ID,Name,Average
20,"Flouflou",84
98,"Flouclair",87
23,"ClairClair",98
11,"Sinclair",92
```

With the `writer` class, we can iterate through the list of students, and then each element can be written as a **csv** line.

Listing 9.12 demonstrates how to write all the lines in the **grades.csv** file, for example, without considering the header. We can observe that the `writer` object has been instantiated with the default parameters of the `writer` class.

Listing 9.12: Writing to csv

```
import csv
# List of grades
student_grades = [[20, 'Flouflou', 84],
[98, 'Flouclair', 87],
[23, 'ClairClair', 98],
[11, 'Sinclair', 92]]
```

```
# Writing to file
with open('grades.csv', 'a', newline='') as file_object:
    writer = csv.writer(file_object)
    for line in student_grades:
        writer.writerow(line)
```

In listing 9.12, we used a list of student data. Next, the file was opened in **append** mode, and the **newline** parameter was specified to avoid extra newline characters.

The **writerow** method takes a list of student data as a parameter and converts it into a `str` line in the file. The default encoding values are used. The output file will have the following content.

Output in execution mode

```
20,Flouflou,84
98,Flouclair,87
23,ClairClair,98
11,Sinclair,92
```

We notice that the names of the students, which are character strings, are not surrounded by apostrophes. In this case, the parameters of **writer** can be changed as shown in listing 9.13.

Listing 9.13: Writing to csv with parameter usage

```
import csv
# List of grades
student_grades = [[20, 'Flouflou', 84],
[98, 'Flouclair', 87],
[23, 'ClairClair', 98],
[11, 'Sinclair', 92]]

# Writing to file
with open('grades.csv', 'a', newline='') as file_object:
    writer = csv.writer(file_object, delimiter='|',
    ↪ quoting=csv.QUOTE_NONNUMERIC)
    for line in student_grades:
        writer.writerow(line)
```

With these parameter changes, the character strings will be surrounded by the delimiter "|", and in this example, the symbol "|" is used.

Output in execution mode

```
20|"Flouflou"|84
98|"Flouclair"|87
23|"ClairClair"|98
11|"Sinclair"|92
```

9.4.4 Using DictWriter

In certain situations, the data is available in the form of a dictionary with keys corresponding perfectly to the **csv** columns of the file. This is the ideal case for using the `DictWriter` class.

In listing 9.14, we can see that we have created the writer object based on the `DictWriter` class.

An important parameter here is **`fieldnames`**, which indicates the keys available in the dictionary.

Listing 9.14: Writing with DictWriter

```python
import csv
# List of column names
csv_fields = ['ID', 'name', 'grade']
student_grades = [{'ID': 20, 'name': 'Flouflou', 'grade': 84},
                  {'ID': 98, 'name': 'Flouclair', 'grade': 87},
                  {'ID': 23, 'name': 'ClairClair', 'grade': 98},
                  {'ID': 11, 'name': 'Sinclair', 'grade': 92}]

# Writing to file
with open('grades.csv', 'a', newline='') as file_object:
    writer = csv.DictWriter(file_object, fieldnames=csv_fields,
    ↪  delimiter='|', quoting=csv.QUOTE_NONNUMERIC)
    for line in student_grades:
        writer.writerow(line)
```

In the output file, we obtain lines corresponding to the values of the dictionary keys for each element.

Output in execution mode

```
20|"Flouflou"|84
98|"Flouclair"|87
23|"ClairClair"|98
11|"Sinclair"|92
```

9.5 Quick summary

This quick summary highlights the essential points to consider when working with files in Python:

- The Python standard library provides various methods for reading from and writing to files.
- Text and binary files can be manipulated using appropriate methods.
- Several methods are available for reading and writing files, allowing flexibility in handling different data structures.
- For files in **csv** (Comma-Separated Values) format, Python's standard library provides the **csv** module, offering convenient functions for efficient file handling.

9.6 Quiz

Please answer the following questions. There may be one or more correct answers.

1. The steps to extract data from a file are:
   (a) Open
   (b) Read
   (c) Close

2. If the open mode of a file is not specified, it will be in read mode only.
   (a) True
   (b) False

3. The `readlines()` method reads the contents of a file as:
   (a) List of character lines
   (b) Dictionary of character lines
   (c) A complete line of characters

4. The `split()` method accepts a parameter that specifies the separator between the words of a character string.
   (a) True
   (b) False

5. The `join()` method concatenates `str` or string elements from a list.
   (a) True
   (b) False

6. You can handle not only text files but also binary files with the standard Python library.
   (a) True
   (b) False

7. Consider the following code:

```
with open('data.txt') as fin:
    line = fin.readline()
    print(line)
```

   The file is considered to contain 5 lines. Executing the code leads to the following result:
   (a) Display of the first line of the file

(b) Display of the fifth line of the file
(c) Display of all the lines of the file

8. After opening and manipulating a file, one should close it with:
   (a) The **finish()** method
   (b) The **close()** method
   (c) By using an exception

9. Execution of the following code:

```
open('data.txt','w').write('The fox jumps the barrier')
```

   produces:
   (a) A file called data.txt with the content 'The fox jumps the barrier'
   (b) A file called data.txt
   (c) A line displayed on the console with the content 'The fox jump the barrier'

10. The method to read a complete line until the character `'\n '` is found is:
   (a) **read()**
   (b) **readline()**
   (c) **readlines()**

9.7 Practice problems

PROBLEM 9.1

Consider the file **filein.txt** with the following content:

```
The fox jumps the barrier
The sheeps are lost
```

Write code that reads the content of this file and stores the result in a list where each element is a word from the first line of the file.

```
with open('filein.txt') as fin:
    content = fin.readlines()
    words = content[0].split()

print(words)
```

Output

```
['The', 'fox', 'jumps', 'the', 'barrier']
```

PROBLEM 9.2

Consider the file from problem 9.1. Read the content of this file, convert it to uppercase, and save the result in an output file.

```
# File manipulation
with open('filein.txt') as fin:
    content = fin.readlines()
    # Convert to uppercase and write to output file
    with open("fileout.txt", 'w') as fout:
        for line in content:
            fout.write(line.upper())
```

Output

```
THE FOX JUMPS THE BARRIER
THE SHEEPS ARE LOST
```

9.8 Programming problems

PROBLEM 9.3

Solution provided in the appendix

Let's consider the file **case.txt** with the following content:

```
The fox jumps the barrier.
    The sheeps run in all directions.
    the shepherd whistles and sings without seeing the scene unfolding
    before his eyes.
```

Develop a function **calculate_file_stats()** that takes the file **case.txt** as input and returns the longest line in the file, including leading and trailing spaces.

PROBLEM 9.4

Develop a function **process_case()** that takes two files and copies the content from the first file to the second one, but with the condition of removing lines that start with a lowercase letter.

You will use the file **case.txt** from problem 9.3.

In order to accomplish this task, you can utilize the **process_case()** function. It will read the content from the source file, remove lines starting with lowercase letters, and then write the modified content to the destination file. This function makes it easy to process files while preserving the necessary formatting.

PROBLEM 9.5

Calculate the total hours worked by each employee, as well as the average number of hours per day, considering that employees work 5 days a week. The data is available in the file named **hours.csv** and its content is as follows:

```
123 Flouflou 7.5 7.5 7.8 3.0 5.5
456 Flouclair 7.0 7.6 6.6 5.9 8.5
789 Clairclair 8.5 8.0 7.5 5.0 9.5
```

The output should be in the following format:

Flouflou with Code 123 worked XX.XX hours with an average of XX.XX / day.

Flouclair with Code 456 worked XX.XX hours with an average of XX.XX / day.

Clairclair with Code 789 worked XX.XX hours with an average of XX.XX / day.

To achieve this, you can process the data from the **hours.csv** file and compute the total hours worked and the average hours per day for each employee. The final output will provide a clear overview of each employee's work hours and their average daily contribution.

Chapter 10

Exception Handling

Contents of this chapter

Objectives:

- To understand the advantages of using exception handling
- To use the try-except structure to handle exceptions
- To use the else clause in a try-except structure
- To use the finally clause in a try-except structure
- To use exception propagation
- To define and use custom exceptions classes

10.1 Introduction

So far, we have focused on the normal flow of program execution, where the required data is available for processing operations, and everything goes as planned. However, in most real-world scenarios, we must consider alternative procedures to handle exceptional situations. These exceptional situations may arise due to errors or abnormalities, and it is crucial to handle them effectively to meet our needs.

An exception is an object that describes an abnormal or erroneous situation within a program. When an exception occurs, it is thrown by the program and can be caught and handled by another part of the code.

For developers familiar with languages like Java, an error is also considered an abnormal situation, but it typically should not be handled explicitly. In contrast, both an exception and an error are seen as abnormal situations from Python's perspective. However, an exception is more related to processing issues, while an error is typically associated with functional problems, such as issues with accessing remote servers, databases, or files.

In any case, incorporating exception handling is crucial to manage exceptional situations effectively, whether they are exceptions or errors.

A well-designed program should have two distinct flows: the normal execution flow and the exception execution flow.

There are three main approaches to handle an exception:

- Ignore the exception altogether.
- Handle the exception whenever it occurs within the same section of the code.
- Handle the exception in a different section of the program.

How we choose to handle exceptions should be determined during the program's design phase. If an exception is ignored, the program will terminate abnormally and display an error message.

When an exception occurs, it generates a stack trace, providing valuable information that includes:

- The line number where the exception occurred.
- The sequence of method calls that led to the exception.

Figure 10.1 presents an example of the output displayed when an exception occurs.

```
age = int(input("Please, enter your age:"))
print(age)
```

```
Please, enter your age:fifty
Traceback (most recent call last):
  File "C:\Users\mhafo\PycharmProjects\projet_data\main_fact.py", line 1, in <module>
    age = int(input("Please, enter your age:"))
          ^^^^^^^^^^^^^^^^^^^^^^^^^^^^^^^^^^^^^
ValueError: invalid literal for int() with base 10: 'fifty'
```

Figure 10.1: Error stack.

10.2 The try-except-finally structure

As the program may encounter exceptions during execution, any statement that could potentially raise an exception should be enclosed within a `try` block, as illustrated in listing 10.1.

Listing 10.1: Try-except block

```
try:
    #instructions that may raise an exception
except:
    #code to be executed in case of an error
```

In the `try` block, it is considered good practice to include only statements that might lead to exceptions. These instructions can involve processing operations or functional operations, such as file access.

Within the `except` block, we can add the necessary code to handle the specific exception that occurred. Ideally, this should involve instructions to address the problem or resolve the issue. Additionally, it can involve displaying an alert or logging the error in an error file. Note that the `except` clause is optional.

In general, the complete form of the `try-except` block is as follows:

```
try:
    #instructions that may raise an exception
except SomeError:
    #code to be executed in case of the specific exception
```

Code 10.2 demonstrates the usage of a `try-except` block to handle the `ValueError` exception.

Listing 10.2: Example of try-except block

```
try:
    age = int(input('Please enter your age:'))
    print(age)
except ValueError:
    print('Input error: Invalid age format.')
```

Furthermore, a `try` block can be followed by one or more `except` clauses, as illustrated in code 10.3.

Listing 10.3: Multiple except blocks

```
try:
    #instructions that may raise an exception
except Exception1:
    #Handle this exception
except Exception2:
    #Handle this exception
...
except ExceptionN:
    #Handle this exception
```

Each `except` clause is associated with a specific exception type. This section is known as the exception handler. Given that the `try` block may have multiple potential exception occurrences, there can be various options for exception handlers to deal with specific situations.

The first approach is to use the `Exception` parent class as the primary handler, as demonstrated in code 10.4.

Listing 10.4: Handling with Exception

```
try:
    #instructions that may raise an exception
except Exception:
    #Handle this exception
```

However, the drawback of this method is that all exceptions occurring within the `try` block will be caught by a single handler. Consequently, there is a risk of losing valuable information regarding the nature of the specific exception.

Let's revisit example 10.2 and modify the code to write to a file. We intentionally use a file path that does not exist on the machine in order to cause a system exception.

Listing 10.5: Try-except block with exception

```
try:
    age = int(input('Please enter your age:'))
    f = open('E:\output.txt', 'a')
    f.write(str(age) + '\n')
    f.close()
except Exception as e:
    print(e)
```

When running the code and entering an integer, it produces the following result:

```
Please enter your age:35
[Errno 2] No such file or directory: 'E:\\output.txt'
```

On the other hand, if we enter a character string for the age, the output will be:

```
Please enter your age:thirty
invalid literal for int() with base 10: 'thirty'
```

By handling exceptions with the `Exception` parent class, we get a general handling for any type of exception. However, as seen in the outputs, this approach does not provide specific details about the encountered exception, making it less informative for debugging and troubleshooting.

We observe that we have retrieved error messages corresponding to user actions. However, the question arises as to whether the current exception handling is sufficient. It might be beneficial to notify the user differently based on the type of exception encountered.

The second approach involves using specific handlers for different types of exceptions. In listing 10.6, we introduced exception handlers for `OSError` and `ValueError` exceptions.

Listing 10.6: Try-except block with specific exception handlers

```
flag = True
counter = 0
while flag:
    try:
        age = int(input('Please enter your age:'))
        f = open('E:\output.txt', 'a')
        f.write(str(age) + '\n')
        f.close()
        flag = False
    except OSError as e:
        print(e)
        print('File access error. This will be reported to the
        ↪ Admin!')
        flag = False

    except ValueError as e:
        print(e)
        counter += 1
        print('You have made {} attempts'.format(counter))
```

When an exception occurs, the program continues from the `except` block that matches the type of exception thrown. Consequently, for exceptions of the `OSError` type, a notification is displayed before the program terminates. In case of an exception due to an incorrect entry, the number of attempts is displayed, and the user is allowed to retry.

Now, what if we have two exception handlers, and they have an inheritance relationship. For instance, `FloatingPointError` inherits from `ArithmeticError`. In such a scenario, we need to order the handlers from the most specific to the least specific. If we put the most general `except` clause first, it would handle all exceptions of that type, potentially hiding more specific exceptions.

The `try` statement can also have optional clauses denoted by the reserved words `finally` and `else`.

10.2.1 The else clause

The `else` clause follows the `except` clauses in the `try` block and allows statements to be executed when no error occurs within the `try` block. Please note that you can only have one `else` block in this structure.

Listing 10.7: Try-except block with else

```
try:
    #instructions that may raise an exception
except Exception1:
    #Handle this exception
else:
    #series of statements to be executed
```

In listing 10.8, we have included the `else` clause, allowing the age of the person to be displayed once the `try` block is successfully executed without any errors.

Listing 10.8: Try-except block with else

```
flag = True
counter = 0
while flag:
    try:
        age = int(input('Please enter your age:'))
        f = open('D:\output.txt', 'a')
        f.write(str(age) + '\n')
        f.close()
        flag = False
```

```
    except OSError as e:
        print(e)
        print('File access error. This will be reported to the
        ↪ Admin!')
        flag = False
    except ValueError as e:
        print(e)
        counter += 1
        print('You have made {} attempts'.format(counter))
    else:
        print('Your age is:{}'.format(age))
```

With the inclusion of the else clause, the program now displays the age of the person once the try block is successfully executed, providing a clear and informative output to the user.

10.2.2 The finally Clause

The statements within the finally clause are always executed, regardless of whether the try block threw an exception or if the exception was handled within the except clauses.

The modified block structure will look like this:

```
try:
    #instructions that may raise an exception
except Exception1:
    #Handle this exception
else:
    #series of statements to be executed
finally:
    #series of statements to be executed whether there is an error or
    ↪ not
```

If no exception is thrown, the statements in the finally clause are executed after the statements in the try block are completed.

If an exception is thrown, the statements in the finally clause are executed after the statements in the appropriate except block are completed.

10.3 Exception propagation

An exception can be handled at a higher level if it is not appropriate to handle it where it occurred.

Exceptions are propagated through the method call hierarchy until they are caught or reach the **main()** function or the program's entry point.

A `try` block that contains a method call in which an exception is thrown can be used to catch that exception.

If the exception goes all the way back to **main()** or the beginning of the program without being processed, the program's execution will either be halted, or the message associated with the exception (including the stack information described previously) will be displayed.

10.4 Exception hierarchy

Classes that define exceptions are related through inheritance, forming an Exception hierarchy. All error and exception classes are derived from the `BaseException` class.

You can define a custom exception by inheriting from the `Exception` class or one of its subclasses, depending on the specific purpose of the new class.

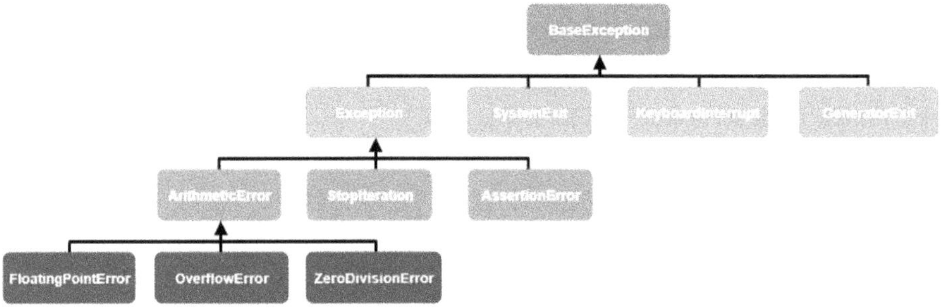

Figure 10.2: Exception hierarchy in Python.

Exceptions are raised using the `raise` statement. This is generally executed implicitly when a problem occurs or explicitly, for example, within an `if` statement. The `if` statement evaluates a condition to determine if an exception should be raised.

To explicitly raise an exception, follow these steps:

- Choose the appropriate type of exception.
- Create an exception object based on this exception class.
- Raise the exception using `raise`.

Table 10.1 provides some examples of exception classes available in Python.

Exception	Description
TypeError	An operation or function is applied to an object of the wrong type
ValueError	An operation or function receives an argument of the correct type but with the wrong value
OSError	A system function returns an error related to the system. The error can be, for example, an error reading files.

Table 10.1: Examples of exception classes.

Listing 10.9: Example of using raise

```
try:
    code = int(input('Enter the code value:'))
    if code > 100:
        # perform some processing
        print('Code is valid')
    else:
        raise ValueError('Invalid code')
except ValueError as v:
    print(v)
```

In this example, the program explicitly raises a `ValueError` when the entered code is not greater than 100, and the error message is displayed accordingly.

10.5 Creating a custom exception class

Python offers a diverse range of exception classes, which are generally effective in handling various situations.

However, there are scenarios where a custom exception class becomes necessary to achieve the desired flexibility, especially when the predefined classes do not fully meet the requirements.

To create a custom exception class, you must inherit from the `Exception` class or one of its subclasses. It is essential to avoid inheriting directly from the `BaseException` class, as it encompasses all exception categories.

As a convention, the name of the custom exception class should end with `Error`.

The basic syntax for declaring a custom class is shown in listing 10.10.

Listing 10.10: Example of a custom exception class

```
class MyError(Exception):
    pass
```

You can further enhance the custom exception class by adding attributes. For instance, we can include a **value** attribute, as shown in listing 10.11.

Listing 10.11: Example of a custom exception class with an attribute

```
class MyError(Exception):
    def __init__(self, value, message):
        super().__init__(message)
        self.value = value

    def __str__(self):
        return super().__str__()+",value:{}".format(self.value)
```

Once this class is defined, we can use the `raise` statement to raise an exception of this custom type as shown in listing 10.12.

Listing 10.12: Using a custom exception class

```
try:
    code = int(input('Enter the code value:'))
    if code > 100:
        # perform some processing
        print('Code is valid')
    else:
        raise MyError(code, 'invalid code')
except MyError as v:
    print(v)
```

10.6 Quick summary

This quick summary highlights the essential concepts in handling exceptions in Python, providing a concise overview of the key elements you have learned:

- An exception is an abnormal condition that may occur while executing Python code.
- We use a `try-except-else-finally` block to handle exceptions.
- The `else` clause allows statements to be executed when the `try` block completes without any exceptions.
- The `finally` clause is used to execute instructions whether an exception occurs within the `try` block or one of the `except` blocks.
- We can create our own custom exceptions by inheriting from one of the classes in

the exception hierarchy.
- You can explicitly raise an exception using the `raise` statement.

These points summarize the fundamental concepts related to handling exceptions in Python. By understanding and effectively using the `try-except-else-finally` blocks, and customizing exceptions when necessary, you can write more robust and reliable code. The ability to raise exceptions explicitly also provides finer control over exception handling in your Python programs.

10.7 Quiz

Please answer the following questions. There may be one or more correct answers.

1. If an exception occurs in a script and no exception handling has been planned, execution stops, and the error stack is displayed.
   (a) True
   (b) False

2. The `raise` statement is used to raise an exception.
   (a) True
   (b) False

3. A `try` block can be followed by multiple `except` blocks.
   (a) True
   (b) False

4. A `finally` block allows you to group instructions that will be executed whether the `try` block completes with or without an exception.
   (a) True
   (b) False

5. If you want to create a custom exception, you can do so by inheriting from an existing exception class.
   (a) True
   (b) False

6. Execution of the following code:

```
age = int(input('Enter your age:'))
age += 5
print(age)
```

   gives the following output for an entered value 'twenty two':
   (a) A `TypeError` message
   (b) A `ValueError` message
   (c) twenty two 5

7. The `else` block is useful for grouping statements that need to be executed after successfully completing the `try` block.
   (a) True
   (b) False

8. Execution of the following code:

```
age = input('Enter your age:')
age += 5
print(age)
```

   gives the following output for an entered value of 10:
   (a) A `TypeError` message
   (b) A `ValueError` message
   (c) 15

9. Instructions that may cause a problem should be placed in the `try` block.
   (a) `else`
   (b) `try`
   (c) `except`
   (d) `finally`

10. You may not put a `finally` block after a `try-except` block.
   (a) True
   (b) False

10.8 Practice problems

PROBLEM 10.1

Develop the required code to perform the division of two real numbers entered by the user. Make sure to capture the exceptions related to incorrect input and the case where the denominator value is equal to 0.

```
try:
    # ask for input values
    num = float(input("Please enter the numerator: "))
    denom = float(input("Please enter the denominator: "))

    # perform the calculation
    result = num / denom
except ValueError:
    print("The input value is not a number.")
except ZeroDivisionError:
    print("Division by zero is not allowed.")
else:
    print("{0:5.2f} divided by {1:5.2f} gives: {2:5.2f}".format(num,
    ↪  denom, result))
```

Output

In case of incorrect input:

```
Please enter the numerator: twelve
The input value is not a number.
```

In case the denominator is equal to 0:

```
Please enter the numerator: 12
Please enter the denominator: 0
Division by zero is not allowed.
```

In case the input values are correct:

```
Please enter the numerator: 12
Please enter the denominator: 3
12.0 divided by 3.0 gives: 4.0
```

PROBLEM 10.2

Redo problem 10.2, but allow the user to correct their input if a message indicates an exception.

```
flag = True
while flag:
    try:
        # ask for input values
        num = float(input("Please enter the numerator: "))
        denom = float(input("Please enter the denominator: "))

        # perform the calculation
        result = num / denom
    except ValueError:
        print("The input value is not a number.")
    except ZeroDivisionError:
        print("Division by zero is not allowed.")
    else:
        flag = False
        print("{0:5.2f} divided by {1:5.2f} gives:
         ↪ {2:5.2f}".format(num, denom, result))
```

Output

```
Please enter the numerator: twelve
The input value is not a number.
Please enter the numerator: 12
Please enter the denominator: 0
Division by zero is not allowed.
Please enter the numerator: 12
Please enter the denominator: 4
12.00 divided by  4.00 gives:  3.00
```

PROBLEM 10.3

Develop the code that allows the user to enter integer numbers. These numbers can only be between 1 and 5 exclusively. Outside of this range, a `ValueError` exception is raised. The code should loop until the input condition is satisfied.

```
flag = True
while flag:
    try:
        val = int(input("Please enter your value: "))
        if not 1 <= val < 6:
            raise ValueError("Error: invalid value")
    except ValueError as v:
        print(v)
    else:
        print("Your value is:", val)
        flag = False
```

Output

```
Please enter your value: 56
Error: invalid value
Please enter your value: 3
Your value is: 3
```

PROBLEM 10.4

Revisit problem 10.3 and improve the error message in case of an exception. It should now be **error: enter your value between 1 and 5 exclusively**.

```
flag = True
message = "Please enter your value between 1 and 5: "
while flag:
    try:
        val = int(input(message))
        if not 1 <= val < 6:
            raise ValueError("Error: invalid value")
    except ValueError as v:
        print(v)
        message = "Error: enter your value between 1 and 5 exclusively:
        ↪  "
    else:
        print("Your value is:", val)
        flag = False
```

Output

```
Please enter your value between 1 and 5: 56
Error: invalid value
Error: enter your value between 1 and 5 exclusively: 3
Your value is: 3
```

10.9 Programming problems

PROBLEM 10.5

Solution provided in the appendix

We want to handle the multiplication of two numbers entered by the user. In this case, there is a potential for non-numeric input, which will raise the `ValueError` exception.

Develop a program to:

- Display the message: **The value entered is not a number** in case of non-numeric input.
- Introduce a loop until the entered values do not cause an exception.

The main objective of the problem is to handle non-numeric input using exception handling and implement a loop for continuous input until valid numeric values are provided.

PROBLEM 10.6

Develop a class that can be used to represent complex numbers.

Complex numbers have a real part and an imaginary part. Your class should provide the appropriate attributes, constructor and methods for manipulating a complex number.

If the user enters a string for either the real or imaginary part of the complex number, raise an exception and handle it by displaying an appropriate message.

Test your class with different values.

PROBLEM 10.7

Solution provided in the appendix

Develop a function **process_case()** that takes two files as parameters and copies the contents of the first file into the second. The lines that start with a lowercase letter will be removed. Let's take the file **case.txt** which contains the following content:

```
The fox jumps the barrier.
    The sheeps run in all directions.
    the shepherd whistles and sings without seeing the scene unfolding
    before his eyes.
```

If there is a problem accessing the files, an error message should be displayed to the user.

PROBLEM 10.8

Revisit problem 10.7 and ensure that if there is a problem accessing the files, the IP address and the username are recorded in a log file.

You can use the following code to retrieve the username, machine name, and IP address.

```
import getpass
import socket

username = getpass.getuser()
hostname = socket.gethostname()
ip = socket.gethostbyname(hostname)
```

PROBLEM 10.9

Develop a class **Employee**. Each employee has a first name, last name, and age. Use a constructor to initialize an employee with a first name, last name, and age.

Create a class **EmployeeList** that will be used to manage employees. Use an attribute of type `list` to store the employees.

In the **EmployeeList** class, include the method **add_employee()** to add an employee to the list and the method **display_employees()** to display the employees in the list, respectively.

Using the employees **Alain, FlouFlou, 25**, **Abdel, FlouClair, 34**, and **Annie, FlouFlou, 22**, develop the necessary code to add these employees to the list and then display them. Notify the user that an employee is already present in the list when trying to add an employee with the same first and last name. In this case, adding the employee will not be allowed.

To signal this duplicate entry, we will use an exception. Following the standard naming conventions, this exception will be called **EmployeeDuplicateError** and will be raised if the employee is detected as a duplicate during the addition process.

Chapter 11

Graphical User interfaces

Contents of this chapter

Objectives:

- To understand the role of the tkinter module
- To understand what a graphical component or widget is
- To use attributes of a widget
- To learn how to position a widget using a layout manager
- To learn how to handle events
- To create graphical user interfaces with various widgets

11.1 The tkinter module

In the previous chapters, we focused on developing Python programs without concerning ourselves with the way data is received and displayed. However, in some cases, it can be beneficial to provide a graphical interface to allow users to interact more effectively.

There are numerous modules available for developing graphical interfaces in Python, also known as GUI (Graphical User Interface). Some of the most popular ones include:

- tkinter
- PyQt
- WxPython
- PyGUI

The Python language comes with the `tkinter` module built-in, which is designed for the rapid development of graphical interfaces. It originated from **Tcl/Tk**, a popular library among developers in the early 90s, known for its simplicity and ease of use.

The `tkinter` module provides a wide range of widgets and tools for creating graphical interfaces. It consists of two parts: `TCL` (Tool Command Language) and `Tk` (Toolkit).

One of the key advantages of `tkinter` is its cross-platform compatibility, as it works on all major operating systems. However, the appearance and rendering of the GUI may vary slightly across different platforms, which could be a limitation for modern applications.

The `tkinter` module offers a variety of classes representing components or widgets, windows, and other support classes for creating GUI interfaces. There is a vast array of components available in `tkinter`, and it is crucial to consult the documentation to use the module effectively.

11.1.1 Developing a GUI

The process of developing a GUI interface follows a standard set of steps, which can be summarized as follows:

- Import the `tkinter` module.
- Create a top-level or root window object that will serve as our application's main window.
- Create all the graphical components and position them within the top-level window.
- Connect the components to the application's code for handling events and user interactions.
- Start the main event loop to handle user input and interactions.

In the following sections, we will go through each of these steps in detail.

Components and Containers

To create a GUI interface, we need two types of elements: graphical components (widgets) and containers.

Widgets are responsible for providing visual support, such as text input fields or buttons, while containers are used to group these components. A container can hold multiple widgets or other containers.

Before being displayed, a widget needs to be associated with a container. Typically, the main window is used as the root container, and it is conventionally named **root**.

Therefore, creating a GUI interface involves designing a hierarchy of widgets and containers, as shown in the example structure in figure 11.1.

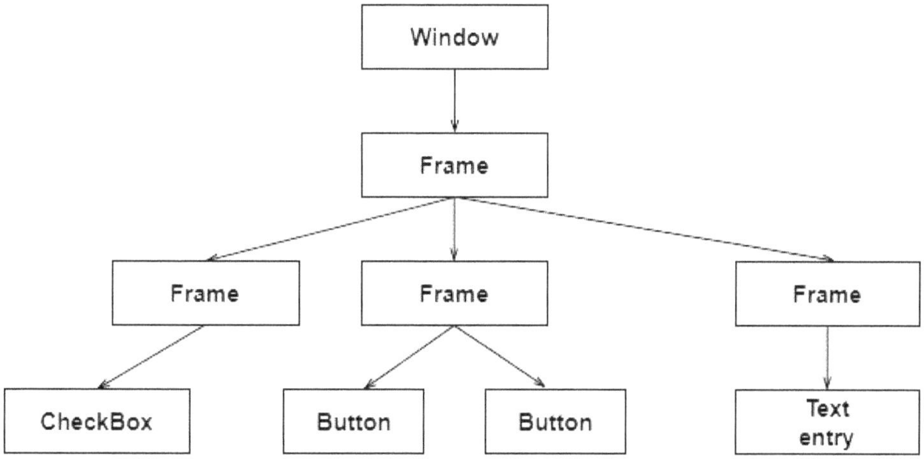

Figure 11.1: Structure of a GUI interface.

This approach leads us to use a placement or layout manager to organize and arrange these components within the window.

Root Window

The root window is the main window that contains all other graphical components. While you can have several top-level windows that can be displayed, only one of them should be designated as the root window.

To create and display the root window, we only need three lines of code, as shown in listing 11.1.

Listing 11.1: Displaying the root window

```
import tkinter as tk
root = tk.Tk()
root.mainloop()
```

The code begins by importing the `tkinter` module with the alias `tk`, as is commonly done. The second line of code instantiates the root window from `tkinter` and assigns it to the variable **root**. The third line, `root.mainloop()`, is crucial as it executes the `mainloop()` method, which keeps the window visible until the user clicks the close button.

Running this code will display an empty window with three basic buttons: minimize, maximize, and close. The window's title will be set to **tk**.

Output in execution mode

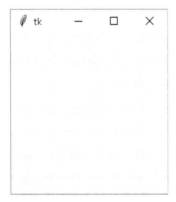

11.2 Components or Widgets

To create graphical GUI interfaces, we need basic graphic components or widgets. Some of the most commonly used ones in Python are:

- **Button**
- CheckBox
- RadioButton
- ComboBox
- **Entry**
- **Label**
- Canvas

We highlighted in bold those that we will use extensively in this chapter.

Widget Attributes

A widget has attributes that define its visual appearance. These attributes are stored in a dictionary and have default values. You can assign values to these attributes when creating the widget or later using the attribute's dictionary and corresponding index.

Listing 11.2 demonstrates the creation of a `Label` widget and its positioning in the **root** window.

Listing 11.2: Example of a graphical component

```
import tkinter as tk
root = tk.Tk()
lbl_hello = tk.Label(root, text='Hello, world!')
lbl_hello['text'] = 'Goodbye, world!'
lbl_hello.pack()
root.mainloop()
```

Output in execution mode

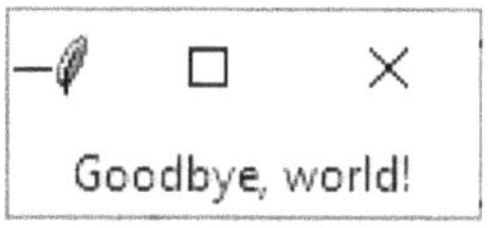

Once the **root** window has been obtained, we create an object of type `Label`. The label obtained, named **lbl_hello**, is placed inside **root**. The `text` parameter is used to set the label's text. The other parameters of the object use default values.

The next line, using indexing with the `text` key, changes the text of **lbl_hello**. To place the label on the window, we use the `pack` layout manager by calling the `pack()` method.

Finally, we call **root**'s `mainloop()` method to start the main event loop.

In general, to add a widget to a container, you can use the code shown in listing 11.3.

Listing 11.3: Link between the graphical component and the container

```
widget_variable = WidgetName(container, **parameters)
```

Here, the **container** parameter represents a container object such as **root**. The ****parameters** parameter represents the dictionary of attributes that can be configured for the widget.

Widget positioning

After creating the widget, we need to physically position it within the visible window for the user. To achieve this, we use placement managers or layout managers.

The `tkinter` module provides three layout managers:

- **Place geometry**: We specify the size of the widget and its exact location on the GUI interface.

- **Pack geometry**: It places the widget within the designated container based on the available space.
- **Grid geometry**: It places the widget on the GUI interface according to a grid with rows and columns.

In this chapter, we will use the `pack` and `grid` managers. Although the `place` manager provides precise control, it is less commonly used due to the variety of display screens. Different screen sizes can cause interfaces designed for one screen to display incorrectly on another screen.

Widget positioning with the pack layout manager

The `pack` layout manager is the easiest to use for positioning widgets. Widgets are placed in the container as they are added, and the manager calculates the available space and positions the widgets accordingly.

However, using the `pack` manager can sometimes lead to quality issues, as it may modify the geometry to accommodate the placement.

When using the `pack` layout manager, the parameters described in table 11.1 are used to determine the placement of widgets.

Parameter	Description	Values
`side`	Widget alignment	`LEFT, TOP, RIGHT, BOTTOM`
`fill`	Specifies whether the widget can grow in size in `X` and `Y` directions	`X, Y, BOTH`
`anchor`	Widget positioning	`nw, n, ne, e, se, s, sw, w, center`
`expand`	Indicates whether the widget can grow	`1/0` or `True/False`

Table 11.1: Parameters for the `pack` layout manager.

Let's consider the window prototype shown in figure 11.2. The widgets used in this prototype are `Entry`, `Label`, and `Button`. `Entry`, `Label` et `Button`.

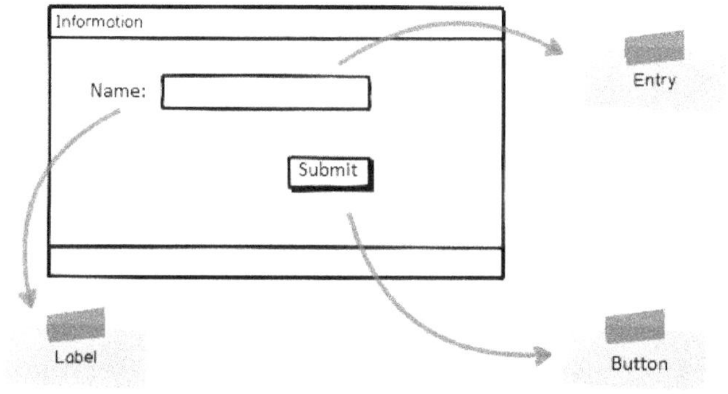

Figure 11.2: Prototype of the input window.

Listing 11.4 produces the requested interface using the default values for each widget.

Listing 11.4: Basic Interface with tkinter

```
import tkinter as tk
root = tk.Tk()

# Create a label
lbl_name = tk.Label(root, text='Name:')
lbl_name.pack()

# Create a text entry field
ent_name = tk.Entry(root)
ent_name.pack()

# Create a button
btn_submit = tk.Button(root, text='Submit')
btn_submit.pack()

root.mainloop()
```

The resulting prototype is shown in figure 11.3.

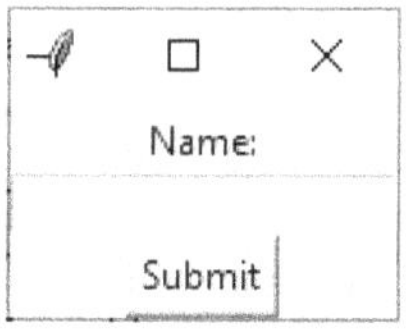

Figure 11.3: Resulting prototype.

Even though the interface in figure 11.3 contains the requested widgets, the layout does not match the prototype shown in figure 11.2. This is because the **pack** layout manager used the default values of the attributes of the widgets, placing each element below the previous one in the order indicated in the code.

To achieve the desired layout, we introduce a **Frame** type container that allows us to group widgets together. This makes it easier to position several widgets simultaneously. In our case, we group **lbl_name** and **ent_name** together in a frame. This results in the code shown in listing 11.5.

Listing 11.5: Using a Frame to group widgets

```
import tkinter as tk
root = tk.Tk()
# Set window size
root.geometry('200x100')

# Create a frame container for label and entry
row = tk.Frame(root)
row.pack(side=tk.TOP, fill=tk.X, padx=5, pady=5)

# Create a label
lbl_name = tk.Label(row, text='Name:')
lbl_name.pack(side=tk.LEFT, anchor='w')

# Create a text entry field
ent_name = tk.Entry(row)
ent_name.pack(side=tk.RIGHT, expand=tk.YES, fill=tk.X, padx=10,
↪    pady=5)

# Create a button
btn_submit = tk.Button(root, text='Submit')
btn_submit.pack(side=tk.TOP, anchor='e', padx=15, pady=5)

root.mainloop()
```

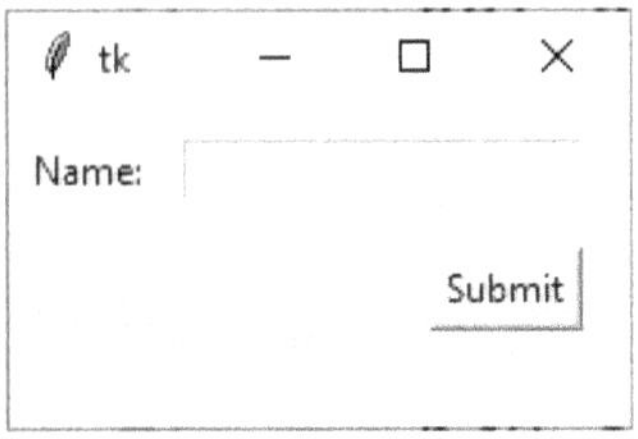

Figure 11.4: Final prototype.

This code requires several remarks regarding the use of the widget parameters shown in table 11.1.

First, we set the size of the window using the `geometry()` method. This method receives the size as a string with the width and height, in this case, 200 and 300, respectively.

A `Frame` type container is created with the following parameters:

- `side`: The chosen alignment is `TOP` to align the label and the input area towards the top in **root**.
- `fill`: The value chosen is `X` to stretch **row** along the width when the window is resized horizontally.
- `padx` and `pady`: We chose the value 5 to add empty space on the `X` and `Y` axes.

For the **lbl_name**, the chosen parameters are:

- `side`: The chosen alignment is `LEFT` with respect to the **row** container.
- `anchor`: We ensure that the label does not move from its position when the window is resized. The chosen value is `w`.

The **ent_name** entry widget is slightly more complicated because it comes right after **lbl_name**. We chose the following values:

- `side`: The chosen alignment is `RIGHT` with respect to the **row** container.
- `expand`: We ensure that the input area increases in size when the window is resized. The chosen value is `YES`.
- `fill`: We indicate that the expansion of the area is done in the `X` direction.
- `padx` and `pady`: We took the value 10 to add empty space on the `X` axis and 5 for the `Y` axis.

The button **btn_submit** is positioned relative to the **root** window. Note that we could have put it in a `Frame` container before adding it to **root**. But since there is only one button, we don't need an additional container.

The parameters used for the button have the following values:

- `side`: The chosen alignment is `TOP` with respect to the **root** container.
- `anchor`: We ensure that the button does not move from its position when the window is resized. The chosen value is `e`.
- `padx` and `pady`: We took the value 15 to add empty space on the `X` axis and 5 for the `Y` axis. To align the button on the left with the input area, we used the value 15 (i.e., 10 for the frame and 5 for the input area).

The resulting window conforms to the prototype. In general, it may take several attempts to fine-tune the values of the parameters to achieve the desired widget placement.

Widget positioning with grid

For more complex GUIs, the `grid` manager is more suitable than the `pack` manager.

In the `grid` manager, the container is divided into a two-dimensional grid with a specified number of rows and columns. Each cell at the intersection of a row and a column can be used to place a widget. If a widget is larger than a single cell, it can span across multiple cells.

The `grid` manager allows for more precise control over the placement of widgets and is especially useful when designing interfaces with many widgets, as shown in figure 11.5.

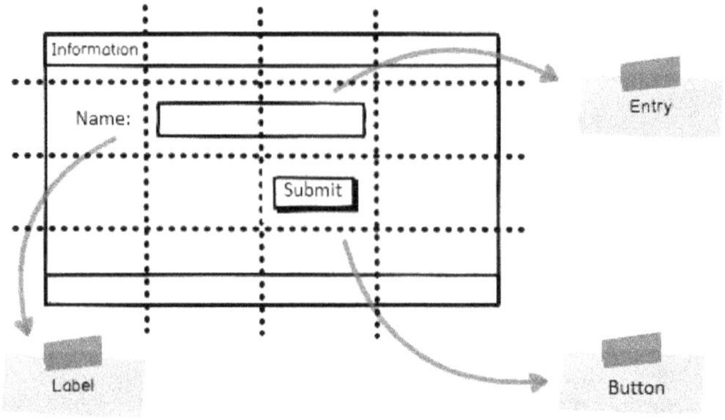

Figure 11.5: Prototype using grid manager.

We observe that the `Entry` widget spans two columns, while the `Button` widget spans one column.

Listing 11.6: Using the grid layout

```
import tkinter as tk
root = tk.Tk()
# Set window size
root.geometry('200x100')

# Create a label widget for "Name"
lbl_name = tk.Label(root, text='Name:')
lbl_name.grid(row=0, column=0, padx=5, pady=5)
```

```
# Create an entry widget
ent_name = tk.Entry(root)
ent_name.grid(row=0, column=1, columnspan=2, padx=5, pady=5)

# Create a button widget
btn_submit = tk.Button(root, text='Submit')
btn_submit.grid(row=1, column=2, padx=5, pady=5, sticky='e')

root.mainloop()
```

The properties to create the prototype shown in figure 11.5 are specific to the `grid` layout manager. Table 11.2 presents some of the properties used in this chapter.

Parameter	Description	Values
`sticky`	Specifies the direction to expand the widget if the cell is larger	`ne, n, nw, e` `sw, s, se` `w, center`
`rowspan`	Indicates whether the widget can span multiple rows	number
`colspan`	Indicates whether the widget can span multiple columns	number
`padx`	Indicates external space to the (X) widget	number
`ipadx`	Indicates internal space to the (X) widget	number
`pady`	Indicates external space to the (Y) widget	number
`ipadx`	Indicates internal space to the (Y) widget	number

Table 11.2: Parameters for the `grid` layout manager.

It is important to mention that we could not utilize the `colspan` property in this prototype because there is only one button positioned below the input area, and it is aligned using `sticky='e'`.

11.3 Events

Events play a crucial role in building graphical interfaces, as they are the foundation of event handling.

When designing interfaces, we have to take into account that users should have the ability to interact with various components. For instance, in the interface shown in

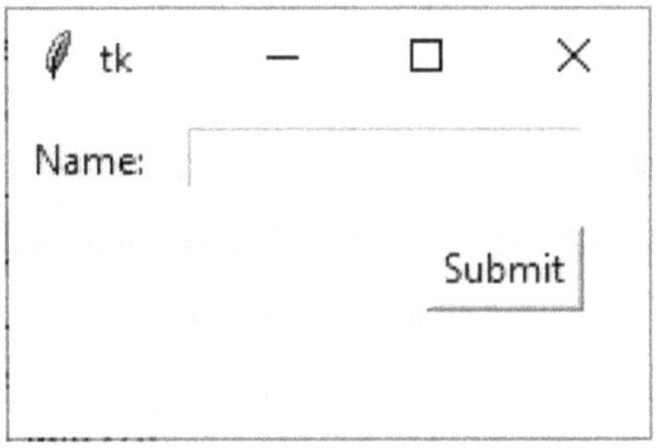

Figure 11.6: Prototype with the grid layout manager.

figure 11.6, the user can click the **Submit** button to trigger name validation. This action generates an event which is the button click event.

The application needs to respond to these user events. It's essential to note that applications can also respond to other types of events that are not directly initiated by the user. For example, a timer object can trigger an event when it reaches its expiration time.

In the model we use, three objects participate in event handling:

- Event source
- Event object
- Event listener

Despite its simplicity, this model can be challenging for beginners because they often confuse the event source with the event itself. It leads to the misconception that a source can only be associated with a single type of event, resulting in a belief that each source widget in the interface needs a separate pair of objects (source, event) for event handling.

However, in reality, a source can generate multiple events, and therefore, multiple event listeners may be needed to capture events from that source.

We will now implement the following steps to manage events at the GUI interface level:

- Declare and instantiate the widget.
- Attach a listener to the widget component, based on the type of event that can be generated by this component and is of interest to the user.
- Develop the task management code to be executed when the event occurs. The code will be supported by the listener.

An event object is created depending on the nature of the event. In Python, there are various event types, such as the **click event**, **mouse event**, and **focus event**, among others.

In the rest of this section, we will delve into the concept of event management by introducing functions commonly referred to as **callbacks**. These callbacks are associated with the events that need to be processed.

Two strategies are employed for implementing callbacks:

- **Command binding**: We use the `command` parameter to specify the callback to be executed. This technique is applicable to widgets that support this parameter.
- **Event binding**: We use the `bind()` method to link the event with the callback responsible for handling event processing.

11.3.1 Command binding

For widgets that have the `command` parameter, we specify the callback to be used at this level.

Can we use the `command` parameter for any event?

The `command` parameter is only supported for specific events, such as left mouse button click and spacebar. The RETURN or Enter key is not supported by this parameter.

Let's consider the interface shown in figure 11.6. In this scenario, we want the entered text to be converted to uppercase when the user clicks on the button. To achieve this, we create the callback function **change_text()**, and its code is provided in listing 11.7.

Listing 11.7: Using callbacks

```
import tkinter as tk
# Command event
def change_text():
    result = ent_name.get().upper()
    ent_name.delete(0, tk.END)
    ent_name.insert(0, result)

root = tk.Tk()
# Set window size
root.geometry('200x100')

# Create a label widget for "Name"
lbl_name = tk.Label(root, text='Name:')
lbl_name.grid(row=0, column=0, padx=5, pady=5)
```

```
# Create an entry widget
ent_name = tk.Entry(root)
ent_name.grid(row=0, column=1, columnspan=2, padx=5, pady=5)

# Create a button widget with a command event
btn_submit = tk.Button(root, text='Submit', command=change_text)
btn_submit.grid(row=1, column=2, padx=5, pady=5, sticky='e')

root.mainloop()
```

If the user types a string, for example 'flouflou' as shown in figure 11.7, and clicks on the button, the string is transformed into uppercase within the input area.

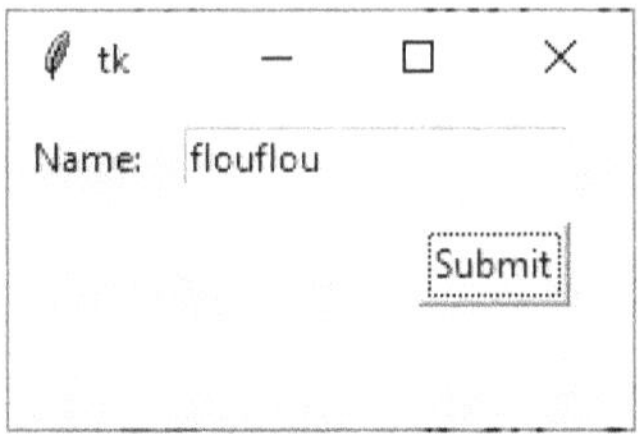

Figure 11.7: Using callbacks.

The result of the callback is displayed in figure 11.8.

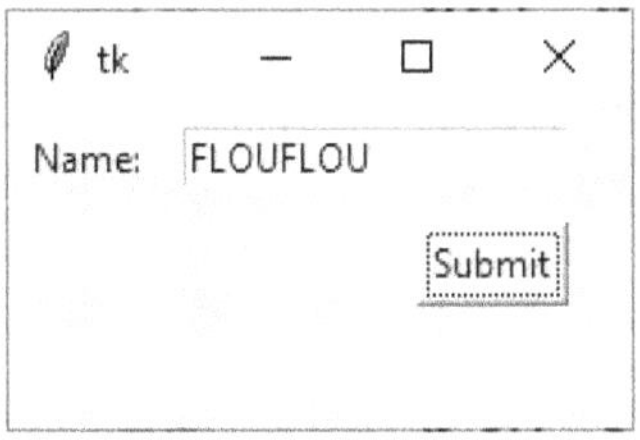

Figure 11.8: Result obtained after using the callback.

we notice in listing 11.7 that a callback was implemented using `command=change_text`. We did not include parentheses because we are passing a reference to the callback function **change_text()** using `command` parameter.

Furthermore, we observe that the function **change_text()** does not require any parameters. If it were otherwise, we would need to use a **Lambda** function[1] for the `command` parameter.

[1] https://python101.pythonlibrary.org/chapter26_lambda.html

11.3.2 Event binding

If the widget does not have the `command` parameter, or if you want to manage events other than the left mouse button click or the spacebar press, you will need to use the **event binding** technique. This involves using the `bind()` method on the widget to handle the events.

The general form of usage is as follows:

```
widget_name.bind(event, handler)
```

Where:

- **event**: denotes the type of event to listen for.
- **handler**: refers to the callback function to execute when the event occurs.

Let's use the interface shown in figure 11.7. However, this time, we want the entered text to change its color to red when the right mouse button is clicked.

Listing 11.8: Using event binding

```
import tkinter as tk
# Command event
def change_color(event):
    ent_name.configure(fg='red')

root = tk.Tk()
# Set window size
root.geometry('200x100')

# Create a label widget for "Name"
lbl_name = tk.Label(root, text='Name:')
lbl_name.grid(row=0, column=0, padx=5, pady=5)

# Create an entry widget
ent_name = tk.Entry(root)
ent_name.grid(row=0, column=1, columnspan=2, padx=5, pady=5)

# Create a button
btn_submit = tk.Button(root, text='Submit')
btn_submit.bind('<Button-3>', change_color) # Binds the right mouse
↪   button click event to the change_color function
btn_submit.grid(row=1, column=2, padx=5, pady=5, sticky='e')

root.mainloop()
```

By clicking with the right mouse button on **Submit**, the entered text transforms into red, as shown in figure 11.9.

Figure 11.9: Using callback with event binding.

The callback function, in this case **change_color()**, takes an `event` object as a parameter. Moreover, in the `bind()` method, the parameter used `'<Button-3>'` corresponds to the right mouse button.

The most common bindings are listed in table 11.3. From this table, we can observe that there are a variety of events that can be linked to the widgets of an interface.

Event	Type	Description
<Button-1>	Mouse	Click on the left button
<Button-2>	Mouse	Click on the middle button
<Button-3>	Mouse	Click on the right button
<ButtonRelease-1>	Mouse	Release of the left button
<Double-Button-1>	Mouse	Double-click on the left button
<Enter>	Mouse	Mouse enters the widget
<Leave>	Mouse	Mouse exits the widget
<FocusIn>	Keyboard	Focus on a widget through the keyboard
<FocusOut>	Keyboard	Focus outside the widget through the keyboard
<Return>	Keyboard	Enter key pressed
<Key>	Keyboard	A key is pressed

Table 11.3: Events related to event binding.

11.4 Quick summary

This quick summary highlights the essential concepts in using the `tkinter` module, providing a concise overview of the key elements you have learned:

- The standard module for creating GUI interfaces in Python is `tkinter`.
- A GUI is composed of various widgets or graphical components.
- Widgets are arranged within a window using a layout manager.
- The most useful placement managers in `tkinter` are `pack` and `grid`.
- To make a widget interactive, you can use an event handler.

11.5 Quiz

Please answer the following questions. There may be one or more correct answers.

1. Is `tkinter` natively available in Python, and do we need to install it?
   (a) Yes
   (b) No

2. Execution of the following code:

```
import tkinter as tk

root = tk.Tk()
```

   produces:
   (a) An empty window
   (b) A window with a `Label` widget
   (c) No result

3. The `grid` layout manager use a cell matrix structure to place components:
   (a) True
   (b) False

4. Execution of the following code:

```
import tkinter as tk

root = tk.Tk()
root.mainloop()
```

   produces:
   (a) An empty window
   (b) A window with a `Label` widget
   (c) No result

5. The `mainloop()` method can be used on components other than the main window:
   (a) True
   (b) False

6. Do each widget in `tkinter` have a number of parameters that have default values suitable for most situations?
   (a) Yes
   (b) No

7. Is it mandatory to use lambda functions for the `command` parameter of a button in `tkinter`?
   (a) Yes
   (b) No

8. Execution of the following code:

```
import tkinter as tk

def display():
    print('Button activated')

root = tk.Tk()
btn = tk.Button(root, text='Display', command=display())
btn.pack()
root.mainloop()
```

   does not give the expected result because:
   (a) We passed the result of the call to the **display()** function through the `command` parameter.
   (b) We did not provide any parameters for the **display()** function.
   (c) It would have been necessary to pass a reference to the **display()** function by removing parentheses from the `command` parameter.

9. Is it possible to use the `place`, `pack`, and `grid` layout managers in the same window in `tkinter`?
   (a) Yes
   (b) No

10. Does the `config()` method allow you to modify the characteristics of a widget in `tkinter`?
    (a) Yes
    (b) No

11.6 Laboratories

11.6.1 Developing a Graphical Interface

Objective

Implement a basic graphical interface for a fruit selection game.

Context

We aim to create a graphical interface to display the name of a fruit.

Functionalities

We will develop the following graphical interface, making sure to adhere to the following points:

- We will use the following list of fruit names: [**'apple'**, **'banana'**, **'orange'**, **'mango'**, **'kiwi'**].
- The display will show a random fruit name using the **change_fruit**() function.
- The verification button will be connected to the **verify_answer**() function. For the time being, we do not provide any functionality for this function.

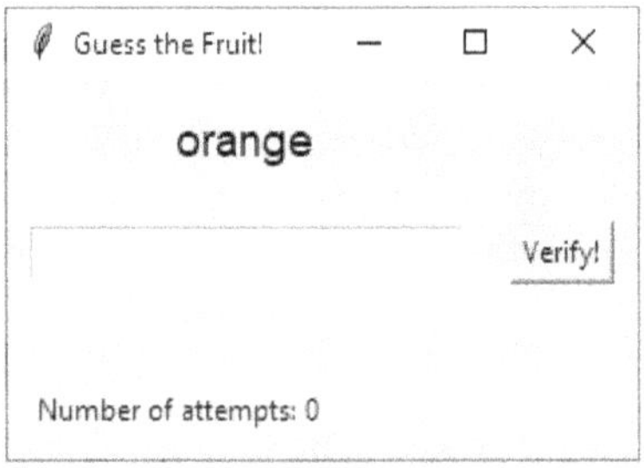

Skills Used

- Using the `tkinter` module
- Utilizing the `grid` layout manager
- Calling functions

Solution

```
import tkinter as tk
import random

# List of fruits
fruits = ["apple", "banana", "orange", "mango", "kiwi"]

# Function to verify the answer
def verify_answer():
    pass

# Function to change the fruit
def change_fruit():
    global current_fruit
    global attempts
    attempts = 0
    current_fruit = random.choice(fruits)
    lbl_fruit.config(text=current_fruit)
    entry.delete(0, tk.END)

# Create the main window
root = tk.Tk()
root.title("Guess the Fruit!")

# Create widgets
lbl_fruit = tk.Label(root, text="", font=("Arial", 14))
lbl_fruit.grid(row=0, column=0, columnspan=2, padx=10, pady=10)

entry = tk.Entry(root, font=("Arial", 12))
entry.grid(row=1, column=0, columnspan=2, padx=10)

btn_verify = tk.Button(root, text="Verify!", command=verify_answer)
btn_verify.grid(row=1, column=2, columnspan=2, padx=10, pady=10)

lbl_result = tk.Label(root, text="")
lbl_result.grid(row=3, column=0, columnspan=3, padx=10, sticky="w")

attempts = 0
lbl_attempts = tk.Label(root, text="Number of attempts: " +
↪   str(attempts))
lbl_attempts.grid(row=4, column=0, columnspan=3, padx=10, pady=10,
↪   sticky="w")
```

```
# Start the game
change_fruit()

# Main window event loop
root.mainloop()
```

11.6.2 Integration of Functions in a Graphical Interface

Objective

Implement the basic code for a fruit selection game.

Context

We propose to create a program that allows the user to learn the name of a displayed fruit on the screen. The user will be asked to enter the name of the fruit in English.

Features

We develop the following graphical interface. We will ensure to respect the following points:

- Display a fruit to the user.
- The user must enter the name of the fruit.
- If the user correctly guesses the name of the fruit, display the message 'Bravo! You have guessed the fruit.' and provide the number of attempts made. If the answer is incorrect, display the error message **Sorry, that's not the right fruit. Try again!**.
- If the answer is correct, display another fruit.

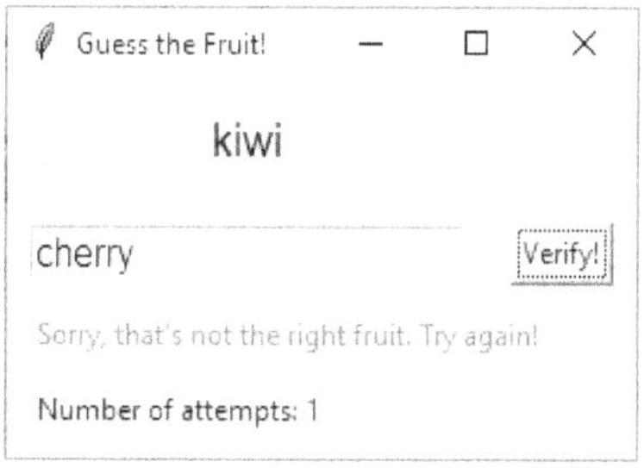

Skills Used

- Using the `tkinter` module
- Utilizing the `grid` layout manager
- Calling functions
- Using variables
- Using the list data structure
- Using predefined functions in Python
- Using Conditional statements

Solution

```
import tkinter as tk
import random

# List of fruits
fruits = ["apple", "banana", "orange", "mango", "kiwi"]

# Function to verify the answer
def verify_response():
    global attempts
    guessed_fruit = entry.get().lower()
    if guessed_fruit == current_fruit:
        lbl_result.config(text="Bravo! You have guessed the fruit.",
        ↪ fg="green")
        change_fruit()
    else:
        lbl_result.config(text="Sorry, that's not the right fruit. Try
        ↪ again!", fg="red")
        attempts += 1

    lbl_attempts.config(text="Number of attempts: " + str(attempts))

# Function to change the fruit
def change_fruit():
    global current_fruit
    global attempts
    attempts = 0
    current_fruit = random.choice(fruits)
    lbl_fruit.config(text=current_fruit)
    entry.delete(0, tk.END)

# Create the main window
root = tk.Tk()
root.title("Guess the Fruit!")

# Create widgets
lbl_fruit = tk.Label(root, text="", font=("Arial", 14))
lbl_fruit.grid(row=0, column=0, columnspan=2, padx=10, pady=10)

entry = tk.Entry(root, font=("Arial", 12))
entry.grid(row=1, column=0, columnspan=2, padx=10, pady=10)
```

```
btn_verify = tk.Button(root, text="Verify!", command=verify_response)
btn_verify.grid(row=1, column=2, columnspan=2, padx=10, pady=10)

lbl_result = tk.Label(root, text="")
lbl_result.grid(row=3, column=0, columnspan=3, padx=10, sticky="w")

attempts = 0
lbl_attempts = tk.Label(root, text="Number of attempts: " +
↪   str(attempts))
lbl_attempts.grid(row=4, column=0, columnspan=3, padx=10, pady=10,
↪   sticky="w")

# Start the game
change_fruit()

# Main window loop
root.mainloop()
```

11.7 Practice problems

PROBLEM 11.1

Develop the code to display a window containing a `Label` with the text **Hello world!**.

```
import tkinter
root = tkinter.Tk()
label = tkinter.Label(root, text='Hello World!')
label.pack()
root.mainloop()
```

PROBLEM 11.2

Using the `config()` method of the `Label` widget, modify the text of problem 11.1 to **Welcome Alain**.

```
import tkinter
root = tkinter.Tk()
label = tkinter.Label(root, text='Welcome World!')
label.pack()
label.config(text="Welcome Alain")
root.mainloop()
```

PROBLEM 11.3

Display the following window that contains a label and a button. By clicking on the button, the window will close (command is `root.quit` if the main window is called **root**).

```
import tkinter
root = tkinter.Tk()
label = tkinter.Label(root, text='Welcome World!')
label.pack()
quit_button = tkinter.Button(root, text='Quit', command=root.quit,
↪  bg='yellow', fg='red')
quit_button.pack(fill=tkinter.X, expand=1)
root.mainloop()
```

PROBLEM 11.4

Display the window shown in figure 11.10 which allows the user to enter values. By clicking on the button, the entered value will be printed on the console. We will use the `Entry` widget and its `get()` method.

Figure 11.10: Entry widget.

```
import tkinter

def print_value():
    print(txt.get())

root= tkinter.Tk()
txt = tkinter.Entry(root)
txt.config(font=('arial', 12))
txt.pack()

show_button = tkinter.Button(root, text='Show', command=print_value)
show_button.pack()

root.mainloop()
```

11.8 Programming problems

PROBLEM 11.5

Create a window with two text areas and a button. When the button is clicked, the text from the first text area should be copied to the second text area.

Hint: use the **Text** widget.

PROBLEM 11.6

Create a window with a dropdown list that displays a list of colors. When a color is selected from the dropdown list, the background of the window should change to that color.

Hint: use the `Combobox` widget that is available through the `tkinter.ttk` module.

PROBLEM 11.7

Solution provided in the appendix

Display the window shown in figure 11.11, which allows you to enter a name and a salary. When you click on the button, the salary value will be read, and the increased value by 1000 will be displayed as shown in figure 11.12. Additionally, the name value

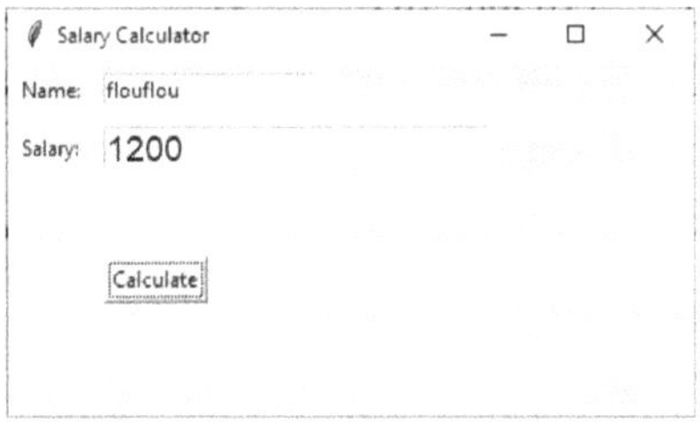

Figure 11.11: Initial window.

will be converted to uppercase.

Figure 11.12: Action on the button.

PROBLEM 11.8

Solution provided in the appendix.

Display the window shown in figure 11.13, which allows the user to enter the name of a sweater, its size, and the requested quantity. The available sizes are: large, medium, and small. Upon clicking the **Display** button, the information string is shown as illustrated

Figure 11.13: Initial window with Combobox.

in figure 11.14.

Figure 11.14: Window displaying the selection result.

Hint: use the `grid` layout manager along with the `Combobox` widget.

PROBLEM 11.9

Consider the window shown in figure 11.15.

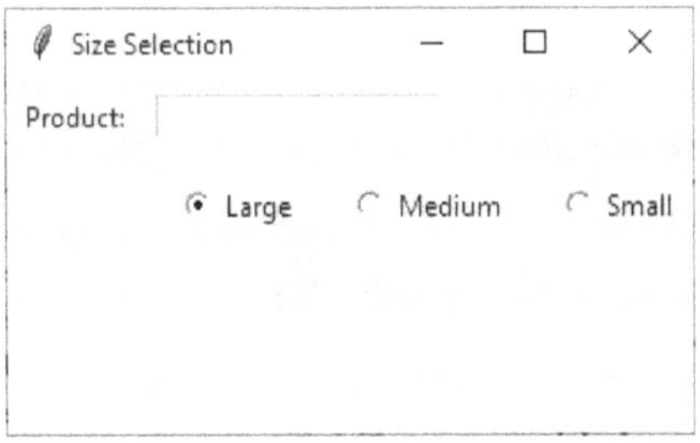

Figure 11.15: Initial window with radio buttons.

Write the code that allows the user to enter the name of a sweater and select its size by clicking on one of the radio buttons.

The available sizes are: large, medium, and small. When a radio button is clicked, the corresponding information should be displayed as shown in figure 11.16.

Hint: use the `grid` layout manager and the `RadioButton` widget.

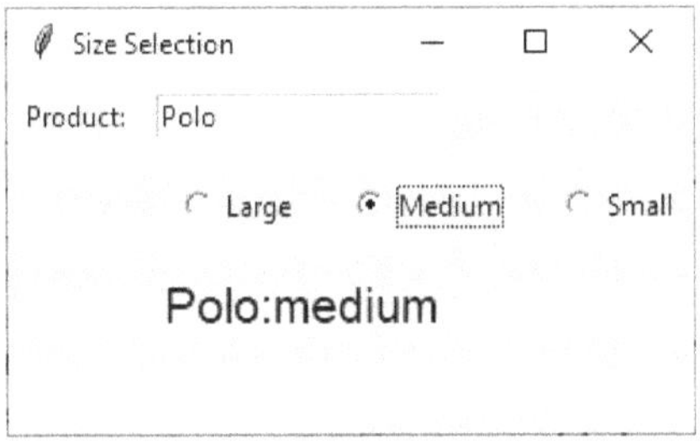

Figure 11.16: Window with the expected result.

PROBLEM 11.10

In this problem, you are required to develop a code that allows the user to modify the text size using the `Scale` widget, as shown in figure 11.17.

To achieve this, you will use the `Scale` widget with the `orient` parameter set to `HORIZONTAL`. To read the value selected by the user from the widget, you will use the `get()` method.

PROBLEM 11.11

Create a window with a text area and a **Save** button. When the button is clicked, the text from the text area should be saved to a text file.

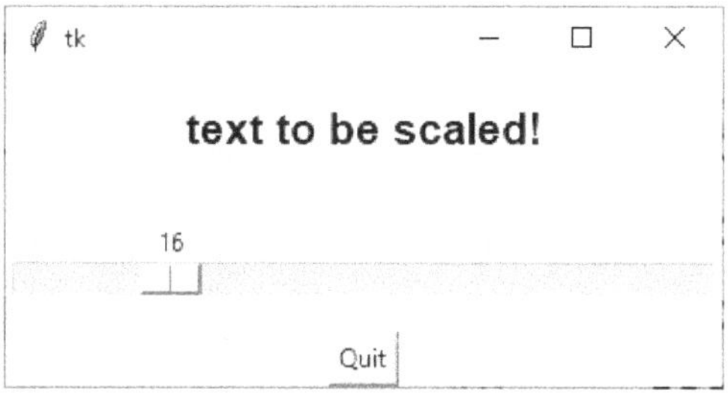

Figure 11.17: Window with the Scale widget.

PROBLEM 11.12

Create a window with a text area and an **Open** button. When the button is clicked, a file selection dialog should appear. After selecting a text file, its content should be displayed in the text area. You can use the file created in problem 11.11.

Chapter 12

Integration Project

12.1 Context

We aim to develop a simple system for calculating the Body Mass Index (BMI). The BMI is calculated using the following formula:

$$BMI = \frac{weight(kg)}{height^2(m)} \tag{12.1}$$

As per Health Canada's website [1], health risks can be assessed based on the BMI values listed in table 12.1.

Classification	BMI Range	Risk of Developing Health Problems
Underweight	< 18.5	Increased
Normal weight	18.5 - 25.0	Lower
Overweight	25.0 - 30.0	Increased
Obesity, Class I	30.0 - 35.0	High
Obesity, Class II	35.0 - 40.0	Very High
Obesity, Class III	> 40.0	Extremely High

Table 12.1: Classification and Risk.

[1] http://www.hc-sc.gc.ca/fn-an/nutrition/weights-poids/guide-ld-adult/bmi_chart_java-graph_imc_java-fra.php

Please note the BMI ranges and their associated risk levels as shown in table 12.1. This information will be crucial for our integration project.

Features

We aim to develop a prototype of this BMI calculator, ensuring the following points are respected:

- Display the Body Mass Index (BMI).
- Display the message regarding the associated health risk and classification.
- If the user does not enter values for height or weight, a message will be shown, indicating that these values are mandatory.
- Initially, the user will have the option to save the calculated BMI value along with a timestamp to a text file.
- The application will be delivered as a GUI and will be developed using the `tkinter` module.

Below is a preview of the user interface for the BMI calculator (figure 12.1).

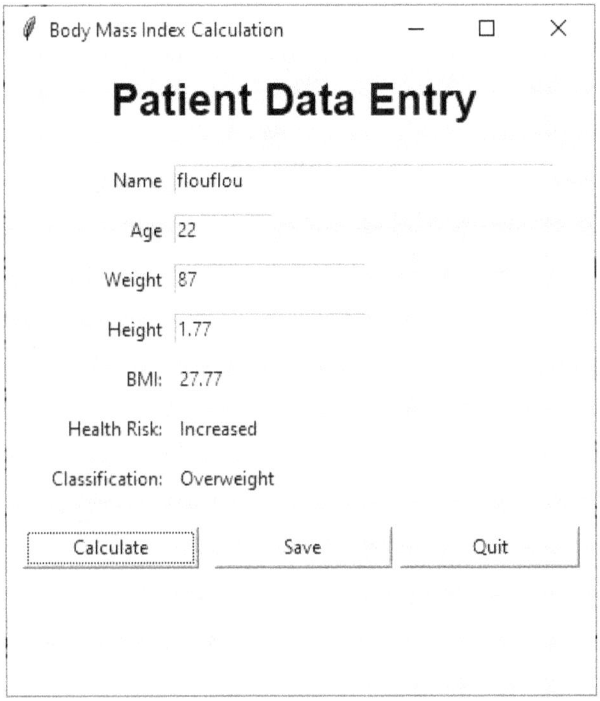

Figure 12.1: BMI calculator.

12.2 Basic module: BMI calculator

Approach

To begin with, we will develop the basic module by asking the user to enter their weight and height. Using these two values, we will calculate and display the BMI (Body Mass Index).

Solution

Since weight and height values can be real numbers, we will convert the entered data to `float` before using them in the BMI calculation. For display purposes, we will show the result with two decimal places. The code is shown in listing 12.1.

Listing 12.1: BMI basic script

```
weight = float(input("Enter your weight (in kg): "))
height = float(input("Enter your height (in meters): "))
# Calculate BMI according to the formula
bmi = weight / height ** 2
print("Your BMI is: {0:7.2f}".format(bmi))
```

Upon execution, the output will be as follows:

Output in execution mode

```
Enter your weight (in kg): 95
Enter your height (in meters): 1.75
Your BMI is:   31.02
```

12.3 Tests and loops

12.3.1 Tests, display of risk and classification

Objective

Develop the part of the application responsible for displaying the associated risk and classification based on a given BMI value.

Features

The BMI value will be displayed along with the messages regarding the associated risk and classification.

Approach

- Initially, we tested the application by asking the user to enter their weight and height. Using these values, we calculated the BMI.
- We will now proceed with displaying the classification and risk based on the calculated BMI value.

Solution

To display the risk and classification, we can use string variables. Depending on the calculated BMI value, we will assign a specific value for both the risk and classification.

In the code shown in listing 12.2, we initialize two lists for the risk and classification values.

We calculate the BMI and then determine the appropriate risk and classification by using the corresponding index and fetching the values from the lists.

Listing 12.2: Display of risk and classification

```
risk = ['Increased', 'Lower', 'Increased', 'High', 'Very High',
↪  'Extremely High']
classification = ['Underweight', 'Normal weight', 'Overweight',
↪  'Obesity, Class I', 'Obesity, Class II', 'Obesity, Class III']

weight = float(input("Enter your weight (in kg): "))
height = float(input("Enter your height (in meters): "))
# Calculate BMI according to the formula
bmi = weight / height ** 2
print("Your BMI is: {0:7.2f}".format(bmi))
```

```
# Determine risk and classification
if bmi < 18.5:
    index = 0
elif bmi < 25:
    index = 1
elif bmi < 30:
    index = 2
elif bmi < 35:
    index = 3
elif bmi < 40:
    index = 4
else:
    index = 5

print('Classification: {}'.format(classification[index]))
print('Risk: {}'.format(risk[index]))
```

Upon execution, the output will be as follows:

Output in execution mode

```
Enter your weight (in kg): 95
Enter your height (in meters): 1.75
Your BMI is:  31.02
Classification: Obesity, Class I
Risk: High
```

12.3.2 Loops, input validation

Objective

Develop the input validation part for the height and weight, which should be greater than 0.

Features

If the user enters a value less than or equal to 0 for either the weight or height, we will inform them that both parameters must have strictly positive values.

Approach

Use a loop to prevent the user from entering a value less than or equal to 0 for the weight or height.

Solution

To ensure that the user enters a value greater than 0 for both weight and height, we initialize the variables to 0. Then we use a loop with the appropriate condition, which in our case is that the variables must be > 0. This gives us the code shown in listing 12.3.

Listing 12.3: Input validation and display of risk and classification

```
risk = ['Increased', 'Lower', 'Increased', 'High', 'Very High',
↪  'Extremely High']
classification = ['Underweight', 'Normal weight', 'Overweight',
↪  'Obesity, Class I', 'Obesity, Class II', 'Obesity, Class III']

weight = 0
while weight <= 0:
    weight = float(input("Enter your weight (in kg):"))

height = 0
while height <= 0:
    height = float(input("Enter your height (in meters):"))

# Calculate BMI according to the formula
bmi = weight / height ** 2
print("Your BMI is: {0:7.2f}".format(bmi))
```

```
# Determine risk and classification
if bmi < 18.5:
    index = 0
elif bmi < 25:
    index = 1
elif bmi < 30:
    index = 2
elif bmi < 35:
    index = 3
elif bmi < 40:
    index = 4
else:
    index = 5

print('Classification: {}'.format(classification[index]))
print('Risk: {}'.format(risk[index]))
```

Upon execution, the output will be as follows:

Output in execution mode

```
Enter your weight (in kg):0
Enter your weight (in kg):95
Enter your height (in meters):-10
Enter your height (in meters):1.75
Your BMI is:  31.02
Classification: Obesity, Class I
Risk: High
```

With this input validation, the user is prompted to enter valid and positive values for weight and height.

12.4 Functions

Objective

Develop the display part for risk and classification, as well as the BMI calculation, using functions.

Approach

We will refactor our code by introducing the following functions:

- **input_value()**: allows user input of values.
- **display_bmi()**: displays the BMI value.
- **display_risk_class()**: displays the classification and associated risk.
- **calculate_bmi()**: calculates the BMI value.
- **main()**: the main program flow.

Solution

The code developed in the previous sections will now be broken down into functions. These functions will be placed in the module **mod_fonctions**. The code is shown in listing 12.4.

Listing 12.4: BMI Basic Script with Functions

```
# BMI Calculation
classification = ["Underweight", "Normal weight", "Overweight",
↪   "Obesity, Class I", "Obesity, Class II", "Obesity, Class III"]
risk = ["Increased", "Lower", "Increased", "High", "Very High",
↪   "Extremely High"]

def input_value(msg, msg_error):
    value = float(input(msg))
    while value <= 0:
        value = float(input(msg_error))
    return value

def calculate_bmi(weight, height):
    return weight / height ** 2

def display_bmi(value):
    print("Your BMI is: {0:7.2f}".format(value))
```

The functions to determine and display the risk and classification are shown in the following code:

```
def determine_risk_class(bmi):
    if bmi < 18.5:
        index = 0
    elif bmi < 25:
        index = 1
    elif bmi < 30:
        index = 2
    elif bmi < 35:
        index = 3
    elif bmi < 40:
        index = 4
    else:
        index = 5

    return index

def display_risk_class(index):
    print("Classification: {0:20s}".format(classification[index]))
    print("Risk: {0:20s}".format(risk[index]))
```

Finally, the main function call will be as follows:

Main Function

```
def main():
    # Enter weight
    weight = input_value("Enter your weight (in kg): ", "Enter weight >
    ↪ 0: ")
    # Enter height
    height = input_value("Enter your height (in meters): ", "Enter
    ↪ height > 0: ")
    # Calculate BMI
    bmi = calculate_bmi(weight, height)
    # Display BMI
    display_bmi(bmi)
    # Determine index
    index = determine_risk_class(bmi)
    # Display risk and classification
    display_risk_class(index)

if __name__ == '__main__':
    main()
```

With this refactored code, we have organized the functionality into functions for better readability and maintainability.

12.5 Class

Objective

Develop a class that models a BMI.

Approach

We will first develop the class to model a patient. For this, we consider the following attributes:

- name: str
- age: int
- weight: float
- height: float

We will add the `__str__()` method to obtain the state of the object. The name of the class will be **Patient**.

- Refactor the code for BMI calculation by ensuring that the `calculate_bmi()` method is available at the **Patient** object level.
- Execute the program by instantiating a **Patient** object. Use this object to calculate the BMI value.

Solution

We now integrate a model class **Patient**. This class will be placed in the module **mod_classes**. The attributes are those defined in the initializer. The code is shown in listing 12.5.

Listing 12.5: Model Class

```
class Patient:
    def __init__(self, name: str, age: int, weight: float, height:
    ↪  float):
        self.name = name
        self.age = age
        self.weight = weight
        self.height = height

    def __str__(self):
        return "Name: {}, Age: {}, Weight: {}, Height:
        ↪  {}".format(self.name,
                                  self.age, self.weight, self.height)
```

```
    def calculate_bmi(self):
        return self.weight / self.height ** 2
```

We modify the **main()** function to create an object of type **Patient**, as shown below in listing 12.6.

Listing 12.6: Main Function

```
def main():
    weight = input_value("Please enter your weight: ", "Please enter a
    ↪ numeric weight greater than 0: ")
    height = input_value("Please enter your height: ", "Please enter a
    ↪ numeric height greater than 0: ")
    name = input("Please enter your name: ")
    age = int(input("Please enter your age: "))

    # Create a Patient object
    patient = Patient(name, age, weight, height)
    # Calculate BMI
    bmi = patient.calculate_bmi()
    # Display BMI
    display_bmi(bmi)
    # Determine index
    index = determine_risk_class(bmi)
    # Display risk and classification
    display_risk_class(index)

if __name__ == '__main__':
    main()
```

With the addition of the **Patient** class, the code is now more organized and follows the principles of object-oriented programming. The BMI calculation is now encapsulated within the class, making it easier to work with patient data.

12.6 Files

Objective

Develop an approach for storing data in a CSV file.

Approach

We will use the **csv** module to write the content of the **Patient** object as a CSV (comma-separated values) string. Each line will be represented by the following sequence of values:

- name: str
- age: int
- weight: float
- height: float

To achieve this, we will develop the **save_bmi(file_name, pat)** method, which takes the file name and a **Patient** object and writes the content to the corresponding file.

The file will be opened in append mode using the `open()` function. The write object will be obtained using the `writer` function from the `csv` module. Writing will be performed using the `writerow()` method of the write object.

Solution

We will now integrate the code for writing to a CSV file using the **csv** module. The function will be placed in the **mod_files** module. The code is shown in listing 12.7.

Listing 12.7: Persistence function

```
import csv
def save_bmi(file_name, pat):
    with open(file_name, "a", newline="\n") as file:
        writer = csv.writer(file, quoting=csv.QUOTE_NONNUMERIC)
        writer.writerow((pat.name, pat.age, pat.weight, pat.height))
```

We modify the **main()** function to include a call to the **save_bmi()** function, as shown below in listing 12.8.

Listing 12.8: Modified main function

```
def main():
    weight = input_value("Please enter your weight: ", "Please enter a
    ↪ numeric weight greater than 0: ")
    height = input_value("Please enter your height: ", "Please enter a
    ↪ numeric height greater than 0: ")
    name = input("Please enter your name: ")
    age = int(input("Please enter your age: "))

    # Create a Patient object
    patient = Patient(name, age, weight, height)
    # Calculate BMI
    bmi = patient.calculate_bmi()
    # Display BMI
    display_bmi(bmi)
    # Determine index
    index = determine_risk_class(bmi)
    # Display risk and classification
    display_risk_class(index)
    # Save to file
    save_bmi("bmi_output.csv", patient)

if __name__ == '__main__':
    main()
```

With the addition of the **save_bmi()** function, the data can now be saved to a CSV file. This allows for the preservation and retrieval of previously calculated BMI data.

12.7 GUI Interface with tkinter

Objective

Develop the GUI module for data input and display.

Approach

- In the first step, we proceed with coding the interface to provide the following features:

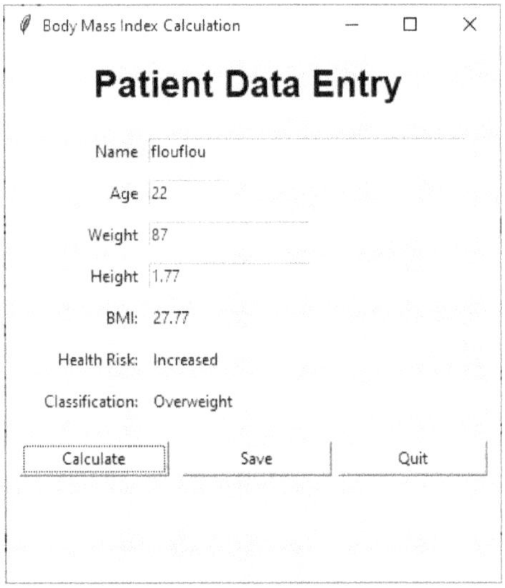

Figure 12.2: The final GUI interface.

- We will use the `grid` manager for the layout of the interface.

Solution

We will now develop the GUI using the tkinter module.

We need to import the necessary modules for the interface. We also define the functions that will be called when the user clicks on the various buttons.

In this implementation, we use a procedural approach to develop the GUI. The functions that will be called are described in listing 12.9.

Listing 12.9: GUI code

```
from tkinter import *

from mod_classes import Patient
from mod_files import save_bmi
from mod_functions import determine_risk_class, risk, classification

def quit():
    root.destroy()

def main_calculate():
    patient = Patient(name.get(), int(age.get()), float(weight.get()),
    ↪   float(height.get()))
    # Call for BMI calculation
    bmi = patient.calculate_bmi()
    # Display BMI, risk, and classification
    lbl_bmi.config(text="{0:5.2f}".format(bmi))
    index = determine_risk_class(bmi)
    lbl_risk.config(text=str(risk[index]))
    lbl_classification.config(text=str(classification[index]))

def save():
    person = Patient(name.get(), int(age.get()), float(weight.get()),
    ↪   float(height.get()))
    # Save to csv
    save_bmi("annual_bmi.csv", person)
```

The code for creating the interface uses the `grid` manager. We create a `Frame` object to contain the window title:

```
# Create the main window
root = Tk()
root.title("Body Mass Index Calculator")
root.geometry("380x400")

# Create a frame for the title
frame_title = Frame(root)
title_font = ('arial', 20, 'bold')
label_title = Label(frame_title, text='Patient Data Entry',
↪  font=title_font)
label_title.grid(row=1, column=1, padx=5, pady=5)
```

A second **Frame** is created to contain the widgets:

Listing 12.10: GUI code

```
# Create a frame for the graphical components
frame_components = Frame(root)
Label(frame_components, text='Name').grid(row=1, column=1, sticky=E,
↪   padx=5, pady=5)
Label(frame_components, text='Age').grid(row=2, column=1, sticky=E,
↪   padx=5, pady=5)
Label(frame_components, text='Weight').grid(row=3, column=1, sticky=E,
↪   padx=5, pady=5)
Label(frame_components, text='Height').grid(row=4, column=1, sticky=E,
↪   padx=5, pady=5)
Label(frame_components, text='BMI:').grid(row=5, column=1, sticky=E,
↪   padx=5, pady=5)
Label(frame_components, text='Health Risk:').grid(row=6, column=1,
↪   sticky=E, padx=5, pady=5)
Label(frame_components, text='Classification:').grid(row=7, column=1,
↪   sticky=E, padx=5, pady=5)

name = Entry(frame_components, width=40)
name.grid(row=1, column=2, columnspan=4, sticky=W)
age = Entry(frame_components, width=10)
age.grid(row=2, column=2, columnspan=4, sticky=W)
weight = Entry(frame_components, width=20)
weight.grid(row=3, column=2, columnspan=4, sticky=W)
height = Entry(frame_components, width=20)
height.grid(row=4, column=2, columnspan=4, sticky=W)

lbl_bmi = Label(frame_components)
lbl_bmi.grid(row=5, column=2, sticky=W)
lbl_risk = Label(frame_components)
lbl_risk.grid(row=6, column=2, sticky=W)
lbl_classification = Label(frame_components)
lbl_classification.grid(row=7, column=2, sticky=W)
```

A third **Frame** is created to contain the buttons:

Listing 12.11: GUI code

```
# Create a frame for the buttons
frame_buttons = Frame(root)
btn_calculate = Button(frame_buttons, text='Calculate', width=15,
↪   command=main_calculate)
btn_calculate.grid(row=1, column=1, padx=5, pady=5)
btn_save = Button(frame_buttons, text='Save', width=15, command=save)
btn_save.grid(row=1, column=2, padx=5, pady=5)
btn_cancel = Button(frame_buttons, text='Quit', width=15,
↪   command=quit)
btn_cancel.grid(row=1, column=3)
```

Finally, the different `Frame` objects are added to the main window.

Listing 12.12: GUI code

```
# Place the frames
frame_title.grid(row=1, column=1, columnspan=3, padx=5, pady=5)
frame_components.grid(row=2, column=1, padx=5, pady=5)
frame_buttons.grid(row=3, column=1, padx=5, pady=5)

root.mainloop()
```

Executing this module will result in the desired window.

Chapter 13

Debugging with PyCharm

13.1 Introduction

Regardless of the development environment used, it is important to know how to debug code. This can be done either to find the cause of an error in the code or simply to evaluate the quality of the code by executing it step by step.

Consider the code 13.1 which includes a function for calculating the factorial.

Listing 13.1: Factorial calculation with error

```
def factorial(n):
    f = 1
    for i in range(0, n+1):
        f *= i
    return f
```

An error has been introduced in this code. The objective is to see how to use the debugging features of PyCharm to find and then correct this error.

We will call the function with the following code.

Listing 13.2: Function call code

```
#### Function Call Code ###
if __name__ == '__main__':
    num = int(input('Please enter a value for factorial: '))
```

```
while num >= 0 and num <= 9:
    facto = factorial(num)
    print('The factorial of {} is {}'.format(num, facto))
    num = int(input('Please enter another value for factorial
    ↪   (0-9): '))
```

Execute the script and verify that the result is not correct.

13.2 Debugging with breakpoints

In order to find the source of the error, we will use one or more breakpoints that we place on the instructions suspected of causing the problem.

We start by placing a **breakpoint** on the line we are interested in. In our case, our interest is in the factorial calculation function, which is:

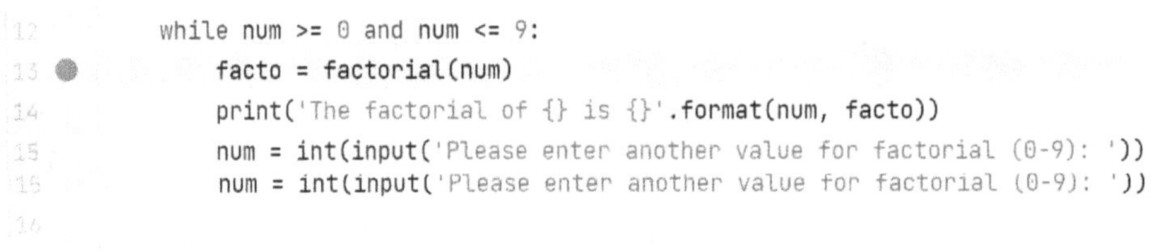
while num >= 0 and num <= 9:
facto = factorial(num)
print('The factorial of {} is {}'.format(num, facto))
num = int(input('Please enter another value for factorial (0-9): '))
num = int(input('Please enter another value for factorial (0-9): '))

Figure 13.1: Breakpoint before the function call.

The breakpoint is activated simply by clicking with the left mouse button in the line number column of PyCharm.

From the PyCharm documentation, it should be noted the following point about breakpoints:

> *Line breakpoints can be set on executable lines. Comments, declarations, and empty lines are not valid locations for the line breakpoints.*

To start debugging, click on the debug option as shown in figure 13.2:

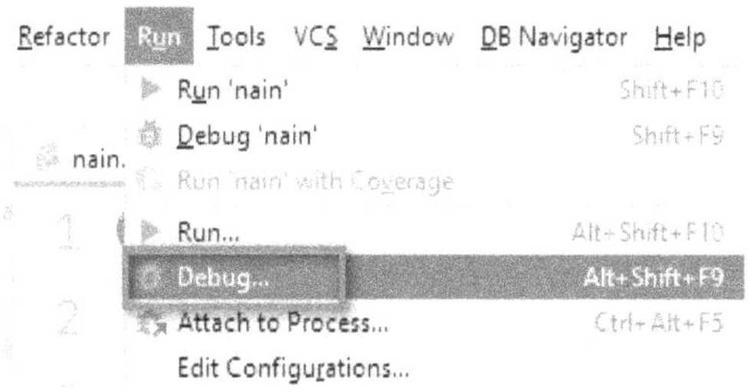

Figure 13.2: Starting a debug session through the menu.

You can also launch the debugging through the toolbar icon, as shown in figure 13.3:

Figure 13.3: Starting a debug session through the toolbar icon.

The execution will pause at the breakpoint. The line becomes blue, and at this point, we can explore the behavior of our code using the step-by-step execution process.

```
if __name__ == '__main__':
    num = int(input('S.V.P, saisir une valeur pour factoriel:'))   num: 8
    while num > 0 or num < 10:
        facto = factorial(num)
        print('Factorielle de {} est {}'.format(num, facto))
        num = int(input('S.V.P, saisir une valeur pour factoriel:'))
```

Figure 13.4: Stopping at a breakpoint.

We will now use the icons in the **stepping toolbar** section. This section is now enabled. Figure 13.5 shows the available icons to access debugging commands.

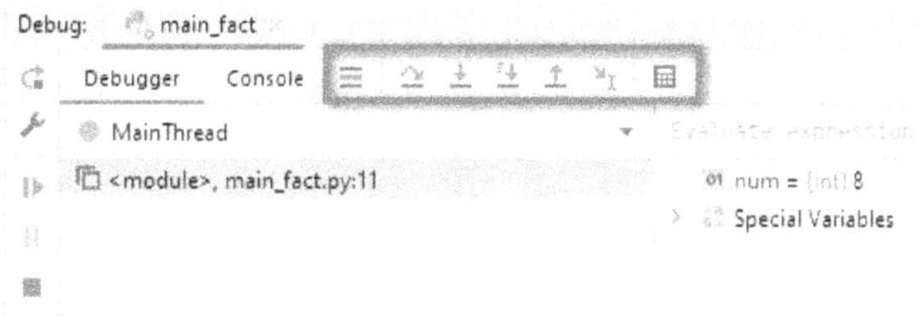

Figure 13.5: Accessing the debugging icons through the toolbar.

If we have not redefined the keyboard mapping, the following commands (from left to right) will be available:

- **Show Execution Point or Alt+F10**: highlights the current execution point.
- **Step Over or F8**: executes the current statement. If there is a method call, it will be executed without diving into its body.
- **Step Into or F7**: when on a method or function call statement, it will navigate into the method or function.
- **Step Into My Code or Alt+Shift+F7**: avoids stepping into the code of libraries or external modules.
- **Step Out or Shift + F8**: continues the execution until the current method or function is finished.
- **Run to Cursor or Alt + F9**: executes all statements until the line where the cursor is placed.
- **Evaluate Expression or Alt+F8**: allows evaluating an expression, which can be helpful when setting up a watch on a variable.

In this case, we want to detect the reason why the factorial is not calculated correctly. The breakpoint has been set at the function call **facto = factorial(num):**.

We will also use the **watch** on the variables **i** and **f**. To do this, start the debugging and then select the variable. Right-click the variable and select the "Add to Watches" option, as shown in figure 13.6:

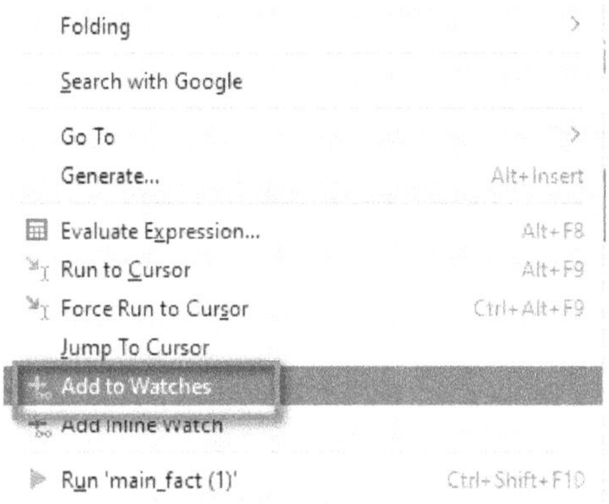

Figure 13.6: Adding a watch on a variable.

Next, use **Step Into or F7** to execute the statements of the function step by step. Check the watch panel, as shown in figure 13.7.

By repeating the process several times, we notice that the variable **f** does not change, as shown in figure 13.8:

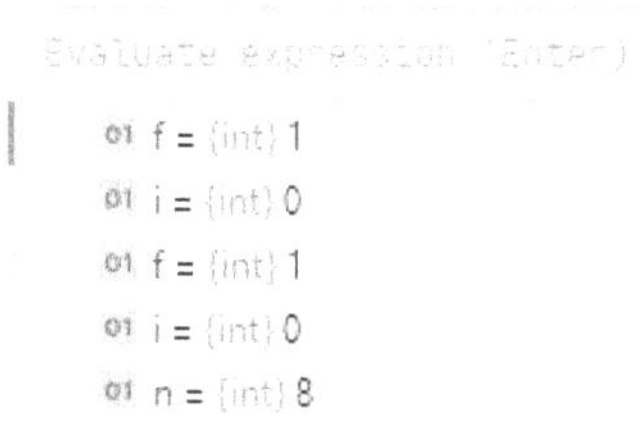

Figure 13.7: Checking the watch on variables.

Figure 13.8: Checking the watch on variables.

Thus, the cause of the incorrect calculation is identified by the fact that **f** has an initial value of 0. This results in the product always being equal to 0.

Modify your code to have:

```
def factorial(n):
    f = 1
    for i in range(2, n + 1):
        f *= i
    return f
```

Verify again, and now we can clearly see that the factorial is calculated correctly, as shown in figure 13.9.

13.3 Using a watch on a variable

Now, we want to identify the reason why the condition for the value range, that is, between 1 and 9, is not being considered. For this, we will add a watch on the variable **num** and the expressions **num > 0** and **num < 10**.

We repeat the same process for the other part of the logical expression. The watches are shown in figure 13.10.

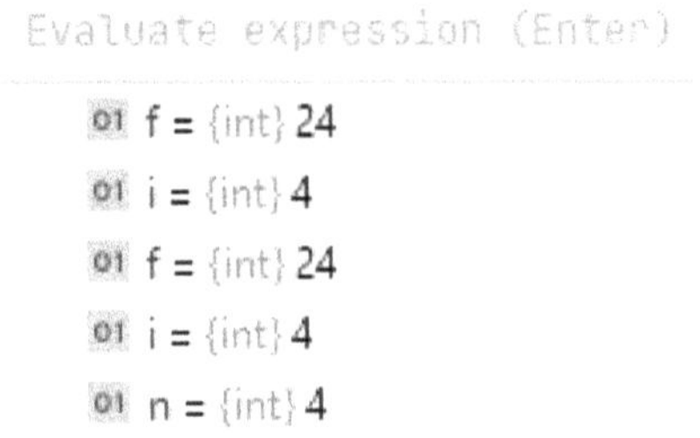

Figure 13.9: Checking watches on variables.

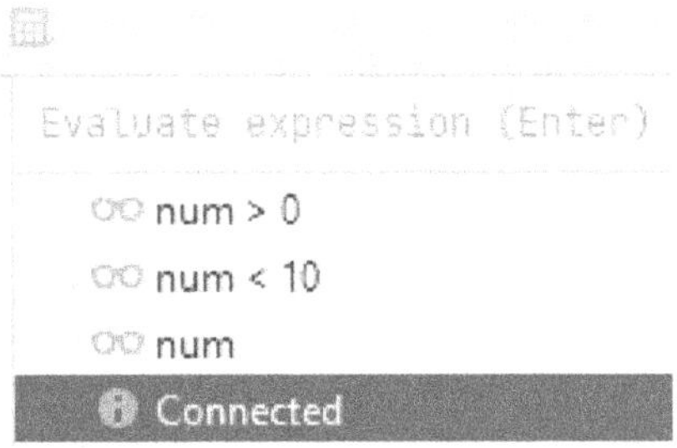

Figure 13.10: Checking watches on variables.

Next, we set a breakpoint on the **while** loop, as shown in figure 13.11.

```
    while num >= 0 and num <= 9:
        facto = factorial(num)
        print('The factorial of {} is {}'.format(num, facto))
        num = int(input('Please enter another value for factorial (0-9): '))
```

Figure 13.11: Breakpoint on the while loop.

Run your script with the value of **num** equal to `0`. The result is shown in figure 13.12.

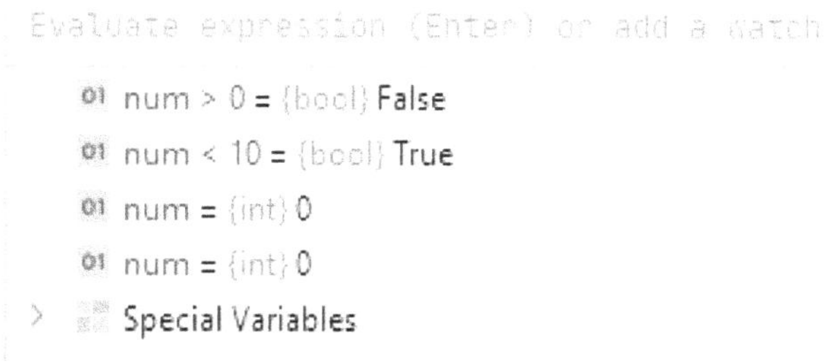

Figure 13.12: Checking watches on variables.

We can see that the logical expression of the **while** loop will be `True` because we used the `or` operator. If we repeat the operation for **num** equal to `15`, we get:

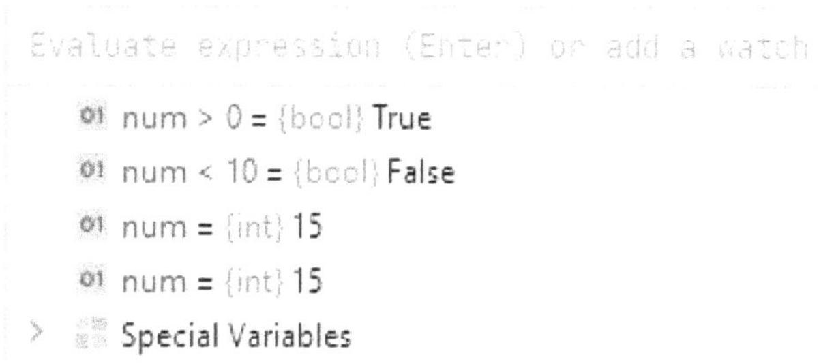

Figure 13.13: Checking watches on variables.

We can test for a value in the range between 0 and 10, and we will see that it evaluates to `True` for both cases. Therefore, the correct operator to use would be `and`. Modify your code to have:

```
while num > 0 and num < 10:
```

Repeat the previous test cases. For **num** equal to 0, the watches are shown in figure 13.14.

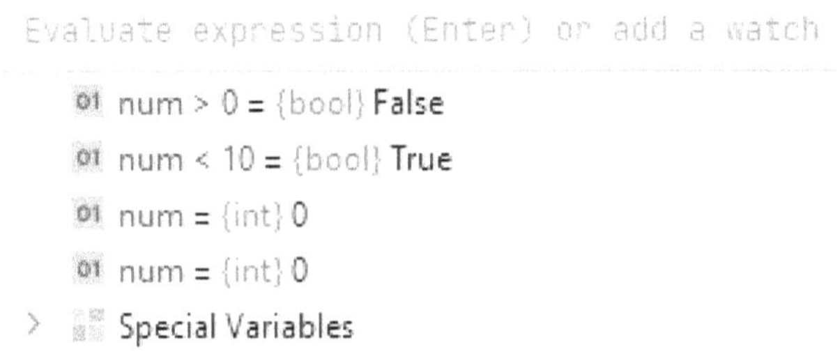

Figure 13.14: Checking watches on variables.

If we wanted to add a watch for the entire logical expression, it would look like this:

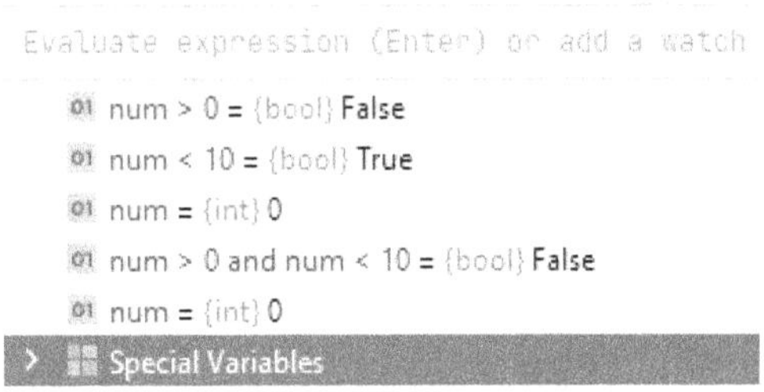

Figure 13.15: Adding a watch for the logical expression.

Through this problem, we saw how to use the debugging features of PyCharm.

Appendix A

Operator Precedence

In section 2.4.2, we briefly mentioned the order of precedence for arithmetic operators. However, it is essential to keep in mind that in many cases, expressions to be evaluated consist of multiple operations that may involve different types of operators.

Therefore, the evaluation order is determined by the rules of precedence and associativity of the operators used. Table A.1 shows Python operators grouped by their precedence level. The operators are listed from the highest precedence level to the lowest.

Consider the example in listing A.1.

Listing A.1: Operator Precedence in an Expression

```
# Operator Precedence in an Expression
parent = "flouclair"
num_children = 1

if parent == "flouclair" or parent == "flouflou" and num_children >=
↪  3:
    print("The parent is eligible for a bonus.")
else:
    print("The parent is not eligible for a bonus.")
```

The output is as follows:

Output in execution mode

```
The parent is eligible for a bonus.
```

In this example, the result is surprising. We might expect the output to be "The parent is not eligible for a bonus." because the number of children is less than 3. However, due to operator precedence, the `and` operator takes precedence over the `or` operator.

As a result, the condition **`parent`** `== "flouflou" and` **`num_children`** `>= 3` is evaluated before being combined with the `or` condition.

This does not quite correspond to what we intended to achieve. Indeed, we wanted to offer a bonus to the parent, either "Flouflou" or "Flouclair," but only if the number of children is greater than or equal to 3. The expected result in this case, given the values of the variables **parent** and **num_children**, should be that the parent is not entitled to the bonus.

To get the desired behavior, we should use parentheses to explicitly define the evaluation order. By adding parentheses, we ensure that the expression inside the parentheses is evaluated first.

Category	Operators
Primary	()
Multiplicative	*, /, //, %
Additive	+ , -
Shift	«, »
Relational	==, !=, >, >=, <, <=
Logical AND	and
Logical OR	or
Logical NOT	not
Bitwise AND	&
Bitwise XOR	^
Bitwise OR	|

Table A.1 - Operator Precedence table.

The modified code will be as indicated in listing A.2.

Listing A.2: Operator precedence in an expression

```
# Operator precedence in an expression
parent = "flouclair"
num_children = 1
if (parent == "flouclair" or parent == "flouflou") and num_children >=
↪  3:
    print("The parent is eligible for a bonus.")
else:
    print("The parent is not eligible for a bonus.")
```

Now the output gives us the expected result:

Output in execution mode

```
The parent is not eligible for a bonus.
```

When multiple operators of the same category are present in an expression, we use the principle of associativity. In this case, most operators are left-associative.

Consider the example in listing A.3.

Listing A.3: Operator precedence in an expression

```
# Left-to-right precedence of operators in an expression
number1 = 15
number2 = 4
number3 = 12
result = number1 + number2 * number3 / 3
print(result)
```

The output gives us the following result:

Output in execution mode

```
31.0
```

The order of operations is thus *, /, +, and then the assignment.

Appendix B

Quiz Solutions

Chapter 1 - Introduction

1. a
2. b,c,d
3. a,b,d
4. a
5. b
6. a
7. d
8. a
9. d
10. b

Chapter 2 - Basic syntax

1. a
2. a
3. b
4. b
5. b
6. c
7. b
8. c
9. b
10. b

Chapter 3 - Decision Structures

1. a,b
2. b
3. a
4. b
5. c
6. a
7. b
8. b
9. a,c
10. a

Chapter 4 - Repetitive structures

1. a,c
2. a
3. a
4. a
5. c
6. b
7. b
8. d
9. b
10. b

Chapter 5 - Functions

1. a,c	4. a	7. c	10. b
2. b	5. b	8. a	
3. b	6. b	9. b	

Chapter 6 - Sequences and Collections

1. a,b,d,e	4. b	7. b,c	10. b
2. a	5. b	8. a	
3. a	6. b	9. a	

Chapter 7 - Classes and Objects

1. a,b	4. a	7. a	10. b
2. a	5. a	8. a	
3. a	6. a	9. c	

Chapter 8 - Inheritance

1. a,b	4. a	7. b	10. b
2. b	5. a	8. b	
3. a	6. b	9. a	

Chapter 9 - Files

1. a,b,c	4. a	7. a	10. b
2. a	5. a	8. b	
3. a	6. b	9. a	

Chapter 10 - Exception Handling

1. a	4. a	7. a	10. a
2. a	5. a	8. a	
3. b	6. b	9. b	

Chapter 11 - Graphical User Interfaces

1. a	4. a	7. b	10. a
2. c	5. b	8. a c	
3. a	6. a	9. b	

Appendix C

Answers for Selected Problems

Chapter 2

Problem 2.8, page 51

```
user_name = input('Enter your name: ')
print('Hello {}'.format(user_name))
```

Problem 2.9, page 51

```
salary = float(input('Enter your salary: '))
salary += 500
print('Your new salary is: {0:7.2f}'.format(salary))
```

Problem 2.10, page 51

```
#Conversion and calculation
student_name = input('Enter student name:')
mid_term_exam = float(input('Enter mid-term exam grade:'))
final_exam = float(input('Enter final exam grade:'))
student_average = 0.4 * mid_term_exam + 0.6 * final_exam
print('Student name: {} Average: {}'.format(student_name,
↪  student_average))
```

Problem 2.11, page 52

```
#Initializing variables
var_1 = 0
var_2 = 1000000000000
var_3 = -10
var_4 = 10.10
var_5 = '10'
var_6 = True

#Checking variable types
print(type(var_1))
print(type(var_2))
print(type(var_3))
print(type(var_4))
print(type(var_5))
print(type(var_6))
```

Problem 2.12, page 52

```
var_1 = 48.5
result = isinstance(var_1, float)
print(result)
```

Chapter 3

Problem 3.4, page 66

```
###### Solution 1 ######
#Input
a = int(input('Enter a:'))
b = int(input('Enter b:'))
c = int(input('Enter c:'))
max_val = a
min_val = b

if b > a:
    max_val = b
    min_val = a

#Find min and max
if max_val < c:
    max_val = c
elif min_val > c:
    min_val = c

print("Minimum:", min_val, "Maximum:", max_val)
```

Another solution that uses a simultaneous assignment is as follows:

```
###### Solution 2 ######
#Input
a = int(input('Enter a:'))
b = int(input('Enter b:'))
c = int(input('Enter c:'))
max_val, min_val = a, b

if b > a:
    max_val, min_val = b, a
```

```
#Find min and max
if max_val < c:
    max_val = c
elif min_val > c:
    min_val = c

print("Minimum:", min_val, "Maximum:", max_val)
```

Problem 3.5, page 66

```
#Conversion from meters to feet, solution 1
distance = float(input('Enter the distance in meters:'))
distance_converted = distance / 0.3048
print('The distance in feet is:{0:7.2f}'.format(distance_converted))
```

A more elaborate solution that offers a menu for the choice of conversion is as follows:

```
#Conversion from meters to feet and feet to meters
distance = float(input('Enter the distance to convert:'))
option = int(input('Enter option 1 or 2: \n1. Convert meters to
↪   feet\n2. Convert feet to meters\n'))
if option == 1:
    distance_converted = distance / 0.3048
    print('The distance in feet
     ↪   is:{0:7.2f}'.format(distance_converted))
elif option == 2:
    distance_converted = distance * 0.3048
    print('The distance in meters
     ↪   is:{0:7.2f}'.format(distance_converted))
else:
    print('Invalid option chosen')
```

Chapter 4

Problem 4.6, page 83

```
# Generate a random number
import random
unknown_number = random.randint(1, 100)

# Find the number
tries = 1
number = int(input('Guess the number:'))
while number != unknown_number:
    if number > unknown_number:
        print('Your number is greater!')
    else:
        print('Your number is smaller!')
    tries += 1
    number = int(input('Guess the number:'))

print('Congratulations! You found the number {} in {}
↪  attempts.'.format(unknown_number, tries))
```

Problem 4.8, page 83

```
# Determine the total of even numbers needed to reach a given number
a = int(input('Enter a:'))
total = 0
i = 1
while total < a:
    print(2 * i)
    total += 2 * i
    i += 1

print('We need the first {} even numbers'.format(i - 1))
```

Problem 4.11, page 84

```
# Count characters and occurrences of letter 'a'
line = input("Enter a sentence: ")
char_count = len(sentence)
print("Number of characters:", char_count)

letter_a_count = line.lower().count('a')
print("The letter -a- is used", letter_a_count, "time(s).")

letter_a_or_A_count = line.lower().count('a') +
↪  line.lower().count('A')
print("The letter -a or A- is used", letter_a_or_A_count, "time(s).")
```

Problem 4.12, page 84

```
# Suggesting activities based on weather
temperature = float(input("Enter the temperature in Celsius: "))

if temperature >= 25:
    print("Swimming is the suggested activity.")
elif 18 <= temperature < 25:
    print("Tennis is the suggested activity.")
elif 2 <= temperature < 18:
    print("A hike in the woods is the suggested activity.")
else:
    print("Skiing is the suggested activity.")
```

Chapter 5

Problem 5.7, page 106

```
def get_input(message):
    '''
    Returns a value entered by the user

    :param message: The message to display to the user
    :return: The value entered by the user
    '''
    return input(message)

# Calling the function
result = get_input("Enter a value:")
print(result)
```

Problem 5.8, page 106

```
def convert_seconds(seconds):
    '''
    Calculate the number of hours, minutes, and seconds

    :param seconds: The number of seconds to convert
    :return: The tuple containing the number of hours, minutes,
    and seconds
    '''
    hours = seconds // 3600
    minutes = (seconds % 3600) // 60
    remaining_seconds = ((seconds % 3600) % 60)
    return hours, minutes, remaining_seconds

# Calling the function
result = convert_seconds(89568578)
print('Hours: {0}, Minutes: {1}, Seconds: {2}'.format(
    result[0], result[1], result[2]))
```

Chapter 6

Problem 6.29, page 144

An approach without using functions is given by the following code:

```
listing = []
# Input values
for i in range(0, 10):
    listing.append(float(input('Enter a real value: ')))

# Display the values
print('Elements in the list: {}'.format(listing))

# Calculate the average
average = sum(listing) / len(listing)
print('The average of the values is: {:7.2f}'.format(average))
```

An approach using functions is as follows:

```
def input_values(number_of_values, message):
    lst = []
    for i in range(0, number_of_values):
        lst.append(float(input(message)))
    return lst

def calculate_average(lst):
    return sum(lst) / len(lst)

def main():
    # Input values
    listing = input_values(10, 'Enter a real value: ')

    # Display the values
    print('Elements in the list: {}'.format(listing))

    # Calculate the average
    average = calculate_average(listing)
    print('The average of the values is: {:7.2f}'.format(average))

if __name__ == '__main__':
    main()
```

Both approaches will achieve the same result. The second one, using functions, allows for better organization and reusability of code.

Problem 6.30, page 144

```
# version 1

def input_values(value_count, message):
    lst = []
    for i in range(0, value_count):
        lst.append(float(input(message)))
    return lst

def calculate_list_product(list1, list2):
    # Check the length of both lists
    if len(list1) != len(list2) or len(list1) == 0:
        print('Calculation impossible')
        return None
    else:
        result = []
        for i in range(0, len(list1)):
            result.append(list1[i] * list2[i])
        return result

def calculate_list_sum(list1, list2):
    # Check the length of both lists
    if len(list1) != len(list2) or len(list1) == 0:
        print('Calculation impossible')
        return None
    else:
        result = []
        for i in range(0, len(list1)):
            result.append(list1[i] + list2[i])
        return result
```

The calling code for this function is as follows:

```
def main():
    list_1 = input_values(5, 'Enter a real value:')
    print('Elements in the list:{}'.format(list_1))
    list_2 = input_values(5, 'Enter a real value:')
    print('Elements in the list:{}'.format(list_2))

    # List with each element as the sum
    list_sum = calculate_list_sum(list_1, list_2)
    # Display the result
    print('List with each element as the sum:{}'.format(list_sum))

    # List with each element as the product
    list_product = calculate_list_product(list_1, list_2)
    # Display the result
    print('List with each element as the
    ↪  product:{}'.format(list_product))


if __name__ == '__main__':
    main()
```

Chapter 7

Problem 7.5, page 168

The model class is given by the following code:

```
# Class Student
class Student:
    """Initializer"""
    def __init__(self, last_name, first_name, gender, address,
    ↪  student_code, final_grade):
        self.last_name = last_name
        self.first_name = first_name
        self.gender = gender
        self.address = address
        self.student_code = student_code
        self.final_grade = final_grade

    def __str__(self):
        return "Student  last name: {:<10} first name: {:<10} " \
               "gender: {:<7} address: {:<20} code: {:<8} " \
               "final grade: {:<8}".format(self.last_name,
               ↪  self.first_name, self.gender,
                                          self.address,
                                          ↪  self.student_code,
                                          ↪  self.final_grade)

    def do_homework(self):
        print("I am a diligent student")
```

The code for creating an object of this class and utilizing its attributes and methods is provided below:

```
def main():
    """Instantiate objects"""
    obj1 = Student(first_name="Alain", last_name="Flouflou",
    ↪  gender="M", address="14 Park Street", student_code="118907",
                   final_grade=78)
    print(obj1)
```

```
    # Call the method do_homework
    obj1.do_homework()

if __name__ == '__main__':
    main()
```

Problem 7.6, page 168

```
# Stock Class and Operations
class Stock:
    """Constructor"""
    def __init__(self, symbol, title, closing_price, current_price):
        self.symbol = symbol
        self.title = title
        self.closing_price = closing_price
        self.current_price = current_price

    def __str__(self):
        return "Stock  Symbol: {:<5} Title: {:<20} " \
               "Closing Price: {:7.2f} Current Price: {:7.2f} " \
               .format(self.symbol, self.title, self.closing_price,
               ↪  self.current_price)

    def percentage_change(self):
        return ((self.current_price / self.closing_price) - 1) * 100
```

The code for creating the object and using its members is as follows:

```
def main():
    """Instantiate an object"""
    stock1 = Stock(title="Microsoft", symbol="MSFT",
    ↪  closing_price=123.24, current_price=127.04)
    print(stock1)

    # Display the percentage change
    percentage = stock1.percentage_change()
    print('Percentage change: {:7.3f}'.format(percentage))

if __name__ == '__main__':
    main()
```

Problem 7.9, page 170

The model class is given by the following code:

```
# Car Class
class Car:
    """Initializer"""
    def __init__(self, title, distance, consumption, fuel_cost):
        self.title = title
        self.distance = distance
        self.consumption = consumption
        self.fuel_cost = fuel_cost

    def __str__(self):
        return "Title: {:<10s} Distance: {:7.2f}, Consumption: {:7.2f},
        ↪  " \
               "Fuel Cost: {:7.2f}  " \
            .format(self.title, self.distance, self.consumption,
            ↪  self.fuel_cost)

    def calculate_trip_cost(self):
        return (self.distance * self.consumption * self.fuel_cost) /
        ↪  100.0
```

The code to create an object and use its attributes is as follows:

```
def main():
    """Instantiate object"""
    title = input('Enter the car name:')
    distance = float(input('Enter the distance:'))
    fuel_cost = float(input('Enter the fuel cost:'))
    consumption = float(input('Enter the car consumption:'))
    car1 = Car(title=title, distance=distance,
               consumption=consumption, fuel_cost=fuel_cost)
    print(car1)

    # Calculate the trip cost
    total_cost = car1.calculate_trip_cost()
    print('The total cost of the trip is: {:.2f}'.format(total_cost))

if __name__ == '__main__':
    main()
```

Chapter 8

Problem 8.4, page 201

```
# Contact Management with Inheritance
class Contact:
    def __init__(self, name, email):
        self.name = name
        self.email = email

    def __str__(self):
        return "Name: {0:<15s} and Email: {1:<15s}".format(self.name,
        ↪  self.email)

class Supplier(Contact):
    def __init__(self, name, email, supplier_code):
        super().__init__(name, email)
        self.supplier_code = supplier_code

    def place_order(self, order):
        print('The order is for: {}'.format(order))

    def __str__(self):
        return super().__str__() + " Supplier Code:
        ↪  {0:25s}".format(self.supplier_code)


obj1 = Contact("Alain Flouflou", "a.flouflou@monsite.com")
print(obj1)

objF = Supplier("Annie ClairClair", "a.clairclair@monsite.com",
↪  "1234")
print(objF)
```

Problem 8.5, page 201

The classes **Contact** and **Supplier** are presented below.

```
# Contact Management with Inheritance
class Contact:
    def __init__(self, name, email):
        self.name = name
        self.email = email

    def __str__(self):
        return "Name: {0:<15s} and Email: {1:<15s}".format(self.name,
        ↪ self.email)

class Supplier(Contact):
    def __init__(self, name, email, supplier_code):
        super().__init__(name, email)
        self.supplier_code = supplier_code

    def place_order(self, order):
        print('The order is for: {}'.format(order))

    def __str__(self):
        return super().__str__() + " Supplier Code:
        ↪ {0:25s}".format(self.supplier_code)
```

The class **ContactRegister** provides methods for manipulating objects of type **Contact**, as follows:

```
class ContactRegister:
    def __init__(self, name, register=()):
        self.name = "contact list"
        self.register = list()

    def search_contact(self, keyword):
        results = list()
        for contact in self.register:
            if keyword in contact.name:
                results.append(contact)
        return results
```

```
    def display_contacts(self):
        print("Number of contacts: {:<4d}".format(len(self.register)))
        for tmp in self.register:
            print(tmp)

    def add_contact(self, contact):
        self.register.append(contact)
```

The code for creating and manipulating objects is as follows:

```
# Create the contact register
listing = ContactRegister("contact list")

obj1 = Contact("Alain Flouflou", "a.flouflou@monsite.com")
# print(obj1)
listing.add_contact(obj1)

objF = Supplier("Annie ClairClair Inc", "a.clairclair@monsite.com",
↪  "1234")
# print(objF)
listing.add_contact(objF)

# Display the content of the register
listing.display_contacts()

# Search for a contact
keyword = "Clair"
results = listing.search_contact(keyword)
print("*" * 25)
print("Elements found")
print("*" * 25)
for res in results:
    print(res)
```

Chapter 9

Problem 9.3, page 224

```
# Solution returning only the length
def calculate_file_length(file):
    maximum = ""
    for line in open(file):
        if len(line) > len(maximum):
            maximum = line
    return len(maximum)

# Solution returning both length and the line itself
def calculate_file_stats(file):
    max_line = ""
    for line in open(file):
        if len(line) > len(max_line):
            max_line = line
    return len(max_line), max_line

def main():
    max_length = calculate_file_length("case.txt")
    print("Maximum length:", max_length)

    max_length, max_line = calculate_file_stats("case.txt")
    print("Maximum length:", max_length)
    print("Line with maximum length:", max_line)

if __name__ == '__main__':
    main()
```

Chapter 10

Problem 10.5, page 244

The first solution does not include exception handling.

```
# Multiplication of two numbers without exception handling
number_1 = float(input('Enter number 1:'))
number_2 = float(input('Enter number 2:'))
result = number_1 * number_2
print('The product of {} and {} is: {}'.format(number_1, number_2,
↪ result))
```

In the second solution, we include basic exception handling. However, if an exception occurs, the user does not have the opportunity to re-enter the values.

```
# Multiplication of two numbers with basic exception handling
try:
    number_1 = float(input('Enter number 1:'))
    number_2 = float(input('Enter number 2:'))
except ValueError as e:
    print('The value entered is not a number!')
else:
    result = number_1 * number_2
    print('The product of {} and {} is: {}'.format(number_1, number_2,
    ↪ result))
```

A more comprehensive solution including a loop allows the user to re-enter the values in case of an exception.

```
# Multiplication of two numbers with exception handling and loop
flag = True
while flag:
    try:
        number_1 = float(input('Enter number 1:'))
        number_2 = float(input('Enter number 2:'))
    except ValueError as e:
        print('The value entered is not a number!')
    else:
        result = number_1 * number_2
        print('The product of {} and {} is: {}'.format(number_1,
        ↪ number_2, result))
        flag = False
```

Problem 10.7, page 244

```
def process_case(input_file, output_file):
    with open(input_file) as fi:
        with open(output_file, 'w') as fo:
            for line in fi:
                if not line.strip().islower():
                    fo.write(line)


if __name__ == '__main__':
    process_case('case.txt', 'output.txt')
```

Another solution that takes into account the exception on the file is given by the following code:

```
def process_case(input_file, output_file):
    try:
        with open(input_file) as fi:
            with open(output_file, 'w') as fo:
                for line in fi:
                    if not line.strip().islower():
                        fo.write(line)
    except FileNotFoundError as e:
        print('File access problem')

if __name__ == '__main__':
    process_case('case.txt', 'output.txt')
```

Chapter 11

Problem 11.7, page 274

Using the **grid** layout manager, the following application provides a GUI so that we capture data from the user and then perform and display results.

```
import tkinter as tk
def calculate():
    name_text = ent_name.get().upper()
    ent_name.delete(0, tk.END)
    ent_name.insert(0, name_text)
    salary = float(txt_salary.get()) + 1000
    lbl_result.config(text=str(salary))

# Create the root window
root = tk.Tk()
root.geometry('400x200')
root.title('Salary Calculator')

# Add name section
lbl_name = tk.Label(root, text='Name:')
lbl_name.grid(row=1, column=1, sticky='w', padx=5, pady=5)
ent_name = tk.Entry(root)
ent_name.grid(row=1, column=2, sticky='w', padx=5, pady=5)

# Add salary section
lbl_salary = tk.Label(root, text='Salary:')
lbl_salary.grid(row=2, column=1, sticky='w', padx=5, pady=5)
txt_salary = tk.Entry(root, font=('arial', 14))
txt_salary.grid(row=2, column=2, sticky='w', padx=5, pady=5)

# Result display
lbl_result = tk.Label(root, font=('arial', 14), fg='red')
lbl_result.grid(row=3, column=2, sticky='w', padx=5, pady=5)

# Add the calculate button
btn_calculate = tk.Button(root, text='Calculate', command=calculate)
btn_calculate.grid(row=4, column=2, sticky='w', padx=5, pady=5)

# Display the window
root.mainloop()
```

A breakdown of the code is as follows:

- **calculate Function**: A function named **calculate** is defined. This function capitalizes the entered name, updates the corresponding entry field, computes the salary by adding 1000 to the provided salary, and displays the result.
- **Root Window Creation**: The root window is created using the `tk.Tk()` method. The window dimensions are set to 400x200 pixels, and it is given the title **Salary Calculator.**
- **Name Section**: A label and entry field are added to input the user's name. The label **Name:** is positioned in the first row and first column, and the entry field is positioned next to it.
- **Salary Section**: A label and a larger entry field are added to input the salary. The label **Salary:** is positioned in the second row and first column, and the entry field is placed beside it.
- **Result Display**: A label is set up to display the calculated salary result. The label's font size is adjusted, and the text color is set to red. It is positioned in the third row and second column.
- **Calculate Button**: A button labeled **Calculate** is incorporated. When clicked, it triggers the calculate function. The button is positioned in the fourth row and second column.
- **Window Display**: The constructed GUI is displayed using the `root.mainloop()` function.

Problem 11.8, page 275

```
import tkinter as tk
from tkinter import ttk

def display():
    product = txt_product.get()
    quantity = float(txt_quantity.get())
    size = size_combobox.get()
    result = 'Product: {}, Size: {}, Quantity: {}'.format(product,
    ↪  size, quantity)
    lbl_result.config(text=result)

# Create the root window
root = tk.Tk()
root.geometry('450x200')
root.title('Sweater Selection')
```

```
# Add product section
lbl_product = tk.Label(root, text='Product:')
lbl_product.grid(row=1, column=1, sticky='w', padx=5, pady=5)
txt_product = tk.Entry(root)
txt_product.grid(row=1, column=2, sticky='w', padx=5, pady=5)

# Add size section
lbl_size = tk.Label(root, text='Size:')
lbl_size.grid(row=2, column=1, sticky='w', padx=5, pady=5)

# Combobox creation
size_var = tk.StringVar()
size_combobox = ttk.Combobox(root, width=10, textvariable=size_var)
# Values
size_combobox['values'] = ('Large',
                           'Medium',
                           'Small')
size_combobox.current(1)
size_combobox.grid(row=2, column=2, sticky='w', padx=5, pady=5)

# Add quantity section
lbl_quantity = tk.Label(root, text='Quantity:')
lbl_quantity.grid(row=3, column=1, sticky='w', padx=5, pady=5)
txt_quantity = tk.Entry(root)
txt_quantity.grid(row=3, column=2, sticky='w', padx=5, pady=5)

# Result display
lbl_result = tk.Label(root, font=('arial', 14), fg='red')
lbl_result.grid(row=4, column=2, sticky='w', padx=5, pady=5)

# Add the display button
btn_display = tk.Button(root, text='Display', command=display)
btn_display.grid(row=5, column=2, sticky='w', padx=5, pady=5)

# Display the window
root.mainloop()
```

Index

-Symbols-
ArithmeticError 232
BaseException 234
Error 235
Exception 234
FloatingPointError 232
OSError 231
ValueError 229
else 232
except 232
finally 232, 233
raise 234
try 229

- -
C 5

-A-
algorithm 3
attributes 148

-B-
base class 174
boolean 28, 36, 54, 57, 59

-C-
C++ 5, 148
child 172, 174
class
    child 172
    parent 172
constructor 149
csv 211

-D-
decision 28
dict 111

-E-
exception 227, 228
exit 16

-F-
for 69, 136
Fortran 5

-G-
global 93

-I-
id 27
IDLE 9
if 54
if-eles 57
if-elif 59
inheritance 173
    multiple 185
    simple 174
initializer 150
input 10
instance 152, 155

-J-
Java 5, 148

-K-
KeyError 125

-L-
len() 119
list 111
local 90, 93
loops 69

-M-

mainloop 249
max() 119
methods 152
min() 119
MRO 185

-N-

None 29

-O-

object 150
- attribute 148, 151
- method 149
- state 149

operator 34
- addition 35
- and 37
- assignment 34
- binary 34
- division 35
- exponentiation 35
- floor division 35
- modulo 35
- multiplication 35
- not 38
- or 38
- relational 36
- subtraction 35
- ternary 34
- unary 34

OSError 231

-P-

parent 172
pass 57
polymorphism 182
print 10
problems
- practice 49, 64, 80, 102, 133, 165, 198, 223, 240, 272
- programming 51, 66, 83, 106, 144, 168, 201, 224, 244, 274

PyGUI 247
PyQt 247

-Q-

Quiz 11, 47, 61, 77, 99, 131, 163, 195, 221, 238, 264

-R-

range() 73
return 88

-S-

self 150
set 111
stack 228
subclass 174
super class 174

-T-

tkinter 247
try-except 229
tuple 111
type 27

-U-

UML 157

-V-

ValueError 229, 231
variable 26
- boolean 28
- float 30
- int 30
- name 26
- None 29
- str 30

venv 22

-W-

while 69
WxPython 247

www.ingramcontent.com/pod-product-compliance
Lightning Source LLC
Chambersburg PA
CBHW080615060326
40690CB00021B/4702
* 9 7 8 1 7 3 8 0 6 2 7 0 6 *